GODDESSES AND QUEENS

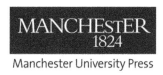

MANCHESTER
1824

Manchester University Press

Goddesses and queens: the iconography of Elizabeth I

Edited by

Annaliese Connolly and Lisa Hopkins

Manchester University Press
Manchester and New York

distributed exclusively in the USA by Palgrave

Published by Manchester University Press
Oxford Road, Manchester M13 9NR, UK
and Room 400, 175 Fifth Avenue, New York, NY 10010, USA
www.manchesteruniversitypress.co.uk

Distributed in the United States exclusively by
Palgrave Macmillan, 175 Fifth Avenue,
New York, NY 10010, USA

Distributed in Canada exclusively by
UBC Press, University of British Columbia, 2029 West Mall,
Vancouver, BC, Canada V6T 1Z2

British Library Cataloguing-in-Publication Data is available

Library of Congress Cataloging-in-Publication Data is available

ISBN 978 0 7190 9011 0 paperback

First published by Manchester University Press in hardback 2007

This paperback edition first published 2013

The publisher has no responsibility for the persistence or accuracy of URLs for any external or third-party internet websites referred to in this book, and does not guarantee that any content on such websites is, or will remain, accurate or appropriate.

Printed by Lightning Source

Lisa Hopkins
For Chris and Sam

Annaliese Connolly
For my mother and Glyn

Contents

Illustrations

The illustrations appear between pages 148 and 149

Acknowledgements

We would like to thank, in particular, Matthew Steggle for his thorough reading of the entire manuscript and for his practical and good-humoured advice. Thanks also to the anonymous reader for their considered comments and to the inter-library loan staff of the Mary Badland library at Collegiate Crescent, Sheffield Hallam University.

Notes on contributors

Jayne Elisabeth Archer is Lecturer in Medieval and Renaissance Literature at the University of Wales, Aberystwyth. She is a Postdoctoral Research Fellow with the John Nichols project, an editorial project of which the principal outcome will be an old-spelling edition of John Nichols's collection of Elizabethan progress entertainments, *The Progresses and Public Processions of Queen Elizabeth I (1788–1823)*. She has also published articles on Elizabethan and Jacobean masques and on the court culture of Queen Henrietta Maria.

Carol Blessing is a Professor of Literature at Point Loma Nazarene University, San Diego, where she also teaches in the Women's Studies Minor and specialises in medieval and Renaissance studies and women in the church. She earned her doctorate at the University of California, Riverside, writing her dissertation on women and the law in the plays of John Webster; the Shakespeare Theatre of Washington, DC, also commissioned her to write an essay on *The Duchess of Malfi*. She has presented papers on Elizabeth I at several conferences.

Helen J. Burgess is Assistant Professor of English at Washington State University Vancouver, where she teaches in the Digital Technology and Culture program.

Heather Campbell is Associate Professor in the Department of English at York University in Toronto. She has published articles on Shakespeare and Marvell, and is currently working on autobiographical writings by women in early modern England and New England.

Annaliese Connolly is currently studying for her doctoral thesis at Sheffield Hallam University. In addition to teaching, she has written for *The Year's Work in English Studies*, *Early Modern Literary Studies* and *Renaissance Journal*. She has also published a study guide for Cliffnotes on *Romeo and Juliet*.

Lisa Hopkins is Professor of English at Sheffield Hallam University. Her most recent publications include *The Female Hero in English Renaissance Tragedy* and *Writing Renaissance Queens: Texts by and about Elizabeth I and Mary, Queen of Scots*.

Scott L. Newstok is Assistant Professor of English at Gustavus Adolphus College. Beyond English Renaissance thanatology, his work examines how Shakespearean drama (and authority) gets translated into American culture through figures such as Willa Cather, Orson Welles, and George W. Bush. He is currently editing a volume of Kenneth Burke's writings on Shakespeare for Parlor Press.

Ben Spiller is a graduate of Warwick University where he gained a BA and MA in Theatre Studies and was president of the student drama society while he directed a number of plays. He is an Arts Council England Theatre Adviser and works for the British Shakespeare Association. He has written for *Early Modern Literary Studies*, *Shakespeare Bulletin* and the *Renaissance Journal*, recently taught at Oxford and Warwick Universities, and is currently working on his doctoral thesis with Professor Lisa Hopkins at Sheffield Hallam University. Ben is Artistic Director of 1623 theatre company, which performs and workshops Shakespeare in non-traditional theatre spaces.

Matthew Steggle is Senior Lecturer in English at Sheffield Hallam University. His publications include *Richard Brome: Place and Politics on the Caroline Stage* (Manchester University Press, 2004) and the commentary on *Cynthia's Revels* for the forthcoming *Cambridge Works of Ben Jonson*.

Deanne Williams is Associate Professor of English at York University, Toronto. She is the author of *The French Fetish from Chaucer to Shakespeare* (Cambridge, 2004) and co-editor of *Postcolonial Approaches to the European Middle Ages: Translating Cultures* (Cambridge, 2004). Current projects include a study of Shakespearean medievalism.

Introduction

In the spoof history *1066 and All That* the section devoted to Elizabeth I describes her as follows:

> Although this memorable Queen was a man, she was constantly addressed by her courtiers by various affectionate female nicknames, such as Auroraborealis, Ruritania, Black Beauty (or Bête Noire), and Brown Bess.[1]

This account of Elizabeth, despite its comic intent, is telling, as it speaks not only to her anomalous position as a female ruler, who remained unmarried, but to the strategies employed by both the queen and her public in order to respond to her position. The summary of Elizabeth, in sending up the large number of personae that were adopted and created for her both during and after her reign, is acknowledging both their range and influence, from the contemporary mythical figures of, for example, Belphoebe and Gloriana in Spenser's *The Faerie Queene* to the more recently popular sobriquet 'Good Queen Bess'.[2] The extract from *1066 and All That* acknowledges the myth-making about Elizabeth, whilst also pointing to the reasons for it, as her position as the head of a patriarchal society meant that she had to combine the qualities of both a king and a queen. Elizabeth's ability to manipulate her two bodies is summarised in the famous description of Elizabeth by Cecil to John Harington that she had been 'more than a man, and in troth, sometimes less than a woman';[3] indeed Courtney Lehmann provocatively declares that 'Elizabeth I, I would argue, is the original cyborg'.[4]

It is perhaps because of the suggestivity and ambiguity of her image that Elizabeth has found so ready a home on the screen. There have been over twenty films which focus on her, beginning in 1912 with Sarah Bernhardt as the queen in *Elisabeth, Reine d'Angleterre*. A selective list of these films illustrates the popularity of Elizabeth and her reign with cinemagoers and includes a roll-call of some of the finest stage and screen actresses (and actors). Bette Davis starred as the queen twice in *The Private Lives of Elizabeth and Essex* (1939) and *The Virgin Queen* (1955). Jean Simmons starred as the queen in *Young Bess* (1953), with Jenny Runacre taking the role as Elizabeth in Derek Jarman's *Jubilee* in 1977, while Quentin Crisp provided a camp Queen in *Orlando* in 1992. Elizabeth has also been a familiar face on the small screen, with the landmark

television series *Elizabeth R* in 1971 starring Glenda Jackson, followed by a more
irreverent portrait of the Queen in *Blackadder the Second* with Miranda Richardson as the
tantrum-throwing Queenie.[5] Television series about Elizabeth have also been produced
to coincide with the launch of book-length biographies of the queen. The 2000 Channel
Four series *Elizabeth* starring Imogen Slaughter, which was presented by David Starkey,
accompanied the publication of his biography of the same name in that year.

The more recent films about the queen have been *Elizabeth* by Shekhar Kapur in
1998, starring Cate Blanchett, and *Shakespeare in Love* with Dame Judi Dench in 1999.[6]
Julianne Pidduck suggests that the release of these two films about the Elizabethan age
reflected a particular zeitgeist in England in the late 1990s. The popularity of Elizabeth
and Shakespeare in the cinema was partly a result of the success of films by Kenneth
Branagh such as *Henry V* (1989), *Much Ado About Nothing* (1993), *Love's Labour's Lost*
(1999), and Baz Luhrmann's *William Shakespeare's Romeo + Juliet* (1996), coupled with
significant developments in the Elizabethan heritage industry such as the completion
of the reconstruction of the Globe theatre in 1997.[7]

To confirm the continuing popularity of Elizabeth (she and Princess Diana were
the only females in the Top Ten Great Britons poll held in 2001 by the BBC),[8] there
have been several new big-budget television series screened in Britain in 2005 and
2006. The first was the two-part drama *Elizabeth I* for Channel Four, directed by
Tom Hooper, which appeared in the autumn of 2005. It starred Helen Mirren as the
queen, and began in 1579 when Elizabeth had reigned for fifteen years and was forty-
six years old. The two episodes are concerned with her relationship with two men:
Robert Dudley, Earl of Leicester, played by Jeremy Irons, and Robert Devereux, Earl
of Essex, played by Hugh Dancy.[9] In the spring of 2006 the BBC produced a four-
part mini-series called *The Virgin Queen*, with Anne-Marie Duff in the title role. The
series begins, as Kapur's film does, in the reign of Mary Tudor (played by Joanne
Whalley), charting Elizabeth's imprisonment in the Tower and eventual accession.
The second episode explores Elizabeth's relationship with Robert Dudley and Mary,
Queen of Scots. The third and final episodes move forward to the Armada, the death
of Dudley and the emergence of the Earl of Essex. The series was a strange mixture
of ostentatious research and anachronisms such as the reference to 'entrepreneurial
spirit' and the rendering of the beginning of the Armada speech as 'I think foul scorn
that Spain or any prince of Europe ...'.[10] This glut of Tudor drama on the television
is shortly to be added to in the cinema with the release of Shekhar Kapur's sequel to
Elizabeth, *The Golden Age*, which has been billed as focusing on the relationship between
Elizabeth and Sir Walter Ralegh.

One feature which many of these films and dramatisations tend to have in common
is that the Elizabeth they present is categorically *not* a virgin. This is demonstrated
particularly in Kapur's *Elizabeth* and the more recent television series. Elizabeth,
particularly in the films which begin before she becomes queen, and in the early years
of her reign, is shown enjoying a physical relationship with Robert Dudley. Indeed
Kapur is anxious to present a vision far removed from her popular image as a Virgin

Queen, in order to chart the creation of the icon known as Elizabeth I.[11] The film presents the less familiar face of the young queen, whose youthfulness is reflected in her costume and flowing hair. Personal and political treachery underlines the tension between public duty and individual happiness and we see, in the final shots of the film, Elizabeth developing the iconic face of a queen who must rule. Carole Levin and Jo Eldridge Carney identify the resonance of this choice for a twentieth-century audience:

> In certain ways the Elizabeth of the film appears a modern woman trying to figure out whether she can balance her personal and public lives or be forced to choose between her personal relationships and her career.[12]

Courtney Lehmann identifies *Elizabeth* as one of a group of films which

> purport to dramatize striking exceptions to Renaissance rules of gender decorum, presenting us with heroines who succeed as politicians, poets, and even players. However, the kaleidoscopic view of female subjectivity purveyed by these films is eclipsed by their more powerful fetishization of sex – the power to deny or to enjoy it – as the heroine's only legitimate means of career advancement.[13]

Another notable point is that, as Renée Pigeon points out, 'Although Elizabeth's reign lasted 45 years, the popular image of both the queen and the Elizabethan period belongs to the last ten or fifteen years of that reign'.[14] The films *Elizabeth* and *Shakespeare in Love* offer two strikingly different approaches to this popular image, with Kapur, as we've noted, beginning his film with Elizabeth the princess and her virginity as a construct rather than a reality. Judi Dench's role as an older queen, with a sweet tooth and the decay to prove it, is more in keeping with the ruffed and bewigged Elizabeth of her portraits and classroom history. Despite this it is Dench's portrayal of the queen that critics have responded to most favourably. For Pigeon, for example, Dench's Elizabeth succeeds in at least grasping some of the queen's strength and self-sufficiency.[15] In general, for all the interest she apparently commands, the Elizabeth of film is a thin shadow of her historical self, reduced to a pitifully small range of roles and poses.

The chapters in this book, in contrast, address the full range of the queen's extraordinary iconographical repertoire, focusing specifically on its development during Elizabeth's forty-five-year reign. The most familiar representations of Elizabeth are those in which she is presented as a female deity or ruler, such as the Virgin Queen, Diana, or the Fairy Queen. Elizabeth's iconographical repertoire also made use of less well-known examples: for instance Arthur Gorges wrote to Sir Robert Cecil that 'Sir W. Ralegh will shortly grow to be Orlando Furioso if the bright Angelica [i.e. the queen] persevere against him a little longer',[16] aligning her with a character from Ariosto's epic poem *Orlando Furioso*. It is even possible that Lodowick Lloyd's 'A Dittie to the tune of Welsh Sydannen' was inspired by the fact that 'Sidanen' means 'the silken-fair' and may arise from Elizabeth's reputation as 'the first who wore Silk-stockings in England', in 1561.[17] Elizabeth is also figured as male when she is presented as St George, Solomon, David, Arthur, or Aeneas in the Sieve portrait.[18] Some of these images are less familiar, partly because they are to be found in speeches and sermons rather than the visual representations of the queen. For example, William Leigh, vicar of Standish in Lancashire, preached a sermon on three successive Accession Days in which he compared Elizabeth not only to David but also to Joshua and Hezekiah, in order to praise her defence of the Protestant faith in the face of the Catholic threat.[19]

Iconographical crossdressing was not unknown amongst Renaissance rulers, as in the famous image of Francis I of France dressed as the Roman goddess Minerva, but, although she often gendered herself male in her writing, the only time Elizabeth physically presented herself in the figure of a man was at Tilbury in 1588, when she addressed her troops before the arrival of the Armada.[20] In this instance Elizabeth draws on the discourse of the sovereign's two bodies, which she had previously utilised to acknowledge the frailty of her own female body natural, whilst indicating through images of masculinity her role as king in the body politic. Elizabeth was therefore able to style herself as both queen and king, a mother to her people and a prince married to her kingdom. This strategy enabled Elizabeth to present a positive role model for a female ruler as well as negotiating the pressure from her Parliament to marry. As Leah Marcus has argued, however, Elizabeth's strategy of adopting masculine characteristics, particularly in dressing as a military leader, also had the effect of suggesting the threatening female sexuality of an Amazon, together with the fluidity of gender roles, something which threatens the emasculation of her male subjects.[21]

The queen herself was also a significant participant in the manufacturing of her own image, although it is ironic that, for such a prolific producer of speeches and letters, Elizabeth displayed extreme nervousness about both. One of her mottoes was 'video et taceo' – 'I see and keep silent'[22] – and she repeatedly refers to her own uncertainty about whether to speak or to keep silent: in a Latin oration at the University of Oxford in 1566 she began 'For a long time, truly, a great doubt has held me: Should I be silent or should I speak? If indeed I should speak, I would make evident to you how uncultivated I am in letters; however, if I remain silent my incapacity may appear to be contempt';[23] and she concluded a speech to Parliament in 1576 with

> And thus as one which yieldeth you more thanks – both for your zeal unto myself and service in this Parliament – than my tongue can utter, I recommend you to the assured guard and best keeping of the Almighty, who will preserve you safe, I trust, in all felicity. And wish withal that each of you had tasted some drops of Lethe's flood to deface and cancel these my speeches out of your remembrance.[24]

Similarly in her second reply to Parliament on their urging that Mary, Queen of Scots, should be executed,

Then her majesty turned to the lords and said that she never had a greater strife within herself than she had that day, whether she should speak or be silent, lest if she should speak, in showing her affection she might seem to dissemble, and if she should be silent she might do them wrong in not answering their expectations.[25]

Sometimes the queen tried to suppress discussion altogether: the editors of the *Collected Works* note that 'There is recurrent evidence that Elizabeth made efforts to keep most of her verses out of general circulation', and she forbade debate about the succession in Parliament.[26]

In part this urge to reticence is attributable to the fact that, as a young princess in particular, Elizabeth was acutely aware of the difficulties attendant upon self-expression. Writing to her brother Edward VI, she declares, 'it is (as your majesty is not unaware) rather characteristic of my nature not only not to say in words as much as I think in my mind, but also, indeed, not to say more than I think'. Cordelia-like, she also tells him 'What cause I had of sorry when I heard first of your majesty's sickness all men might guess but none but myself could feel, which to declare were or might seem a point of flattery, and therefore to write it I omit'.[27] Elizabeth was well aware that any communicative process could be potentially treacherous, as is shown in a slightly later letter to her sister Queen Mary protesting that

> as for the traitor Wyatt, he might peradventure write me a letter, but on my faith I never received any from him. And as for the copy of my letter sent to the French king, I pray God confound me eternally if ever I sent him word, message, token, or letter by any means, and to this my truth I will stand to my death.

Even fluency could be dangerous, as is sharply registered in her letter to the Lord Protector 'as concerning that point that you write – that I seem to stand in mine own wit in being so well assured of mine own self – I did assure me of myself no more than I trust the truth shall try'.[28] Silence, though, was an equally perilous course. In the letter to Mary protesting her innocence with regard to Wyatt, the editors note that 'Diagonal lines fill the interval between the body of the letter and its ending to prevent unwanted insertions'. It then concludes 'I humbly crave but one word of answer from yourself': at all costs the dialogue must be kept open.[29]

Not least because of the perils posed by the Mary, Queen of Scots, situation, Elizabeth as a queen continued to be as much concerned about speech and its reliability as she had been as a princess. She feared above all the interpretative process that might be applied to her words. In her annotation of a subsidy bill sent to her by Parliament she wrote tartly that

> I know no reason why any my private answers to the realm should be made for prologue to a subsidies. But neither yet do I understand why such audacity should be used to make, without my license, an act of my words. Are my words like

lawyers' books, which nowadays go to the wire-drawers to make subtle doings more plain? Shall my princely consent be turned to strengthen my words that be not of themselves substantives?[30]

Bitter experience taught her that this was a serious fear, as when she had to write to James of Scotland in May 1586 that 'I muse much, right dear brother, how possibly my well-meant letter, proceeding from so faultless a heart, could be either misliked or misconstered'.[31] Whether she is writing herself as princess, queen, or even as king, Elizabeth always shows herself acutely aware that controlling the image she presents is a crucial strategy both for rule and, ultimately, for political and personal survival.

This book concentrates in particular on the multivalent nature of the queen's identity in literature, portraiture, sermons, pamphlets, and speeches, to explore the ways in which Elizabeth's iconography is used to address the thorny question of her gender and role as a female monarch. While some of the figurings we examine, such as Cynthia and the Fairy Queen, are well known, they take on a new complexion here in the light of recent scholarship, and we attend, too, to some significantly less familiar images of the queen as the Babylonian Queen Semiramis, and Lady Alchymia, the presiding deity of alchemy, as well as to how representations of the queen are utilised not only in colonialist discourse but on particular expeditions to the New World.

Scholarship on the iconography of Elizabeth is indebted to and has developed out of the ideas of Frances Yates and Roy Strong, who argued for the existence of a Cult of Elizabeth.[32] Recent historicist criticism has extended and contested their ideas that Elizabeth was able to create and disseminate an image for herself as a replacement for the Virgin Mary in post-Reformation England and that this served as a successful political tool to consolidate her position and overcome the difficulties concerning her gender.[33] The chapters in *Goddesses and Queens* are both informed by and engage with this fine work, and develop it in sophisticated explorations of the complex interaction between the queen, her image and her public, mapping on the one hand the degree of Elizabeth's agency in the formulation and dissemination of those iconic personae such as Cynthia and the Virgin Queen, and on the other those less proverbial, such as Deborah, the paradigmatic female ruler from the Old Testament.

The chapters are also concerned with the wider responses to these images of the Queen. One of the threads of discussion that runs throughout the book is the way in which, despite Elizabeth's best efforts, she was unable to exert complete control over her image and its circulation. Susan Doran has noted one subtle example of this lack of control in the portraits of the queen which were commissioned not by Elizabeth herself but by her courtiers.[34] Christopher Hatton, for example, had the Sieve portrait of c.1583 painted by Quentin Massys the Younger, to praise the queen's chastity and her commitment, like Aeneas, to founding an empire rather than to considerations of love. These emblems would have been pleasing to Elizabeth, but the portrait also reveals Hatton's own political agenda, as his sign is identified on the sleeve of the courtier in the background of the painting. Hatton was opposed to the proposed marriage between Elizabeth and the Duke of Anjou.[35] In this way the purpose and reception of the queen's image was far from homogenous. As these chapters testify, the queen's image was interpreted and appropriated by a range of audiences, to create a tradition of panegyric in which praise could serve the double purpose of eulogy and criticism, as well as producing a competing, negative discourse about the queen.[36]

This book falls into three sections. In Part I the chapters look at the diverse range of religious and quasi-religious images that were employed by and about Elizabeth, such as Deborah, the Jewish female leader from the Old Testament and one of the many Old Testament figures to whom Elizabeth was compared, the unlikely but suggestive parallel with Joan of Arc, and finally Lady Alchymia, the female deity in alchemical treatises.

The Biblical figure of Deborah is one example of a figuring of the queen used by both Elizabeth and her clergy.[37] The relationship between each of their uses of the figure of Deborah reveals how this idealisation of Elizabeth as a means of flattering her could in fact be used as a double-edged weapon, containing covert reminders to the queen when she appeared to fall short of the ideal and was perceived to be failing to defend the Protestant faith.[38] In 'Elizabeth I as Deborah the Judge: Exceptional Women of Power', Carol Blessing explores this tension. On the one hand, Deborah appears to be an ideal model for Elizabeth I, as she is presented as both a political and a spiritual leader, whose role as judge involved the interpretation and adjudication of Hebrew law. Deborah was also involved in the commissioning of troops for battle against the Canaanites and then composing a hymn of victory. The parallel between Deborah and Elizabeth was made particularly at the beginning of Elizabeth's reign, indeed one of her coronation pageants makes this connection explicit. The emphasis here is that, like Deborah, Elizabeth should govern with true judgement and in close consultation with her parliament.

> In the fifth was a seat royal, wherein was placed Deborah, a Queen of the Jews that ruled Israel eleven years, having about her all her counsellors to talk and consult of the realm and benefit of the conmmonwealth.[39]

On the other hand, Deborah's status as a female governor and wife and mother meant that she could be used, particularly by her clergy and Commons, to offer a critique of the queen's behaviour as her reign progressed. As it became increasingly likely that the queen would not marry and produce children, the use of Deborah in sermons and speeches took on an increasingly coercive and ironic edge.[40]

Ben Spiller, in 'Warlike Mates? Queen Elizabeth, and Joan La Pucelle in *1 Henry VI*', examines how the famous address at Tilbury established and perpetuated her iconic status as a king-like queen, not only by claiming that her heart and stomach were of a decidedly masculine constitution, but by her rallying of her army while mounted upon a horse.[41] The cultural significance of Elizabeth's decision to partly mirror the appearance of her male soldiers and establish herself as an iconic woman war leader is recalled in 1590 by the dramatist(s) of *1 Henry VI*. Although in the play the female soldier is the French Catholic Joan La Pucelle, apparent antithesis to England's Protestant monarch, her self-assured leadership of her army and display of intense patriotism come dangerously close to being possible echoes of the queen's conduct and speech two years earlier. Spiller argues that Elizabeth's self-fashioning of iconic warrior queen in 1588 made sufficient impact on the late Elizabethan imagination to invite the first audiences of *1 Henry VI* to draw potential parallels between Joan La Pucelle and the English queen, and that, at the same time, it exposes some of the darker potential undercurrents of ostensibly laudatory iconography.[42] Spiller develops this argument by considering how the relationship between Joan and Elizabeth was established in the Royal Shakespeare Company production of *1 Henry VI* in 2000.

The gradual transformation of Elizabeth's image from *chaste* virgin to *perpetual* virgin has been the discussion of much recent criticism on Elizabeth I (and is an idea similar to that explored in the Shekhar Kapur film).[43] This process of changing oneself to bring a new identity into existence has much in common with the discourse of Alchemy. Elizabeth's own transformation therefore offers analogies with the alchemical process, something reinforced by her own representation in alchemical treatises as its presiding deity Lady Alchymia. Again, however, this association offers a negative reading of the queen and her own self-fashioning, since alchemy was regarded as a pseudo-science, something with which the gullible could be tricked out of money. The alchemical processes involved in the quest for the Philosopher's Stone, which offered the key not only to eternal life but also to the knowledge of how to transform metals into gold, were couched in religious terminology. The appropriation of such language offered less than flattering parallels with the Queen and the strategies of her own cult. It is perhaps most famously satirised in Ben Jonson's *The Alchemist*, first published in 1610, in which Dol Common disguises herself as the Queen of Fairy. One year earlier, in 1609, the first Folio edition of *The Faerie Queene* was published; *The Alchemist* seems, therefore, to be alluding to *The Faerie Queene* and its particular place within the tradition of royal panegyric. Jonson, it seems, in Dol's rendering of the Fairy Queen and in her attempts to gull Dapper, is deliberately sending up Elizabeth and her cult.[44]

In '"Rudenesse it selfe she doth refine": Queen Elizabeth I as Lady Alchymia', Jayne Archer contends that alchemy provided one of the most important imaginative and intellectual frameworks through which Elizabethans saw, interpreted, and reshaped their worlds. Tracing back the idea of the interdependency of philosophers and monarchs to Plato's *Republic*, Archer argues that this relationship was particularly fraught during the latter half of the sixteenth century, when a vital aspect of any monarch's ability to wield and to control power in others was seen to lie in his or her ability to control alchemical knowledge. Alchemists such as William Blomfild and John Dee, for example, approached the queen in their bids for patronage; each promised the imminent discovery of the Philosopher's Stone, and, with it, absolute power and eternal life. And each imagined their queen as Lady Alchymia, the presiding deity of alchemy. Archer makes the case that Queen Elizabeth's representation as Lady

Alchymia is a significant, although largely overlooked, aspect of the iconographic arsenal upon which subjects could draw in order to reimagine their queen and themselves. She examines Queen Elizabeth's representation as Lady Alchymia in order to argue that, by figuring Queen Elizabeth as the muse of alchemy, natural philosophers and alchemists were able to petition the queen on behalf of their own experiments and schemes, and also to serve a surprising range of cultural and political purposes. In the hands of alchemists such as William Blomfild, for example, this use of iconography was, in part, a coercive strategy, motivated by self-interest and by an explicitly Protestant agenda. In the writings of John Dee and poets such as John Davies, more subtle meanings are encoded, and the figure of Lady Alchymia is used to interrogate the nature of the patron/client relationship. Their work also examines the notion, common in alchemical literature, that women possess a unique, privileged and unsettling knowledge of the secrets of Nature.

Part II turns to one of the major enterprises of the Elizabethan era, the attempt to colonise the New World, during which the eastern seaboard of America was renamed Virginia in celebration of the Virgin Queen. The naming of the land in this way reveals the complex relationship between the discourse of gender and power and the ways in which Elizabeth's body became key in the ideological underpinning of England's imperialist project.

It has been suggested that, particularly in the paintings of the queen after 1570, the emphasis on Elizabeth's virginity is a response to specific political events such as England's relations with Spain and the succession.[45] In this way Elizabeth's virginity becomes an important quality in presenting England as a powerful nation. In the Ditchley portrait (figure 4), for example, painted around 1592 for Sir Henry Lee, the identification between the body of the Virgin Queen and her island nation is made explicit. Here Elizabeth the inviolate virgin stands on a map of England, protecting it beneath the skirts of her dress; both she and the land she governs are impenetrable. The unity between land and body in this painting recalls Elizabeth's Tilbury speech in which she deliberately employs the trope of land as feminine, when she describes the threat of Spanish invasion in terms of rape:

> I ... think foul scorn that Parma or Spain, or any Prince of Europe should dare to invade the borders of my realm, to which rather than any dishonour shall grow by me, I myself will take up arms.[46]

The overriding sense in both examples is of Elizabeth as both the protector of and ruler over her people. The sheer size of the towering figure of the queen, with her ageless face, presents an image of the superhuman. The Ditchley potrait is the largest painting of Elizabeth and its influential role in the official propaganda of empire can be seen in the way in which the queen's image is used by those she authorised to carry out the colonisation of the Americas. In 1595 for example, when Sir Walter Ralegh embarked on the first Guiana voyage in the hope of locating El Dorado, he took with him a picture of the queen. During his stay in Trinidad, when he sacked the capital of the island, San Jose, and captured the Spanish governor, Ralegh then produced a picture of Elizabeth and offered her protection to the native tribes of the island:

> I made them understand that I was the servant of a Queene, who was the great Casique of the north and a virgin, and had more Casiqui under her then there were trees in their Iland: that she was an enemy to the Castellani in the respect of their tyrannie and oppression, and that she delivered all such nations about her, as were by them oppressed, and having freed all the coast of the northern world from their servitude had sent me to free them also, and with al to defend the countrey of Guiana from their invasion and conquest. I shewed them her majesties picture which they so admired and honored, as it had beene easie to have brought them Idolatrous thereof.[47]

The contrast between the anticipated scale of the success of the English colonial enterprise and the image of Elizabeth used by Ralegh to legitimise his project in Guiana is something which is explored in this section. The first chapter, Deanne Williams's 'Elizabeth I: size matters', considers the development of the iconography of Elizabeth as a collaborative enterprise, through the examination of some of the most famous paintings of Elizabeth, paying particular attention to *The Ditchley portrait*, the Siena *Sieve Portrait* and the *Rainbow Portrait*. The chapter documents the dialectic between images of the great and the small in these paintings and other cultural artefacts, which Williams argues provided a potent metaphor for the relationship between tiny England and the increasingly vast empire which it aspired to control.

Next, Heather Campbell in '"And in their midst a sun": Petrarch's *Triumphs* and the Elizabethan Icon' notes that a good deal has been written on the subject of Elizabeth's identification with Petrarch's Laura, but that the emphasis tends to have been placed on the Laura of the sonnets. Campbell contends, however, that before 1558 *I Trionfi* was by far the more popular of Petrarch's vernacular works and, in both the pageantry and the portraiture, it is with the Laura of *I Trionfi* that Elizabeth consistently identifies herself. The most notable texts are the Coronation Procession, the Siena Sieve portrait, the Ermine portrait and the Procession to Blackfriars, which are discussed in detail, but *I Trionfi* is also invoked repeatedly and consistently in the progresses, in woodcuts and even in posthumous portraits. Campbell argues that the evocation of *I Trionfi* was calculated to appeal to the established and respectable courtiers, the old guard whose support Elizabeth emphatically needed, in a move which is closely parallel to the repeated use of the image of the Roman empire to validate the desired attempt to construct an English one. As the lady of the sonnets she would figure as desirable, chaste and unattainable, certainly, but the romantic vocabulary for the text would have been limiting, and potentially damaging to her political credibility. Her identification with Laura the triumphator recuperated the potential of the lady of the sonnets, but added the desired imperial dimension, with its quasi-masculine implications of power. The vocabulary of victory and the evocation of Rome supported her position as monarch, neutralising the problems inherent in her gender at the same time as the Laura-image exploited her feminine potential.

Finally, Helen Burgess in '"Nature without labor": Virgin Queen and Virgin Land in Sir Walter Ralegh's *The Discoverie of the Large, Rich and Bewtiful Empyre of Guiana*' takes as her text Sir Walter Ralegh's *The Discovery of Guiana*, which was first published in 1596, following a disastrous voyage to the Orinoco basin in search of the legendary 'El Dorado', or City of Gold. Ralegh's *Discovery of Guiana* is not only a historical account of the voyage but it also allows us to explore the relationship between Elizabeth the 'Virgin Queen' of England, and her virtual counterpart, Guiana, the 'virgin land' Ralegh proposes to conquer in her name. Burgess argues that in Ralegh's rhetoric, Elizabeth's virginity and the virginity of Guiana are linked through the images of wise management and sustainability of resources. These 'virgin' tropes may help justify Ralegh's presence in Guiana, but they also provide the justification for her projected conquest. Despite Ralegh's protestation that he comes to protect the land from the marauding Spaniards, the land is already figured as a body implicitly ripe for plunder. The link between the body of the queen and her wise use of resources ultimately covers up England's desperate need for a 'virgin land' in the face of a country already beginning to suffer the effects of deforestation and 'excess manurance'. England, despite Elizabeth's careful husbandry, is not a sustainable environment. Once again, then, an apparently celebratory image of Elizabeth as a Virgin Queen proves to throw a dark shadow.

Part III focuses on the ways in which the classical world was plundered for modes of imaging and figuring the queen. The continuing prestige of the classical world, and the enduring myth of the *translatio imperii*, made it an obvious *locus* to turn to for appropriate figurings of legitimate and desirable rule. This too, however, was an iconographical manoeuvre that was not without its attendant difficulties, since, though the classical world certainly afforded many memorable female rulers, most notably Cleopatra, Dido, and Semiramis, these presented considerable difficulties because all these queens were as notorious for the extravagance of their love-lives as famous for the fact of their rule.

Chapter 7, 'The dark side of the moon: Semiramis and Titania', Lisa Hopkins explores a particularly problematic precedent, Semiramis, who posed considerable iconographical difficulties because her story included so many elements and encompassed such extremes. She was said variously to be the epitome of valour and discretion and a woman crazed with lust, whose passions allegedly extended even to bulls and horses; to have been transformed into a dove; to have dressed as a man; to have built Babylon; to have slept with her own son; and to have invented castration. Because of the alleged infatuation for a bull, she was sometimes coupled with Pasiphaë or Lais, other emblems of female lust, but equally she was frequently presented as a nonpareil. Despite this instability in her role, however, references to her are frequent in writing of the earlier part of Elizabeth's reign, and Hopkins explores the ways in which these texts range across the spectrum of the cultural meanings that could be made of Semiramis.

One of the many plays that glances at Semiramis is Shakespeare's *A Midsummer Night's Dream*, which has a reference to the tomb of her husband Ninus and features a fairy queen who becomes infatuated with a man with the head of a donkey. In 'Evaluating virginity: *A Midsummer Night's Dream* and the iconography of marriage', Annaliese Connolly argues that Shakespeare's play is infused with the myth of Dido, Queen of Carthage, and that Shakespeare is, in fact, deliberately referring to Marlowe's *Dido, Queen of Carthage*, making use of words found elsewhere only in Marlowe's play to purposely signal the thematic links between *Dido* and *A Midsummer Night's Dream*. Dido's other name of Elissa made her an obvious emblem of Elizabeth; Connolly argues, however, that Shakespeare invokes *Dido* primarily to align himself with its satirical treatment of courtly entertainment, whilst underlining the importance of the humour of Marlowe's play. In a play that ostensibly celebrates its queen, some rather darker meanings can in fact be discerned.

In Chapter 9, 'Cynthia waning: *Cynthia's Revels* imagines the death of the queen', Matthew Steggle examines Cynthia, the virgin moon-goddess, who was one of the most important avatars of Elizabeth, featuring in works ranging from *The Faerie Queene* to court pageants, and from Lyly's drama to Ralegh's lyric. As recent critics have noted in connection with Elizabethan panegyric, the moon stands problematically on the celestial border between a sublunary, mortal world, subject to time and death, and the unchanging heavens above: there is a growing tension in lunar representations of the ageing Elizabeth in the last decades of her reign, as the prospect of her death and succession become more thinkable. Furthermore, at the accession of James, ideas of Elizabeth as Cynthia are transferred into a narrative in which James is figured as the sun-god Apollo, bringing true day after Cynthia's night. Steggle's chapter locates the latest Elizabethan figurations of Elizabeth as Cynthia, in Jonson's *Cynthia's Revels*, in the political context of its first performance in 1600–1601, to examine how this text can seen as anticipating that ideological shift. Steggle argues that, while her representation as Cynthia in Jonson's play may contain panegyric of the queen, it also encodes expectations and ideological figurations of both her death and the succession.

Finally, Scott L. Newstok in '"Turn thy Tombe into a Throne": Elizabeth's Death Rehearsal' provides a coda to the book by considering Elizabeth's initial figuration of her virginal intentions in her first speech to Parliament. Newstok argues that this speech, which ended with a coy but forceful epitaphic gesture, effectively inaugurated a pattern of subsequent manifestations as Diana, Cynthia, Gloriana, and the Virgin Mary. His analysis focuses on this gesture as a rhetorical and performative move that, by creating a statement of supposedly retrospective *fact*, thereby helps *consolidate* the very state purportedly *described*. This peculiar manner of deathly self-projection became prevalent in the Elizabethan period, partly in response to the Protestant reformations of memorial practices (which perhaps led to increased anxiety about presenting one's own epitaph). Indeed, Elizabeth appears to have been the first major public figure in

England to declare this kind of anticipatory retrospection. Playing out this epitaphic tension in the public sphere was somewhat risky; the 1352 Statute of Edward III explicitly defines treason to include even merely 'compassing or imagining the King's death'. By invoking the iconography of epitaphic virginity, was Elizabeth allowing others to imagine or compass the iconography of her own death? Newstok begins by examining at length the versions of her first speech to Parliament (including Camden's later revision), and also compares the rhetoric of Elizabeth's epitaphic iconography to the supposed epitaph of Malory's Arthur (which likewise has a curious temporal projection: 'once and future') along with subsequent rulers, including Charles I (and *Eikon Basilike*). Elizabeth inaugurated, in effect, a new kind of speech act: the 'preliminary auto-epitaph', which served as an initial and forceful move to control the attempts of others, as W.C. Fields put it, 'to write your epitaph'. Newstok's chapter thus neatly summarises the enormously wide range of Elizabeth's iconographical repertoire of its appeal, and provides a fitting end to a book which ranges so widely across the allegorical personae of the queen.

Notes

1. W.C. Sellar and R.J. Yeatman, *1066 and All That* (Harmondsworth: Penguin Books 1960), pp. 65–66.
2. See for instance James Knowles, '"To Enlight the Darksome Night, Pale Cinthia Doth Arise": Anna of Denmark, Elizabeth I and the Images of Royalty', in *Women and Culture at the Courts of the Stuart Queens* (Basingstoke: Palgrave Macmillan, 2003), pp. 21–48.
3. See Louis Montrose, '"Shaping Fantasies": Figurations of Gender and Power in Elizabethan Culture', in *Representing the Renaissance*, edited by Stephen Greenblatt (Berkeley: University of California Press, 1988), p. 122.
4. Courtney Lehmann, 'Crouching Tiger, Hidden Agenda: How Shakespeare and the Renaissance are Taking the Rage out of Feminism', *Shakespeare Quarterly* 53.2 (Summer 2002), pp. 260–279, p. 278.
5. See Julia M. Walker, *The Elizabeth Icon 1603–2003* (Houndmills: Palgrave Macmillan, 2004), pp. 185–193.
6. See Michael Dobson and Nicola J. Watson, *England's Elizabeth: An Afterlife in Fame and Fantasy* (Oxford: Oxford University Press, 2002), pp. 257–267.
7. See Julianne Pidduck, '*Elizabeth* and *Shakespeare in Love*: Screening the Elizabethans', in *Film/Literature/Heritage: A Sight and Sound Reader*, edited by Ginette Vincendeau (London: British Film Institute, 2001), pp. 130–135, p. 130, and Daniel Rosenthal, *Shakespeare on Screen* (London: Hamlyn, 2000).
8. See Julia M. Walker, *The Elizabeth Icon 1603–2003* (Houndmills: Palgrave Macmillan, 2004), pp. 201–209.
9. For an interview with Helen Mirren and Nigel Williams, the script writer, see the Channel Four website at: http://www.channel4.com/history/microsites/H/history/e-h/elizabeth102.html
10. For details of the series and an opportunity to watch clips from the series see the BBC website at: http://www.bbc.co.uk/drama/virginqueen/
11. See Thomas Betteridge, 'A Queen for All Seasons: Elizabeth I on Film', in *The Myth of Elizabeth*, edited by Susan Doran and Thomas S. Freeman (Houndmills: Palgrave Macmillan, 2003), pp. 242–259.

12. Carole Levin and Jo Eldridge Carney, 'Young Elizabeth in Peril: From Seventeenth Century Drama to Modern Movies', in *Elizabeth I: Always Her Own Free Woman*, edited by Carole Levin, Jo Eldridge Carney, and Debra Barrett-Graves (Aldershot: Ashgate, 2003), p. 232.

13. Lehmann, 'Crouching Tiger, Hidden Agenda', p. 260.

14. Renée Pigeon, '"No Man's Elizabeth": The Virgin Queen in Recent Films', in *Retrovisions: Reinventing the Past in Film and Fiction*, edited by Deborah Cartmell, I.Q. Hunter, and Imelda Whelehan (London: Pluto, 2001), pp. 8–24, p. 10.

15. Pigeon, '"No Man's Elizabeth", pp. 20–21.

16. Robert Lacey, *Sir Walter Ralegh* (London: Weidenfeld & Nicolson, 1973), p. 170.

17. Sally Harper, '"A Dittie to the tune of Welsh Sydannen": A Welsh image of Queen Elizabeth', *Renaissance Studies* 19.2 (April 2005), pp. 201–228, p. 211.

18. For discussion of Elizabeth as David see Michele Osherow, '"A poore shepherde and his sling": A Biblical Model for a Renaissance Queen', in *Elizabeth I: Always Her Own Free Woman*, edited by Carole Levin, Jo Eldridge Carney, and Debra Barrett-Graves (Aldershot: Ashgate, 2003), pp. 119–130.

19. William Leigh, *Queene Elizabeth, paralleled in her princely virtues, with Dauid, Iosua, and Hezekia ... in three sermons* (1612). Quoted from *Early English Books Online*. Also cited in Alexandra Walsham, '"A Very Deborah?": The Myth of Elizabeth I as a Providential Monarch', in *The Myth of Elizabeth*, edited by Susan Doran and Thomas S. Freeman (Houndmills: Macmillan, 2003), p. 146.

20. Laura Levine, *Men in Women's Clothing: Anti-Theatricality and Effeminization 1579–1642* (Cambridge: Cambridge University Press, 1994), p. 7.

21. Leah Marcus, *Puzzling Shakespeare: Local Reading and Its Discontents* (Berkeley: University of California Press, 1988), pp. 51–105.

22. See Mary Thomas Crane, '"Video et Taceo": Elizabeth I and the Rhetoric of Counsel', *Studies in English Literature* 28 (1988), pp. 1–15, p. 2.

23. Leah S. Marcus, Janel Mueller, and Mary Beth Rose, eds, *Elizabeth I: Collected Works* (Chicago: University of Chicago Press, 2000), p. 90.

24. Marcus et al., *Elizabeth I: Collected Works*, p. 171.

25. Marcus et al., *Elizabeth I: Collected Works*, p. 196.

26. Marcus et al., *Elizabeth I: Collected Works*, pp. xx and 102.

27. Marcus et al., *Elizabeth I: Collected Works*, pp. 16 and 36.

28. Marcus et al., *Elizabeth I: Collected Works*, pp. 42 and 32.

29. Marcus et al., *Elizabeth I: Collected Works*, p. 42.

30. Marcus et al., *Elizabeth I: Collected Works*, p. 103.

31. Marcus et al., *Elizabeth I: Collected Works*, p. 281.

32. See Frances Yates, *Astraea: The Imperial Theme in the Sixteenth Century* (London: Routledge, 1975), and Roy Strong, *The Cult of Elizabeth: Elizabethan Portraiture and Pageantry* (Berkeley: University of California Press, 1977), *Gloriana: The Portraits of Queen Elizabeth I* (New York: Thames and Hudson, 1987).

33. See Louis Montrose, 'The Elizabethan Subject and the Spenserian Text', in *Literary Theory/ Renaissance Texts*, edited by Patricia Parker and David Quint (Baltimore: Johns Hopkins University Press, 1986), pp. 303–340, and '"Shaping Fantasies"'; Philippa Berry, *Of Chastity and Power: Elizabethan Literature and the Unmarried Queen* (London: Routledge, 1989); Susan Frye, *Elizabeth I: The Competition for Representation* (Oxford: Oxford University Press, 1993); Helen Hackett, *Virgin Mother, Maiden Queen: Elizabeth I and the Cult of the Virgin Mary* (Houndmills: Macmillan, 1995); and Levin, Carney and Barrett-Graves, eds, *Elizabeth I: Always Her Own Free Woman*.

34. See Doran and Freeman, eds, *The Myth of Elizabeth*, p. 10.

35. See Susan Doran, 'Virginity, Divinity and Power: The Portraits of Elizabeth I', in *The Myth of Elizabeth*, edited by Susan Doran and Thomas S. Freeman (Houndsmill: Macmillan, 2003), pp. 171–199.

36. See Julia M. Walker, ed., *Dissing Elizabeth: Negative Representations of Gloriana* (Durham: Duke University Press, 1998).

37. See Michele Osherow, '"Give Ear O' Princes": Deborah, Elizabeth, and the Right Word', *Explorations in Renaissance Culture* 30.1 (Summer 2004), pp. 111–119.

38. See Alexandra Walsham, '"A Very Deborah?": The Myth of Elizabeth I as a Providential Monarch', in *The Myth of Elizabeth*, edited by Susan Doran and Thomas S. Freeman (Houndsmill: Macmillan, 2003), pp. 143–168.

39. See Richard Grafton, *Grafton's abridgement of the Chronicles of England. Newly and diligently corrected and finished the last of October 1570* (London: Richard Tottel, 1570) (STC 12151), 178v–179r, in *The Queen's Majesty's Passage & Related Documents*, edited by Germaine Warkentin (Toronto: Victoria University in the University of Toronto, 2004), pp. 110–113.

40. See Donald Stump, 'Abandoning the Old Testament: Shifting Paradigms for Elizabeth, 1578–82', *Explorations in Renaissance Culture* 30.1 (Summer 2004), pp. 89–109, p. 89.

41. Frances Teague, 'Queen Elizabeth in Her Speeches', in *Gloriana's Face: Women, Public and Private, in the English Renaissance* (Hemel Hempstead: Harvester Wheatsheaf, 1992), pp. 63–78.

42. See Marcus, *Puzzling Shakespeare*, pp. 51–105.

43. See, for example, Hackett, *Virgin Mother* and 'Icons of Divinity: Portraits of Elizabeth I', in *Renaissance Bodies: The Human Figure in English Culture c.1540–1660*, edited by Lucy Gent and Nigel Llewellyn (London: Reaktion Books, 1990), pp. 11–35.

44. See Caroline McManus, 'Queen Elizabeth, Dol Common, and the Performance of the Royal Maundy', in *The Mysteries of Elizabeth I: Selections from English Literary Renaissance*, edited by Kirby Farrell and Kathleen Swaim (Amherst: University of Massachusetts Press, 2003), pp. 43–66.

45. See Doran, 'Virginity, Divinity and Power' and Hackett, 'Icons of Divinity: Portraits of Elizabeth I'.

46. See Louis Montrose, 'The Work of Gender in the Discourse of Discovery', *Representations* 33 (1991), pp. 1–41.

47. Sir Walter Ralegh, *The Discoverie of the Large, Rich and Bewtiful Empyre of Guiana*, edited by Neil L. Whitehead (Manchester: Manchester University Press, 1997), p. 134. See also Charles Nicholl, *The Creature in the Map: Sir Walter Ralegh's Quest for El Dorado* (London: Vintage, 1996).

Part I

A world in crisis: Elizabeth's iconography and religious tensions

1

Elizabeth I as Deborah the Judge: exceptional women of power

CAROL BLESSING

When Queen Elizabeth I, the first female Protestant monarch, was enthroned in 1558, male poets, artists, theologians, and statesmen struggled to represent this new phenomenon. They needed to legitimise Elizabeth's power in order to flatter her and maintain national order, yet do it in a guarded manner in order to continue containment of women. The use of classical and Christian precedents, as typical of Renaissance art and writings, often formed the basis of her representations. The classical sources have been addressed at some length: Frances Yates has focused on Elizabeth as Astraea, and Philippa Berry on Elizabeth's association with the goddess Diana.[1] More recently, studies have examined the linkage of female Biblical personages with Elizabeth, notably in the work of Alexandra Walsham and Robert Healey.[2] This chapter will probe further the pairing of Elizabeth with Deborah the Judge, the Bible figure most often used to describe Elizabeth's gynecocracy, to view the cultural constructs of the Hebrew woman who stood in both political and religious authority within Scriptures, and to link those constructions to the era's representations of the English queen.

According to the 1560 Geneva Bible, in verse 4 of chapter 4 of the Book of Judges, 'Deborah a Prophetesse the wife of Lapidoth judged Israel'.[3] This matter-of-fact statement, and the account of her successful years of leadership which follow, are the subjects of controversy and consternation for a great many commentators, in the early modern period as well as today. Deborah is unique in Scripture as a female who holds the post of judge, the precursor to the office of king in ancient Israel. A judge needed to understand, interpret, and adjudicate Hebrew law, an unusual responsibility for a female. While there may be other women who have power or influence in Scripture, Deborah alone is given the title to accompany, legitimise, and reinforce that authority. Deborah's position of judge is combined with the power to commission Barak, the captain of the Israelite army, to prophesy victory over the Canaanites, to lead Barak and his forces, and later to write a hymn of victory (Judges 5) praising God for the outcome (including the killing of Canaanite ruler Sisera by another brave woman,

Jael), making Deborah a true Renaissance woman. Within the Biblical passage Deborah receives high acclaim, for 'the land had reste fourtie years' (Judges 5:31, The Geneva Bible). Although the Biblical example raises hope that views of women's roles might be expanded, more often than not her interpreters relegated her to object status, altered to fit dominant religious and political modes of her day. Further, she seems ideal as a positive model for Elizabeth I; yet, their linkage often served not to elevate the position of women but to reinforce these two as anomalous females, thus limiting for both their power and influence.

Elizabeth's political position paralleled Deborah's; her single status, however, diverged from Deborah's roles of wife and mother. In her volume on Elizabethan entertainments, Jean Wilson notes that explicit connections between the two women occurred mainly in the beginning of Elizabeth's reign, possibly anticipating a future marriage and children for the queen.[4] The Hebrew Bible scholar J. Cheryl Exum, however, finds that the Hebrew for 'the wife of Lappidoth' could also be rendered 'fiery woman', and Deborah's title of mother might be interpreted metaphorically to describe her relationship to her people (she is a 'mother in Israel'),[5] which more closely captures Elizabeth's portrayal as mother of England.

A noticeable change in both the number and type of references to Deborah in fact occurred during the earlier part of Elizabeth's reign. Elizabeth was referred to as 'England's Deborah', and apologists for women, theologians, writers of fiction, and creators of masques glorified the image of Deborah and Elizabeth to demonstrate not only the legitimacy of the right of Elizabeth, as woman, to rule, but the importance of the biblical example of Deborah. As she became the champion of Protestantism, Elizabeth's comparison to Deborah was seen as an important religious reinforcement for the queen's authority. Both Holinshed's account and the accounts anthologised by Nichols of the coronation pageants record the enactment of Elizabeth as Deborah, complete with palm tree (so labelled for the benefit of the non-tropical British onlookers) under which to rule. While Phillippa Berry interprets the coronational references to Deborah as emphasising Elizabeth's military role,[6] the implications extend further. The connection of England with Israel as God's chosen land was tied to Elizabeth as initiating a divine form of rule. Above the head of the 'seemelie and meet personage richlie apparelled in parlement robes' representing Elizabeth was another sign which read 'Debora the judge and restorer of the house of Israell: Judic. 4'. This figure was faced by players representing the nobility, clergy, and the commoners, who had before them a sign reading 'Debora with hir estates consulting for the good government of Israell'. Finally, a child came forward to 'open the meaning of the pageant', whose speech is recorded by Holinshed as follows:

> Jabin of Canaan king,
>   had long by force of armes.
> Opprest the Israelites,
>   which for God's people went:

But God minding at last.
        for to redresse their harmes,
The worthie Debora.
        as judge among them sent,
In warre she through Gods aid,
        did put hir foes to flight,
And with the dint of sword.
        the band of bondage brast.
In peace she, through Gods aid,
        did alwaie mainteine right,
And judged Israell.
        till fortie yeares were past.
A worthie president,
        o worthie queene thou hast,
A worthie woman judge,
        a woman sent for staie:
And that the like to us.
        indure alwaie thou maist,
Thy loving subjects will.
        with true harts and toonges praie.[7]

Holinshed's concluding commentary emphasises Elizabeth's need to share powers with a male Parliament, as he says

> The ground of this last pageant was, that for somuch as the next pageant before had set before hir graces eies the flourishing and desolate states of a commonweale, she might by this be put in remembrance to consult for the worthie governement of hir people, considering God oftentimes sent women noblie to rule among men, as Debora, which governed Israell in peace the space of fortie yeares: and that it behoveth both men and women so ruling to use advise of good councell.[8]

The coronation pageant exemplifies the hope placed in Elizabeth that she will not be a second Queen Mary, that she will serve her people as Deborah served Israel. Holinshed's commentary, however, reminds the new queen and her subjects as audience that she must listen to male counsel to rule properly, ignoring for the most part the issue of a woman's right of religious office, glossing over the woman's right to rule, and concentrating on her ability to receive counsel, a point peripheral to the Biblical account of Deborah. He subtly separates Deborah from the male Israelite judges by denying her autonomy, as he hints at Elizabeth's need for male thought to augment her own.

Elizabeth's visit to Norwich in 1578 prompted two more pageants presented in her honour, as recorded in Bernard Garter's *The Joyfull Receyving of the Queenes most excellent*

Majestie into hir Highnesse Citie of Norwich. Again using Deborah as a representation of the Queen, the second pageant emphasised the warlike aspect of the female judge's character, as the person portraying Deborah says:

> But he that neyther sleepes nor slackes such furies to correct,
> Appointed me Debora for the judge of his elect:
> And did deliver Sisera into a womans hande.
> I slewe them all, and so in rest his people helde the lande.[9]

Israel as the elect, God's chosen nation, becomes England in this enactment. The anticipation of rest for England under the female sovereign depends upon her appointment by God and her destruction of its enemies.

Spenser and Shakespeare also allude to Deborah in their works, invoking her military strength in possible deference to the Elizabethan coronation pageants. Spenser cites Deborah as a model woman for her bravery in Book III of *The Faerie Queene*, one with whom contemporary women cannot compare. As he asks, 'Where be the brave atchievements doen by some [women]?' he complains, 'But when I read, how stout Debora strake proud Sisera … I swell with great disdaine' (III.4.7–9).[10] The Dauphin Charles, in *1 Henry VI*, compares Joan of Arc favourably to Deborah in possessing 'the spirit of deep prophecy' and in showing courage, as he says: 'Stay, stay thy hands! Thou art an Amazon, / And fightest with the sword of Deborah', pledging her his 'heart and hands' after her demonstration of valour in battle (I.2.104–12).[11] The play's condemnation of Joan as a witch who killed Englishmen obviously negates the positive qualities of La Pucelle, and subtly undermines the role model of Deborah. Holinshed, Shakespeare's most likely source, however, condemns the comparison of Joan with Deborah and other Biblical women, as he brands Pussell 'a damnable sorcerer suborned by satan' (III, p. 172).[12]

The English defeat of the Spanish Armada in 1588 further reinforced Elizabeth as the military Deborah leading her people to victory, celebrated in Oliver Pigge's 1589 *Meditations*[13] and raising a crucial point: who were England's enemies that Elizabeth, in her role of Deborah, was supposed to fight? If they did not actually exist, would they have been created to strengthen Elizabeth's association with Deborah? The Protestant reformers saw evil as the menace of Catholicism from within the country and Church practices. With the Armada attack, the threat of Spanish usurpation was raised, layering a national difference to the religious danger. Spanish invasion mirrored the Canaanite tyranny overcome by Deborah. One item of the Judges account was consistently overlooked in the parallel: the Israelites' sins had caused God to allow Jabin, King of Canaan, power over them.[14] No Elizabethan account of the story mentions the sins of the English as Deborah's people. The evil is seen as purely outside of the Anglican mainstream. Interestingly, Elizabeth chose to write one of her few works referring to herself as Deborah using Spanish, in a prayer in translation here from Marcus, Mueller, and Rose's important collection:

Oh my God, O my father, whose goodness is infinite and whose power is immense, who art accustomed to choose the weak things of this world in order to confound and destroy the strong, persist – persist for the glory of Thy name, for the honor of thy Son, for the repose and quietitude of Thine afflicted Church – in giving me strength so that I, like another Deborah, like another Judith, like another Esther, may free Thy people of Israel for the hands of Thy enemies. Lord, rise up and judge Thy cause.[15]

Why was the English Church perceived by Elizabeth and English Protestants as the afflicted one? Certainly, within England, the Catholic Church was the one under scrutiny and endangered. Within Europe the Reformation had created a division between Catholic and Protestant, forming competing notions of chosen nationhood. The divisions were headed by Spain and England, imperialism and religious domination merging into a cause aptly represented by competing iconography: Philip II as the Spanish Solomon versus Elizabeth I as the English Deborah. The idea of a perceived national and religious threat created greater cohesion, a greater purpose. The identification of Elizabeth with Deborah from her reign's inception solidified the nation's self-image. As Deborah had led God's chosen Israelites to defeat Sisera's Canaanite army, so Elizabeth would thwart the threatening Catholic infidels through Protestant leadership. With the Armada invasion of 1588, Elizabeth's saviour status had reached its peak. In the language of her enemies, Elizabeth prays for their defeat.

Religious writing, including Bible commentaries, glosses, and sermons wrestled with interpreting Deborah before, during, and after Elizabeth's reign, although her era created a marked increase in interest. The Catholic writings that predated Elizabeth usually presented Deborah as prophetess, suppressing her role as judge, thus limiting her position and power. The theological commentator Ian Maclean has linked the tradition that women have the power of prophecy with their greater proclivity to devotion, which, as he says, St Thomas Aquinas attributes to the females' shortage of rational thought.[16] Thus, the gift of prophecy is seen in some ways as a less positive attribute than that of humanity's God-given reason. Although Aquinas cites the example of Deborah in his discussion of prophets, he limits the contemporary female prophet to testifying in private rather than public spheres: 'Hence women, if they have the grace of wisdom or of knowledge, can administer it by teaching privately but not publicly.'[17]

Protestant reformers tread lightly in dealing with Deborah, their reverence for the authority of Scripture making it impossible for them to ignore passages that seemingly contradicted their own notions of gender roles. Many, as mentioned previously, worked to incorporate Elizabeth into their outlook. John Calvin's commentary on 1 Timothy 2:12, which states 'But I suffer not a woman to teach, nor to usurp authority over the man, but to be in silence', acknowledges the contradictory evidence presented by the example of Deborah. Calvin both legitimises the example and declares it an anomaly not to be repeated in his contemporary Church, in an argument often repeated by other Protestant commentators upon the passage.

If any one bring forward, by way of objection, Deborah (Judges iv. 4) and others of the same class, of whom we read that they were at one time appointed by the command of God to govern the people, the answer is easy. Extraordinary acts done by God do not overturn the ordinary rules of government, by which he intended that we should be bound. Accordingly, if women at one time held the office of prophets and teachers, and that too when they were supernaturally called to it by the Spirit of God, He who is above all law might do this; but, being a peculiar case, this is not opposed to the constant and ordinary system of government.[18]

Calvin's discussion betrays his bewilderment at God's use of female agency. His word choice of 'extraordinary', 'supernaturally', and 'peculiar' underlines the contrast to what he considers 'constant and ordinary' gender roles for issues of both religion and government.

One of the works that labours at more length to rewrite the Deborah story is John Knox's 1558 *The First Blast of the Trumpet Against the Monstrous Regiment of Women*. Here Knox acknowledges the account of Deborah in Judges, but denies that her example has any broader significance; it was, as he says, an isolated case, unusable as a precedent to support female political authority. Knox wishes to prove that Catholic Queen Mary's gender should void her claim to English rule, as he declares: 'it is more than a monster in nature that a woman shall reign and have empire above man'.[19]

Knox concedes that the example of Deborah, and also that of the prophetess Huldah (from 2 Chron. 34), did indeed exist in the Old Testament. He, however, argues against using these females' behaviour as examples for his own day, saying that 'particular examples do establish no common law',[20] and continues:

The causes were known to God alone: why he took the spirit of wisdom and force from all men of those ages and did so mightily assist women, against nature and against his ordinary course, that the one [Deborah] he made a deliverer to his afflicted people of Israel ... With these two women, I say, did God work potently and miraculously; yea, to them he gave most singular grace and privilege. But who hath commanded that a public, yea, a tyrannical and most wicked law be established upon these examples?[21]

This interpretation emphasises the power of God to violate his own pattern in creating the roles of these anomalous women. Knox points out that Deborah did not inherit her position through a royal lineage but through Divine appointment. Of course he fails to note that all the judges of Israel were similarly empowered, since the line of royal blood had yet to be established in this pre-king period:

For they are never able to prove that either Deborah, or any other godly woman, having the commendation of the Holy Ghost within the Scriptures, hath usurped authority above any realm or nation by reason of their birth and blood. Neither yet did they claim it by right or inheritance. But God, by privilege, favor, and grace, exempted Deborah from the common malediction given to women in that behalf; and against nature he made her prudent in counsel, strong in courage, happy in regiment, and a blessed mother and deliverer to his people.[22]

Deborah's example is counter to nature, says Knox, particularly her masculine attributes of prudence, strength, and leadership, as he underscores the 'common malediction given to women'. Within the context, the word 'malediction' refers to woman's inability to participate in patriarchal succession, her God-given weak character, or her curse, but Knox also unwittingly acknowledges the common malediction, in terms of perceptions, stereotypes, and prejudices directed towards women by men, a point reinforced by his entire missive. Even though Deborah clearly holds the office of judge, Knox rejects her precedence for his contemporary setting:

> If any stick to the term, alleging that the Holy Ghost saith that she judged Israel, let them understand that neither doth the Hebrew word, neither yet the Latin, always signify civil judgment or the execution of the temporal sword, but most commonly is taken in the sense which we have before expressed ... And so I doubt not but Deborah judged, what Israel had declined from God, rebuking their defection and exhorting them to repentance, without usurpation of any civil authority.[23]

Finally, says Knox, Deborah shares her power with Barak, who served as commander of Israel's army, thus diluting the representation of Deborah as leader of the triumphal army. Her authority was possible only in conjunction with a male's. 'She spoileth herself of all power to command', writes Knox of Deborah's appointment of Barak as captain to her troops.[24]

Robert Healey writes of John Knox's dissatisfaction with Elizabeth in religious decisions: failing to establish the all-encompassing reformation he had hoped for, 'the Deborah who appeared in Elizabeth Tudor did not meet Knox's standards'.[25] As previous studies have discussed, Deborah became linked through Elizabeth with the Protestant cause, symbolically cleansing England as Israel of its Canaanite enemies, the Catholics. What Healey asserts, however, is that Elizabeth's moderate religious views did not match the anti-Catholic zeal of Knox and others who desired a purging of papist practices within the English Church, not the compromised system Elizabeth authorised.

Knox's declamation against female rulers was answered by John Aylmer's 1559 work *An Harborowe for Faithfull and Trewe Subjectes, agaynst the late blowne Blaste, concerninge the Government of Wemen*, which was politically correct in upholding the authority of the new female monarch, Elizabeth. Women, says Aylmer, might more probably show God's power precisely because of what Knox criticised them for, their weaknesses, which can then be used an illustration of 2 Corinthians 12:9, 'My strenthe is moste perfight when you be moste weake'. Deborah becomes one of Aylmer's main points of scriptural argumentation, as Aylmer refutes Knox's attempts to isolate and undermine her account. One example is indeed sufficient to prove a case, says Aylmer, as he goes on to list other anomalies in Scripture that have been accepted. He upholds Deborah as in fact the best biblical example of woman's authority.

> Deborah shal marche in the first ranke and have the first place both for the antiquite of the tyme, the authoritie of the story, and the happy successe of hir reigne. Deborah (saieth the scripture) judged the people of Israell, and the people resorteth unto hir, she delyvered them out of thraldome, and set them at libertie. In this womans doinges is playnie set out that she both governed in peace and in war, and so did consequently al that any ruler by civil authorite might, or is wont to do. She judged saith the scripture ... This woman is counted of some of the Hebrues to be Barakes wife, and yet sent she him to the warre, gave him his commission and made him the generall, whereby appeareth that to be true, which we saide before: that a woman as a wife must be at commaundement, but a woman as a magistrate may lawfullye commaunde.[26]

The passage continues to reinforce the traditional Pauline domestic hierarchy of husband over wife, yet here permits civil authority of a woman, an interesting twist in logic when added to the English depictions of Elizabeth as wife to her country. A.N. McLaren's study cautions further that Aylmer's work cannot be read as unreservedly endorsing female governance, but allows for rule while still under a type of male headship, concluding 'Aylmer proposes loyalty to queen and council, to the queen insofar as she has been counselled – and counselled by men who are themselves godly'.[27] Elizabeth's coronational pageants, discussed earlier, dramatically enact the necessity for male counsel through Parliament.

Another Bible commentary dealing at some length with the 'Deborah issue' was the Italian reformer Pietro Martira Vermigli's painstaking phrase-by-phrase volume written in 1560 and translated into English circa 1564. Vermigli says God used Deborah as an illustration of how He could work despite weak human agency, as he also attempts to reinterpret the term judge, saying that the word 'oftentime signifieth to revenge, and to set at liberty'.[28] Vermigli then guardedly concedes Deborah's and, by extension Elizabeth's, leadership role: 'But if any man wil have the word of judgement to signify to set lawes, or to geve sentence of controversies, I wil not be much against it',[29] continuing 'But bicause Deborah was not onely a Prophetesse, but also in setting at liberty, governed civil things, I might therfore demaund, whether a woman may be appoynted to govern a pub:wealth'.[30] Vermigli's argument supports Elizabeth, whom he backed as a defender of Protestantism, while reinforcing Deborah's exceptionality. God may appoint a female monarch in lieu of the more desirable male heir, as the female judge was raised up only because no suitable males were available.

Deborah was also a popular subject in Elizabethan female praise books, books which, as Linda Woodbridge has successfully argued, often work against rather than for women by representing ideals not humanly achievable, or by holding out a few anomalies which are negated by contemporary behaviour.[31] A more recent essay by Alexandra Walsham similarly works to 'recognize the extent to which flattery can be a subtle but insistent form of exhortation and instruction'.[32] Walsham cogently theorises that identifying Elizabeth with Deborah and other biblical leaders serves to provide a means of control over the female Protestant monarch, by providing examples to follow, rather than actually reflecting Elizabeth's mode of rule and religious piety. Deborah, who should provide a liberating model, is shaped into a restrictive exemplum.

Deborah was discussed in the print dialogue concerning women prior to Elizabeth's reign, although there was a marked increase in the number and types of references to the female Hebrew judge during and even after the British gynecocracy. Among the authors who applauded Deborah were Henricus C. Agrippa, in *A Treatise of the Nobilitie and excellencye of women kynde*, translated by David Clapam circa 1534; Edward Gosynhill in *The prayse of all women / called mulieru pean*, written around 1544; C. Pyrrye, in *The Praise and Dispraise of Women*, 1569; I.G., in *An Apologie for Womenkinde*, 1605; and Lodowick Lloyd, in *The Choyce of Jewels*, 1607.[33] The example of Deborah was also ammunition for the satirical pamphlet wars precipitated by Joseph Swetnam's *The arraignment of lewde, idle, froward, and unconstant women*.[34] Ester Sowernam's *Ester hath hang'd Haman: or an Answere to a lewd Pamphlet, entitled The Arraignment of Women* lists Deborah among those used by God as 'instruments to derive his benefits to mankind'.[35] In *A Mouzell for Melastomus*, Rachel Speght particularly applauds Deborah for writing a hymn of thanksgiving to God, and Mary Tattle-well and Joan Hit-him-home use Sisera, the evil ruler whom Deborah and the Israelites defeated, as an example of a tyrannical male ruler in their work *The Women's Sharpe Revenge*.[36]

Thomas Bentley's 1582 *The Monument of Matrones: conteining seven severall Lamps of Virginitie* describes Deborah in glowing terms as a woman of both prophecy and at least partial power. Emphasising Deborah's prophetic rather than political skills, Bentley uses the phrase 'judged … by the spyrit of prophecy', a twisting of the Biblical account which separates the roles of judge and prophet, and thus once again subtly differentiates her appointment as judge from the males who held the same office.[37] Apparently he takes his interpretation from the 1560 edition of the Geneva Bible, which contained a gloss defining Deborah as acting 'by the Spirit of prophecie, resolving of controversies, & declaring the wil of God'. Anthony Gibson's *A Womans Woorth, defended against all the men in the world*, published in 1599, also mentions Deborah among other Biblical females as examples surpassing the virtue of men:

> Deborah, Judith and Hester, wrought mervailes for conservation of their people, even to the enterprise of so high actions, as the issue of them could not be apprehended, their beginnings were so dreadfull, their effects beyond comparison, and their vertue bounded within no equalitie, to the confusion of men, amazement of the Gods, and perpetuall memorie of the feminine sex.[38]

Despite Gibson's use of hyperbole, his assessment accurately captures the perplexity often expressed during the period by those trying to explain the example of Deborah, especially that her role is recorded in Scripture 'to the confusement of men'.

Other flattering books which used the example of Deborah continued well into the seventeenth century. Thomas Heywood's 1640 *The Exemplary Lives and Memorable Acts of Nine of the Most Worthy Women of the World* asserts that the illustration of Deborah was used in part by God to help keep men humble, as well as to build up women. Heywood atypically attributes all of the roles scripturally ascribed to Deborah without equivocation, those of prophet, judge, woman, wife, and mother.

> Whilst these things were thus in agitation, and the *Isrealites* were in this dejection, there lived Deborah who was a Prophetess, a woman of great sanctity and excellent knowledge, to whom the people resorted, not onely to heare those sacred and divine Oracles which she spake from God; but they also brought before her all differences and controversies, how dificult and doubtfull soever, which by her great wisedome, she reconciled and ended, insomuch that she lived as a Princesse or governesse; For as the Text reporteth of her, shee judged *Isreal*. This excellent woman dwelt in Mount Ephraim, under a Palme tree, betweene Ramah and Bethel, whether (as to our Courts of Justice) all the people of what condition or estate soever customably came to have their causes heard, and by her great wisdome decided.[39]

Heywood subsequently goes on to describe her as a 'godly Matron and gratious mother in Isreal'.[40] Further, the engraving included with his text portrays the heroine as a military victor, in Roman garb, and she is described as 'out-braving danger, and standing the brunt of the battell, against many thousands'.[41] Heywood's account of Deborah jointly compares her to Roman matrons and the goddess Minerva while creating remembrance of Elizabeth's Armada victory.

Because so much of what was seen of Deborah comes through the dominant culture's, i.e. male, viewpoint, it is interesting therefore to have another woman's perspective on her, as Aemilia Lanyer provides in her 1611 *Salve Deus Rex Judaeorum*. Lanyer chastises men for overlooking women's positive qualities when creating their vituperative accounts. Biblical heroines, says Lanyer, are divinely placed so as not only to remind males of the virtues of females but also to keep the men from becoming overly conceited, as divine correctives. Lanyer asserts that God

> gave power to wise and virtuous women, to bring down their [men's] pride and arrogancie. As was cruell Cesarus by the discreet counsell of noble Deborah, Judge and Prophetesse of Isreal ... All which is sufficient to inforce all good Christians and honourable minded men to speake revently of our sexe, and especially of all virtuous and good women.[42]

Lanyer's viewpoint is, however, undermined by Puritan commentaries and supporters of James I's patriarchal politics who once again rewrote Deborah, this time without having to worry about pleasing a female monarch. Richard Rogers's 1615 *A Commentary Upon the Whole Booke of Judges* draws upon the interpretations of Calvin, Knox, and Vermigli in presenting an anomalous woman. Rogers is quick to point out that Deborah's example is overturned by Paul's New Testament writings regarding the place and purpose of women, as he goes on to explain:

> Therefore wee must also heere take heed, that wee bring not that into example which the Lord hath wrought extraordinarily, when it hath pleased him: For wee are tied by Pauls rule, set downe to the Corinthians, to wit, that women keepe silence in the congregation. He addeth a reason, because they must bee subject to their husbands. But the teachers office is to have authority over those which are taught by them, and to governe them also as well as to instruct them, which is not permitted to the wife over her husband, neither over other men.[43]

Rogers exceeds the Pauline restrictions to extend the headship of women to all men, rather than limiting it to their husbands, as the subsequent silencing of Deborah and of all women follows the end of Elizabeth's rule. No female instruction of men would eliminate all semblance of political and spiritual authority for women, as Rogers's commentary employs slippage, moving from discussing ecclesiastical matters to civil leadership. The passage voices anxiety that claiming the Jewish heroine's example would undermine the structure of the Christian family as well as the Church. The fact that Elizabeth had no husband would not have exempted her from Rogers's logic, if she were not allowed headship over any man; the Puritan commentator seems to suffer from historical amnesia as he forgets his previous monarch's governance.

In contrast to Rogers's Puritanism, the circa 1610–1625 writer of *The 10 Pagean of Gedeon*, thought to be a Catholic priest, emphasises the roles of prophetess and mother in his portrayal of Deborah. The work is part of a group of seventeenth-century mystery plays known as the Stonyhurst Pageants. Interestingly, Deborah is depicted not only in the feminine role of comforter and nurturer but also in the position of priest and confessor. The chorus reports that the people of Israel 'to the prophetesse Debbora go for counsell in their misery & what comfort they shall receive from her shall streight be knowne'.[44] Then the Israelites cry out to her 'Mother Debbora we sory are that god we have offended', to which she responds in a manner that absolves them, 'And for the same by hym you shall from you foes be delivered'.[45] Clearly, Deborah is treated here as a prototype of Mary, as a mother and an intermediary between the Israelites and God. It is certainly possible that the pageant reinvokes nostalgia for the dead mother of England, Elizabeth.

With this play ends the large quantity of Deborah references, as the memory of Elizabeth I fades. What this study shows is how plastic the figure of this Biblical heroine was, and how her example and gender as a whole could be shaped in order to fit the female more comfortably into established patriarchal norms. Rewritten by Catholic authors into a prototype of Mary or a prophetess very much in the tradition of the female medieval mystics, Deborah loses the power to decide issues of law, and, often, to command the army of Israel. Reformed by Puritan males, Deborah changes into either a pseudo-judge unable to wield the authority held by male judges or a female whose aberrational example must be explained away with the words of Paul in order to forbid women from repeating her roles in contemporary times. She is viewed as a threat to established patterns of power, and the claim that she is an exceptional woman, whom God empowered only in exceptional circumstances, serves only to reinforce stereotypes of women as weak, domestic, and unable by nature to administer, govern, or show courage. Even the books and pamphlets intended to flatter women often treated Deborah as an exceptional example of virtue, and their use of exaggerated language often belied their supposed purpose.

Judith Butler's well-known discussion of the performative qualities of gender is applicable in this study, with a twist.[46] It is the Biblical commentators who see Deborah as a female masquerading in male roles of judicial and military leadership. Thus, their essentialist views of her as a woman are undisturbed by the traditionally masculine behaviours she exhibits. Likewise, the English queen becomes a female wearing the male guise of authority as a garment, and her parallels with Deborah are cited as means to reinforce this artifice. Elizabeth's own words in her speech at Tilbury, with its ringing proclamation that she has 'the harte and stomack of a king' despite having 'the body butt of a weake and feble woman' served to strengthen this perception.[47] The identification of Elizabeth with Deborah served to codify the idea that the queen of England was an extraordinary, rather than exemplary, female and thus limit the amount of influence she had in changing perceptions of women.

The appearance of Deborah in Scripture was obviously an issue with which early modern Englishmen had to grapple, as the period often drew from biblical antecedents in order to justify or establish male-dominated hierarchies pertaining to the family, the State, and the religious structures of the day. She is viewed as a threat to established patterns of power, and the claim that she is an exceptional woman, whom God empowered only in exceptional circumstances, serves to reinforce stereotypes of women as weak, domestic, and unable by nature to administer, govern, or show courage. Susan Frye argues convincingly, however, that Elizabeth is not a passive victim of her contemporary male constructs, asserting that 'Although Elizabeth was fashioned by her culture's complex expressions of gender roles and distinctions, those expressions were unstable enough to be inverted, extended, and contested in the public performance of herself as ruler of England'.[48] To what extent Elizabeth enjoyed, benefited from, and manipulated her pairing with Deborah is not evident in the queen's own works. None the less, the fact that Deborah and Elizabeth were a threat and a puzzle to men in early modern England served at least to create a small hole in the seamless fabric of the universe that they had created, one which held to patriarchal power modes of Church, State, and family. Although many of the writings on Elizabeth as Deborah attempted to restrain her authority and contain her, perhaps her own example helped disrupt the male mythology of kingship.

Notes

1. Frances Yates, *Astraea: The Imperial Theme in the Sixteenth Century* (London: Routledge and Kegan Paul, 1975); Philippa Berry, *Of Chastity and Power: Elizabethan Literature and the Unmarried Queen* (London: Routledge, 1989).

2. Alexandra Walsham, "'A Very Deborah?' The Myth of Elizabeth I as a Providential Monarch', in *The Myth of Elizabeth*, edited by Susan Doran and Thomas S. Freeman (Houndmills: Palgrave Macmillan, 2003), pp. 143–168; Robert M. Healey, 'Waiting for Deborah: John Knox and Four Ruling Queens', *Sixteenth Century Journal* 25.2 (1994), pp. 371–386.

3. Other English Bibles translated the verse similarly. The Wycliffe Bible stated.'Forsothe Delbora was a prophetesse, wijf of Laphidoth, that demyde [judged] the puple in that tyme', and the 1611 Authorised Version said 'And Deborah a prophetesse, the wife of Lapidoth, shee judged Israel at that time'. All following Biblical references are taken from the Geneva Bible.

4. Jean Wilson, *Entertainments for Elizabeth* (Totawa, NJ: Rowman & Littlefield, 1980), p. 7.

5. J. Cheryl Exum, '"Mother in Israel": A Familiar Figure Reconsidered', in *Feminist Interpretation of the Bible* (Philadelphia: Westminster Press, 1985), p. 85.

6. Berry, *Of Chastity and Power*, pp. 85–86.

7. Raphael Holinshed, *Holinshed's Chronicles of England, Scotland, and Ireland*, vols 3 and 4 (London: 1808), IV, p. 171.

8. Holinshed, *Chronicles*, IV, p. 171.

9. David Galloway, ed., *Norwich 1540–1642*, vol. 5 of *Records of Early English Drama* (Toronto: University of Toronto Press, 1984), p. 258.

10. Edmund Spenser, *The Faerie Queene*, edited by Thomas P. Roche, Jr (New Haven: Yale University Press, 1981), III.2.7–9.

11. William Shakespeare, *The First Part of King Henry VI*, edited by Andrew S. Cairncross (London: Methuen, 1962), I.2.104–112.

12. Holinshed, *Chronicles*, III, p. 172.

13. Oliver Pigge, *Meditations* (1589), cited in Walsham, '"A Very Deborah?"', p. 153.

14. Judges 4:1–3.

15. Leah S. Marcus, Janel Mueller, and Mary Beth Rose, eds, *Elizabeth I: Collected Works* (Chicago: University of Chicago Press, 2000), p. 157.

16. Ian Maclean, *The Renaissance Notion of Women* (Cambridge: Cambridge University Press, 1980), p. 21.

17. St Thomas Aquinas, *Summa Theologica*, 22 vols (London: Burns Oates & Washburne Ltd, 1935), vol. 14, p. 90.

18. John Calvin, *Commentaries on the Epistles to Timothy, Titus, and Philemon* (Edinburgh: Calvin Translation Society, 1856), p. 67.

19. John Knox, *The First Blast of the Trumpet Against the Monstrous Regiment of Women*, in *The Political Writings of John Knox*, edited by Martin A. Breslow (Washington, DC: Folger Library, 1985), p. 38.

20. Knox, *First Blast*, p. 65.

21. Knox, *First Blast*, p. 65.

22. Knox, *First Blast*, p. 67.

23. Knox, *First Blast*, pp. 69–70.

24. Knox, *First Blast*, p. 70.

25. Healey, 'Waiting for Deborah: John Knox and Four Ruling Queens', p. 386.

26. John Aylmer, *An Harborowe for Faithfull and Trewe Subjectes, agaynst the late blowne Blaste, concerninge the Government of Wemen, wherein be confuted all such reasons as a straunger of late made in that behalfe, with a breife exhortation to Obedience* (London, 1559), B3v.

27. A.N. McLaren, 'Delineating the Elizabethan Body Politic: Knox, Aylmer and the Definition of Counsel 1558–88', *History of Political Thought* 17.2 (Summer 1996, pp. 224–252, p. 245.

28. Pietro Martira Vermigli, *Most fruitfull & learned Commentaries of Doctor Peter Martir Vermil Florentine, Professor of Devinitie, in the Universitye of Tygure, with a very profitable tract of the matter and places in holy scripture* (London, 1564), fol. 93v.

29. Vermigli, *Most fruitfull & learned Commentaries*, fol. 93v.

30. Vermigli, *Most fruitfull & learned Commentaries*, fol. 93v.

31. Woodbridge writes, 'misogyny was a method of fortifying the male's dominant position against the incursions of increasingly libertarian women. The same can probably be said of the defense: attacks and defenses were complementary efforts at keeping women housebound, nurturing, chaste, modest, and silent.' Linda Woodbridge, *Women and the English Renaissance: Literature and the Nature of Womankind, 1540 to 1620* (Urbana: University of Illinois Press, 1984), p. 57.

32. Walsham, '"A Very Deborah?"', p. 144.

33. Henricus C. Agrippa, *A Treatise of the Nobilitie and excellencye of women kynde*, trans. David Clapam (London, c.1542); Edward Gosynhill, *The praise of all women/called mulieru pean* (London, c.1542); C. Pyrrye, *The Praise and Dispraise of Women, very fruitfull to the well disposed minde, and delectable to the readers therof* (London, 1569); I.G., *An Apologie for Womenkinde* (London, 1605); Lodowick Lloyd, *The Choyce of Jewels* (London, 1607).

34. Joseph Swetnam, *The arraignment of lewde, idle, froward, and unconstant women* (London, 1615).

35. Simon Shepherd, *The Women's Sharp Revenge: Five Women's Pamphlets from the Renaissance* (New York: St Martin's Press, 1985), p. 96.

36. Rachel Speght, *A Mouzell for Melastomus* (London, 1617), rpt. in Shepherd; Mary Tattle-well and Joan Hit-Him-Home [pseud.], *The Women's Sharpe Revenge: or An answer to Sir Seldom Sober that writ those railing Pamphlets called the Juniper and Crabtree lectures, etc.* (London, 1640), rpt. in Shepherd, pp. 159–193.

37. Thomas Bentley, *The Monument of Matrones: conteining seven severall Lamps of Virginitie, or distinct treatises; whereof the first five concerne praier and meditation: the other two last, precepts and examples, as the woorthie works partlie of men, partlie of women; compiled for the necessarie use of both sexes out of the sacred Scriptures, and other approoved authors* (London, 1582).

38. Anthony Gibson, *A Womans Woorth, defended against all the men in the world. Prooving them to be more perfect, excellent and absolute in all vertuous actions, then any man of what qualitie soever. Written by one that hath heard much, seene much, but knowes a great deale more* (London, 1599), p. 7.

39. Thomas Heywood, *The Exemplary Lives and Memorable Acts of Nine of the Most Worthy Women of the World: Three Jewes. Three Gentiles. Three Christians. Written by the Author of the History of Women* (London, 1640), pp. 9–10.

40. Heywood, *Exemplary Lives*, p. 18.

41. Heywood, *Exemplary Lives*, p. 19.

42. Aemelia Lanyer, *Salve Deus Rex Judaeorum* (London, 1611), f4.

43. Richard Rogers, *A Commentary Upon the Whole Booke of Judges* (London, 1615), p. 197.

44. Carleton Brown, *The Stonyhurst Pageants* (Baltimore: The Johns Hopkins Press, 1920), p. 116.

45. Brown, *Stonyhurst Pageants*, p. 116.

46. Judith Butler, *Gender Trouble: Feminism and the Subversion of Identity* (New York: Routledge, 1990).

47. Felix Pryor, *Elizabeth I: Her Life in Letters* (Berkeley: University of California Press, 2003), pp. 98–99.

48. Susan Frye, *Elizabeth I: The Competition for Representation* (New York: Oxford University Press, 1993), p. 7.

2

Warlike mates? Queen Elizabeth, and Joan La Pucelle in 1 Henry VI

BEN SPILLER

Accounts of Elizabeth I's visit to her naval troops at Tilbury in 1588, shortly before the arrival of the ill-fated Spanish Armada, have established and perpetuated her iconic status as a warrior queen. Elizabeth at Tilbury is a moment in history, legend, or myth, regardless of how apocryphal it may or may not be,[1] that recalls the oration of Henry V as he rallies together his 'band of brothers' before the impending battle at Agincourt. In this chapter I will argue that the cultural significance of the queen's decision to visit her loyal soldiers, and possibly mirror their appearance by wearing a costume of armour, is recalled approximately two years later by the dramatists of 1 Henry VI.[2] While in the play the female military leader is the French Catholic Joan La Pucelle, apparent antithesis to England's Protestant monarch, Joan's self-assured leadership of her army in I.6 and her display of intense patriotism in III.3 are possible echoes of the queen's reported conduct and speech two years earlier. When the play was first performed – c.1590 – Elizabeth's visit to Tilbury, or, more accurately, what was believed to have taken place at Tilbury, appears to have been fresh in the minds of London play-makers and, in turn, possibly their eager audiences. Elizabeth's reputation as iconic warrior queen in 1588 made sufficient impact on the late Elizabethan imagination to invite the first audiences of 1 Henry VI to draw parallels between a theatricalised French witch and a living English heroine. In addition I will consider how the play simultaneously vilifies Joan, invites admiration for her, and allows her to be seen as something of a scapegoat. The notion of national identity will also form an integral part of my chapter, as the cloudy distinction between the French and English in 1 Henry VI problematises the depiction of the two nations.

Nina S. Levine puts forward the notion that, if the Joan of the play is to be read as an allegorical Elizabeth, then the parallels 'may revise the earlier assessments of the play's patriotism, transforming a post-Armada play into a potentially seditious celebration of aristocratic warriors triumphing over unnatural female dominance'.[3] Susan Bassnett, too, interprets the proximity between Elizabeth and Joan as a particularly negative view of the queen, her leadership and the condition of her country.[4] Indeed, Nicola J. Watson and Michael Dobson identify the 'animosity' that Shakespeare – one of a number of playwrights who collaborated on *1 Henry VI* – appears to have felt towards Elizabeth in the latter stages of her reign, through his portrayal in *Hamlet* of Gertrude, 'another post-menopausal queen at the centre of a succession crisis'. Watson and Dobson also point to the similarity between Joan, Richard II, and Elizabeth to fuel their argument that Shakespeare was anything but in love with the queen.[5]

It may indeed be true that Shakespeare, and a number of other playwrights, felt angered by Elizabeth both in the wake of the Armada defeat and in the more general context of her reign. As Susan Frye explains, 'to those alive in 1588, England must have seemed anything but united'. England was a nation divided by religion, Elizabeth ruled 'only with the consent of a powerful aristocracy and city leadership', credit on the continent dried up owing to opposition from Philip II, the treasury was shrinking fast, and the Privy Council continued to appeal for loans and guarantees from the coastal towns most threatened by the Spanish. Elizabeth's Tilbury visit may have provided only 'ineffectual pageantry, for she performed before unpaid and ill-equipped and even hungry soldiers, many of whom, we know from royal proclamation, tried to sell their armour the moment they were disbanded'.[6]

There are a number of other commentators on *1 Henry VI* who have found an anger in the play directed primarily towards the queen. For example:

It has been argued … that his [Shakespeare's] savage depiction of the fraudulent Amazon Joan of Arc in *Henry VI Part 1* vents his frustration with Elizabeth's handling of Baron Willoughbie's French expedition of 1589–90 and the Earl of Essex's Rouen mission of 1591–2; that this hostility is further expressed by the bestial humiliations to which Shakespeare subjects her fellow Faerie Queen, Titania, in *A Midsummer Night's Dream*.[7]

The majority of criticism on *1 Henry VI* that draws parallels between Elizabeth and Joan has perceived the connection as a reflection of the playwrights' dissatisfaction with the queen, and there are indeed aspects to Joan's personality, as portrayed in the play, that seem far from flattering to Elizabeth if Joan is perceived as her onstage alter-ego. For example, Joan is portrayed momentarily as a preposterous fraud when she claims she is of royal parentage (V.3.36–41), asserts she has fallen pregnant while remaining a virgin (V.3.62–4 and V.3.49–53), and proceeds to name two men as the father of her unborn child (V.4.73–78).

While it is true that Elizabeth was rumoured to have conceived at least one illegitimate child,[8] the more positive connection between the queen and Joan, in the instance of the latter's desperate claim of motherhood, is their shared natural instinct to survive. Joan's fiery execution is a matter of seconds away and Elizabeth's vehement enemies might strike at any moment, yet both display determination to prevent the victories of their antagonists. Titania returns as Elizabeth's theatrical counterpart in

Thomas Dekker's early Jacobean play *The Whore of Babylon* (c.1606), which celebrates the queen's conduct at Tilbury through a thinly veiled faerie-world code. Furthermore, it is possible to view the Elizabeth-like Joan in *1 Henry VI* as a more positive comment on the queen and her expedition to Tilbury, with their shared defiance in the face of adversity – particularly snarling misogyny in the form of threatened male soldiers and anxious male advisers, respectively – and each has the interest of her motherland at heart. It is rumoured that Elizabeth was instructed not to journey to Tilbury, as it is claimed she began her militant address with:

> My loving people, we have been perswaded by some, that are careful of our safety, to take heed how we commit our self to armed multitudes for fear of treachery: but I assure you, I do not desire to live to distrust my faithful, and loving people.[9]

While the obstinacy behind such resistance appears somewhat more level-headed and the fuel for a more credible claim than that belonging to Joan, both personalities possess a self-determined resilience, perhaps even an arrogance, which spites an otherwise mighty and fearful opposition; however, ultimately, Joan loses her battle to survive. Questions of nationality and national identity hover over Joan's death, and indeed over that of Elizabeth: who will succeed Joan as the principal defender of a non-English France; and how English will England remain under the rule of Elizabeth's likely successor, the Scottish King James VI?

Carol Blessing's chapter, above, discovers another positive connection between the two figures through a mutual comparison with Deborah the Judge. The Dauphin in *1 Henry VI* exclaims that the young maid Joan 'fight[s] with the sword of Deborah', in the wake of her unexpected – and embarrassing – martial triumph over him.[10] Joan is brought in close proximity to Elizabeth by Blessing, who explains how the English defeat of the Armada 'further reinforced Elizabeth as a military Deborah leading her people to victory'; in other words, Deborah is an iconic intermediary who highlights the women's similarity in terms of judge-like and war-leader characteristics.

Joan of Arc was a controversial figure in France. Her connection with war had subsequently given her the status of national heroine, and the same can be said of the English Elizabeth. Indeed, Joan and Elizabeth may be read as embodiments of France and England, respectively. Joan, as constructed in *1 Henry VI*, is a French Catholic cross-dressing witch. She appears, at first glance, to possess all the qualities that evoked horror in those English Protestants who believed in rigid gender definition and denied the Catholic magic of transubstantiation. However, such a clear distinction between the English and the French is not so apparent in the play. Taking into account the French Civil Wars – or Wars of Religion, depending on a political or religious point of view – that were raging across the continent when the play was first performed, and the play's staging of the beginnings of an English – albeit historical – civil war, the dramatists do seem to make reference to a similarity between the two nations. The chaotic political and religious state of France in the 1590s seems particularly resonant in a theatrical reworking of the first stirrings of the Wars of the Roses, staged in the same decade as the turbulence continued in France. In *1 Henry VI*, the concept of French versus English may well be a code for Spanish versus English. France and Spain were certainly bound together in terms of religion in the 1590s; however, it is important to remember that Catholicism was also the national religion of England when the historical Henry VI was on the throne. By evoking a moment in history when both France and England were united through religion, the playwrights seem less certain of the clear-cut division between England and France (at least in terms of national religion) than subsequent interpreters of Elizabeth have constructed.

By blurring England with its enemy, the play points to the relentlessness of cyclical war per se, regardless of which side is considered. A negative approach to war influences the portrayal of Joan as a theatricalised Elizabeth, who does not receive unconditional support from the playwrights. In addition to the 'shift … in drama, the visual arts, and in historical text during the 1620s and 1630s when Elizabeth's armour and speech first gained importance as the queen's supposed militant Protestantism became an icon of national unity',[11] the image of Elizabeth at Tilbury has also become a myth of nationalist sentiment in subsequent centuries, including our own.[12] While the italics in royal adviser Leonel Sharp's version of Elizabeth's speech represent the commonplace early modern printing practice of emphasising the names of nations and places, they also underline Sharp's manipulation of Elizabeth's words to fuel his campaign, in 1623, against the proposed marriage between Prince Charles and a Spaniard:

> I know I have the bodie, but of a weak and feeble woman, but I have the heart and Stomach of a King, and of a King of *England* too, and think foul scorn that *Parma* or *Spain*, or any Prince of Europe should dare to invade the borders of my Realm.[13]

As Frye explains, Sharp's Tilbury address places emphasis on Elizabeth's 'body, purpose, and personal power'; Sharp's idealised version of Elizabeth 'suggests an England fused into a single entity through Elizabeth'.[14] In other words, the queen is the country, or she embodies it. In III.3 of *1 Henry VI*, Joan personifies France by referring to her country's eyes, wounds, blood, and bosom (III.3.44–57); this echoes the discourse of the human body employed by the English heroes Talbot and Mortimer, who represent the belief that male heroism is displayed through bodily damage.[15] For Joan, her country is like a human body; France lives and breathes and needs attentive nursing in the wake of her battering at the hands of the English.[16] The personified France, who bleeds from her wounds, is akin to an English hero.

The dramatists' decision to provide Joan with the discourse of the human body also echoes Sharp's Tilbury speech. Might not Joan's patriotic speech, here, be interpreted as an alternative, theatricalised version of Elizabeth's Tilbury address? Other examples of the ways in which the playwrights collapse otherwise clear-cut differences between the English and the French are plentiful throughout the play. The concept of clearly-defined nationality is challenged, as the dramatists provide verbal echoes between

French and English personalities. In I.i, Exeter describes the French as 'subtle-witted' before asking whether they are 'conjurers and sorcerors, that, afraid of him [Henry V], / By magic verses have contrived his end?' (I.1.25–27). Bedford attempts to invocate the ghost of Henry V in I.i so it might

> Prosper this realm, keep it from civil broils,
> Combat with adverse planets in the heavens;
> A far more glorious star thy soul will make
> Than Julius Caesar.
>
> (I.1.53–6)

Exeter questions whether the French have brought about Henry V's death through conjuring; and Bedford attempts to conjure a ghost. Later, Joan will evoke fiends from hell. Invocation of the dead and hellish spirits were activities commonly associated with witchcraft in the 1590s, and both are attributed to English and French figures in the play. The third messenger in I.i explains that 'the French exclaimed the devil was in arms' as Talbot mercilessly slaughtered his enemies (I.1.125). After hearing of Talbot's exploits on the battlefield, the Bastard of Orleans exclaims, 'I think this Talbot be a fiend of hell' (II.1.46). In other words, the French equate Talbot with the devil; both sides view their enemy in satanic terms.

By highlighting similarities between the English and the French – or at least having them perceive each other in similarly demonic terms – the dramatists collapse easy, safe distinctions between England and France. England itself – or at least its aristocracy – is unstable in the play; there is little sense of national cohesiveness. Joan's campaign could quite easily have been led by an English commander against a rival English faction, not unlike the treasonous plot of Scroop, Cambridge, and Gray in Shakespeare's later *Henry V*. Perhaps Joan's execution marks a celebration of male dominance over the female war-leader, but it does not give much stability to the English in the play. Instead of bonding the male warriors together against 'the armed woman, the image of disorder and anarchy', the Machiavellian York becomes Talbot's successor in the war against the French and so the discord amongst the self-interested English aristocracy continues. Scapegoating Joan does not bring the English together and strengthen national identity; it marks the end of the campaign against the crossdressing girl-warrior, but it begins the internal war between contenders for the English throne: the Wars of the Roses. Maybe Elizabeth's failure to bring England together through her visit to Tilbury is alluded to indirectly here.

As Levine points out, Shakespeare (who she believes is sole author) 'radically' alters the chronology of his sources by cutting Talbot's life short 'by nearly a quarter of a century in order to allow Joan to triumph over his death'.[17] Rather than cutting Joan's life short and allowing Talbot to enjoy a moment of triumph over the rebellious war leader's death, the dramatists reserve triumph for Joan and appear at least a little sympathetic towards her. Earlier moments of celebration for Joan include those when she beats the French Dauphin and English Talbot, both in one-to-one combat; there are, therefore, three instances in the play when Joan is given the opportunity to revel in her triumphs and audiences are given the opportunity to celebrate or commiserate the dominance of a female warrior over her male counterparts. Thomas Nashe's *Pierce Penilesse, His Supplication to the Divell* (1592) is the only extant contemporary account of the play. Nashe chooses not to mention Joan at all in his writings; he instead focuses on Talbot's status as national hero. Such an approach to the play is indicative of hundreds of years of literary criticism that has viewed the play as simplistically nationalist, with England embodied in Talbot and France personified by Joan. The latter's three moments of triumph are not taken into account by such readings, which grossly simplify the play's complex approach to national identity. For Michael Hattaway, 'Joan becomes [in I.2] a sexual lure for Charles – who promptly takes the bait – so reinforcing the English audience's prejudices about the sexual depravity of the French'.[18] However, as I have shown, the distinctions between English and French are not so clear-cut in this play. To claim that Joan is a sexual lure is problematic in the first place, as the apparent doubles entendres of her conversation with the Dauphin may well be taken at face value; to claim that she consciously wishes to ensnare him is not to acknowledge that Joan – not unlike Lady Macbeth – may be referring to her femininity to cause the Dauphin embarrassment and so sharpen his resolve to follow her plan, bring together troops and thwart the English enemy. It is the English in the play who presume Joan and the Dauphin have been 'juggling' or 'ingling' (both of which have sexual connotations, the latter a possibility of a gay liaison, maybe a reference to Joan's soldierly appearance, or to the fact that Joan would have been played by a boy or a young man on the Elizabethan stage); this does not mean that the English audience members experiencing this play at the Rose Playhouse in the early 1590s agreed with them.

Joan's accusation as she is face-to-face with a shepherd claiming to be her father is, 'You have suborned this man / Of purpose to obscure my noble birth' (V.3.21–22); she may well have a point because, provoked by disrespectful words and Joan's refusal to kneel before him (admittedly sinful in the early 1590s; compare this to young Talbot's voluntary kneeling to his father at IV.4.32–33), the man proceeds to deliver a diatribe of eleven lines before ordering the English to burn the girl because 'hanging is too good' (V.3.33). There are approximately twenty lines between the man's earlier 'Ah, Joan, sweet daughter Joan, I'll die with thee' (V.3.6) and his fierce command to burn her. In the intervening moments, Joan refuses to acknowledge the shepherd as her father, throws insults – including 'decrepit miser' and 'base ignoble wretch' (V.3.7) – at him and fails to kneel on command. York announces that her life has been 'wicked and vile' (V.3.16), and it does not take the shepherd long to agree with him. York, Warwick, and the shepherd all agree that Joan should be burnt: English and French men unite in their decision to rid themselves of Joan. She is the ultimate scapegoat for insecure men, no matter what their nationality: she refuses to conform to the roles of obedient daughter and docile virgin, by expressing her belief that she is nobler than a shepherd's daughter and by singlehandedly leading an army against the English male troops. Such decisions on Joan's part make her an impossibility in a patriarchy – whether English or French – and the men have her removed, in order to restore stability. Ironically, however, the war that will follow in *2 Henry VI* is one born from fighting amongst the English nobility itself; it does not take an outsider, no matter how French, Catholic, crossdressing or witchlike, to initiate the Wars of the Roses. The problem with Joan is her gender, not her nationality.

Audiences of more recent productions of the play have been given the opportunity to catch a glimpse of the inimitable Boudicca-like Elizabeth through the performance of the actor playing Joan. Indeed, a Royal Shakespeare Company production of the play, directed by Michael Boyd and first performed in 2000, alluded clearly to Elizabeth via the performance of Fiona Bell as Joan. Boyd gave a sense of credibility to Joan's seemingly fraudulent claim that she is of royal parentage when, towards the close of the production, shortly after Bell's Joan was mercilessly lowered into the depths of a fiery pit, the feisty Maid of Orleans re-emerged phoenix-like in the guise of England's future (French) Queen, Margaret. Hattaway, too, draws attention to the indirect relationship between Margaret and Joan when he explains that Margaret makes her first entrance 'immediately after the fiends have left Joan: it is as though the female politician has inherited the power of the heroic Joan as a subtler and more dangerous kind of threat to the English cause'.[19] Boyd, therefore (following a little textual rearrangement), seemed to concur with Hattaway by creating an overt and vivid connection between the intense young army leader and the aristocratic contender for the English throne. Such a relationship brought to mind the possible allusions that the play's first audiences might have understood between the onstage Joan and the offstage Elizabeth, who was raised in the countryside, and was understood by a number of her subjects to yearn for a milkmaid's life rather than that of a queen.[20] Furthermore, the three fiends that Bell's Joan conjured from hell were later developed – with no change to costume – into Margaret's three loyal attendants. Red costuming was emblematic of Englishness, whereas blue clothing linked the wearer to France; as the fiends and the attendants – performed by the same actors – were given long red dresses to wear, not only was the double-casting an indirect link between Joan and Margaret, but it also facilitated an association between the fiends and England. A typographical error in the December 2000 issue of *Theatre Record* misnamed the fiends as Joan's 'friends', which is, paradoxically, a somewhat more accurate description of their function in the production: they were her imaginary English friends who deserted her cruelly once she had asked them to work with her against the troops from England.[21] In a study of *1 Henry VI*, Nina S. Levine makes reference to 'Joan's Elizabethan face', which is a helpful reminder that the representation of Joan – who, historically, lived in the mid fifteenth century – as portrayed in a play first performed in the early 1590s, is not striving for historical authenticity; rather, the dramatists' reworking of Joan, as constructed by previous authors such as the historical chronicler Edward Hall, is underpinned by a number of Elizabethan preoccupations, especially a fear and hatred of all things Spanish, Catholic, and transgressive, particularly in terms of gender and sexuality.[22] Furthermore, 'Joan's Elizabethan face' may also be taken to mean 'Joan's Elizabeth-like face', a useful conceptualisation of the dramatists' vivid blurring of two seemingly disparate yet mutually striking personalities.

An even more direct and immediate link between Joan and Elizabeth was established and developed by the production, and it involved a specific choice on the part of the designer. For the majority of her stage time, Joan was dressed in armour, complete with metal breastplate: a visual reference, it seemed, to Elizabeth's probable appearance at Tilbury. Furthermore, Sîan Thomas's portrayal of Queen Gertrude in Boyd's 2004 RSC *Hamlet* was, in the words of one reviewer, 'got up to look like Queen Elizabeth I'.[23] Therefore, this particular director seems to make a point of alluding to the Queen in his productions; he certainly attempts to catch sight of Elizabeth in Shakespearean figures (certainly in two productions at least). The casting decision of Boyd in 2000 linked together both Joan and Margaret as French leaders and temptresses and, by turning Joan into an earlier version of Margaret, the director made credible Joan's claim that she is of noble blood (V.3.21–22 and 36–41). The only major difference in this instance is that Joan rejects her father to make her claim, an act of defiance of which Elizabeth would have never been guilty.

Joan's more regal attributes (no matter how self-proclaimed) are evident throughout the play. For example, Alençon (a name that evokes Elizabeth's actual wooer) believes that, because 'Puzel hath bravely played her part in this', she 'doth deserve a coronet of gold' (III.4.88–89); as far as the Duke is concerned, Joan is at one with the monarchy (or at least an alternative – or his idealised – version of it). Joan's announcement that 'Of all base passions, fear is most accursed' (V.2.18) echoes Queen Elizabeth's fearlessness in the face of adversity, as explained by Pope Sixtus V in August: 'the Queen of England might only be a woman … and only mistress of half an island, yet she had made herself feared by Spain, by France, by the Empire, and by all'.[24] Elizabeth is also believed to have declared, 'I am not afraid of anything',[25] and, in one of the various accounts of the Tilbury address, William Leigh claims she announced 'little doe I feare their [the Spanish] force'. In the play, as a counterpoint to Joan's earlier refusal to 'yield to any rights of love' (I.2.113), Suffolk explains to King Henry that Margaret of Anjou is 'content to be at your command – / Command, I mean, of virtuous chaste intents – / To love and honour Henry as her lord' (V.4.19–21). While Joan is close to Elizabeth in terms of characterisation (a pair of female war-leaders who, equally vilified by their supporters and enemies, yet hold a belief in their regal status and refuse to play wife), Boyd enhanced Joan's nobility through an association with Margaret, and so bound her more closely to an image of the offstage Elizabeth.

I began this chapter with the claim that the first audiences of *1 Henry VI* had the opportunity to connect Joan and Elizabeth when experiencing the play in performance, in the light of the Tilbury address. However, that claim was after I had experienced the play in performance and drawn a connection between Joan and Elizabeth through a very specific design choice in the costume of the actor playing Joan. Furthermore, the details of Elizabeth's speech and conduct at Tilbury were as much a matter of uncertain and contradictory myth when *1 Henry VI* was first performed as they are today; so those connections belong to the realm of imagination. Therefore, the similarities identified between Joan and Elizabeth, prompted by Fiona Bell's breastplate-wearing Joan in 2000, are not those that may have belonged to a theatre audience in the early 1590s; rather, they are rooted in a direct experience of the play in performance, with hindsight and after the myth of Elizabeth at Tilbury had been initiated and sustained. If *1 Henry VI* were played before the queen shortly after the Armada was defeated (and it is a big 'if'), might she not have thought at some point in the performance (but before Joan's conjuring scene), 'I am Joan La Pucelle, know ye not that?' With their mutual conviction to defend their countries from unwanted foreign invaders and rally their troops to inspire defensive action, Elizabeth may well have recognised herself in Joan, as she is believed to have lamented her similarity to Richard II.[26] However, this quotation is entirely fictional, and is as guilty as the texts of Sharp and the other authors of Elizabeth's various Tilbury speeches of putting words in the Queen's mouth to attempt to strengthen an argument; the quotation is as apocryphal as the image of an armoured, horse-mounted national heroine who, with the passage of time and the willingness of many to believe in such an image, has almost become an unquestionable historical fact. The dramatists of *1 Henry VI* and the director Boyd managed to collapse the distinctions between England and France, by offering textual and performative connections (respectively) between Elizabeth and Joan. The imagined appearance of Joan in the script, and the actual appearance of Joan at the Swan Theatre in 2000, connect the shepherd's daughter and the Queen of England through the iconography of female war leader. In I.2 of the play Joan suggests to the Dauphin that he may wish to 'receive' her for his 'warlike mate'; it is not difficult to imagine Joan proffering a similar suggestion to her military sister in arms. Whether or not Elizabeth would have taken up Joan's offer is an entirely new matter.[27]

Notes

1. See Susan Frye, 'The Myth of Elizabeth at Tilbury', *Sixteenth Century Journal* 23 (1992), pp. 95–114, for a cautious account of the Tilbury visit. Frye revisits the various sources upon which the myth has been based and brings to light the anti-Catholic sentiments of Leonel Sharp, who authored the first known published version of Elizabeth's Tilbury address. However, the image of an armoured Elizabeth on horseback at Tilbury is an image that Elizabethans and Jacobeans believed in (for evidence see the ballads and plays to which Frye refers in her article). A number of our contemporary historians still believe in the image (see note 12 below). Televisual representations of Elizabeth's visit to Tilbury include Glenda Jackson's performance of the monarch in the BBC's landmark drama *Elizabeth R* (1971) and the History Channel's *Elizabeth I, the Virgin Queen* (1996). Both portray Elizabeth dressed in shining armour and mounted on a stallion while orating the famous address recorded avowedly by Leonel Sharp. The more recent *Elizabeth I*, first screened on Channel Four in 2005, portrayed the Tilbury address as a public relations exercise in which Helen Mirren's Elizabeth dismounted her horse and illustrated 'even in the dust' by gathering a handful of earth from by her soldiers' feet. There was no question that the speech belonged to no one but Elizabeth. *The Virgin Queen*, with Anne-Marie Duff as Elizabeth, was first

screened by the BBC in 2006 and presented the speech at Tilbury as a less coherent historical moment: a number of other characters, in addition to Elizabeth, voiced parts of the speech, which gave it a sense of instability and increased its potential meanings. While Sharp was not credited as retrospective author of the speech (next to impossible in a costume drama that focuses specifically on Elizabeth's reign), an opportunity was created for audiences to understand that the voice of the Tilbury address is not exclusively Elizabeth's own.

2. It is now generally accepted that Shakespeare was not sole author of *1 Henry VI*. Edward Burns, editor of the Arden 3 text, employs the term 'the dramatists' when discussing authorship. For a more detailed discussion see *1 Henry VI*, edited by Edward Burns (London: Thompson Learning, 2000), pp. 73–84.

3. Nina S. Levine, *Women's Matters: Politics, Gender and Nation in Shakespeare's Early History Plays* (Cranbury: Associated University Presses, 1998), p. 27.

4. Susan Bassnett, 'Sexuality and Power in the Three Parts of *King Henry VI*', in *Shakespeare: The Elizabethan Plays* (Basingstoke: Palgrave Macmillan, 1993), p. 14.

5. Michael Dobson and Nicola J. Watson, *England's Elizabeth: An Afterlife in Fame and Fantasy* (Oxford: Oxford University Press, 2002), p. 45.

6. Susan Frye, 'The Myth of Elizabeth at Tilbury', p. 114. As Lisa Hopkins points out, by 1591 the Canterbury records show that John Marlowe, father to the playwright Christopher Marlowe, no longer possessed any of the military equipment that he had at the time of the Armada. Lisa Hopkins, *Christopher Marlowe: A Literary Life* (Basingstoke: Palgrave Macmillan, 2001), p. 42.

7. Dobson and Watson, *England's Elizabeth*, p. 45.

8. See Julia M. Walker, ed., *Dissing Elizabeth: Negative Representations of Gloriana* (Durham: Duke University Press, 1998).

9. Frye, 'The Myth of Elizabeth at Tilbury', p. 98.

10. *1 Henry VI*, ed. Burns, I.2.105. All subsequent references are taken from this edition.

11. *1 Henry VI*, ed. Burns, p. 95.

12. For evidence that this sentiment is still current see, for example, Anne Somerset, *Elizabeth I* (London: Phoenix Press, 1991), pp. 590–591 and Antonia Fraser, *The Warrior Queens: Boadicea's Chariot* (London: Phoenix Press, 2002), p. 246.

13. Frye, 'The Myth of Elizabeth at Tilbury', p. 98.

14. Frye, 'The Myth of Elizabeth at Tilbury', p. 95.

15. In Shakespeare's *Coriolanus*, too, damage to the male body indicates male heroism. Menenius asks the citizens to consider Coriolanus's 'warlike service' by thinking 'Upon the wounds his body bears, which show / Like graves i' the holy churchyard' (III.3.49–51). Coriolanus earlier refers to the wounds as 'unaching', which furthers the notion of himself as war hero (II.2.148). References taken from the Arden 2 *Coriolanus*, edited by Philip Brockbank (London: Methuen, 1987).

16. The notion of England fused into a single entity through Elizabeth manifests itself in the iconography of the Ditchley portrait of Elizabeth; Joan's use of human body discourse recalls the Queen's Rainbow portrait.

17. Nina S. Levine, *Women's Matters*, p. 39.

18. *1 Henry VI*, edited by Michael Hattaway (Cambridge: Cambridge University Press, 1990), pp. 23–24.

19. *1 Henry VI*, ed. Hattaway, p. 28.

20. Dobson and Watson, *England's Elizabeth*, pp. 85–86.

21. *Theatre Record*, 2–31 December 2000, p. 1698.

22. Levine, *Women's Matters*, p. 27.

23. Charles Spencer, 'Prince Charmless', Rev. of *Hamlet* by the RSC at Stratford-upon-Avon,

Daily Telegraph, 23 July 2004.

24. Fraser, *The Warrior Queens*, p. 232.

25. Fraser, *The Warrior Queens*, p. 237.

26. 'I am Richard II, know ye not that?' Queen Elizabeth famously declared six months after the Essex rebellion, Craig Rustici, '*Ceste Nouvelle Papesse*: Elizabeth I and the Specter of Pope Joan', in *Elizabeth I: Always Her Own Free Woman*, edited by Carole Levin, Jo Eldridge Carney, and Debra Barrett-Graves (Aldershot: Ashgate, 2003), pp. 131–148, p. 143.

27. Some recent historians – for example, Marina Warner, in *Joan of Arc: The Image of Female Heroism* (London: Weidenfeld & Nicolson, 1981) – have suggested that Joan was a bastard half-sister of the Dauphin. If this were indeed true, then Joan would have also shared the same relationship with Catherine of Valois, who was Elizabeth's great-great-grandmother through her marriage to Owen Tudor. Thanks to Lisa Hopkins for providing me with this reference. Since there is the possibility of a familial connection between Elizabeth and Joan, Elizabeth may have had the opportunity to perceive herself in close proximity to Joan, regardless of *1 Henry VI*. However, theatre audiences in the early 1590s were given the opportunity to connect the two figures through warrior iconography, though perhaps in a much less positive context.

3

'Rudenesse it selfe she doth refine': Queen Elizabeth I as Lady Alchymia

Jayne Elisabeth Archer

Introduction

Seeing that the court has been translated into 'a laboratory, or Alchymists workehouse', Mercurie, the anti-hero of Ben Jonson's *Mercurie Vindicated from the Alchemists at Court* (1616), declares: 'The whole household of 'em are become alchemists'.[1] At this pivotal moment in Jonson's masque, the transmutation of the court is accomplished: King James and Queen Anna become alchemists, *frater mysterium* and *soror mystica*, and Mercurie, the agent of transformation, is identified with the poet himself, Jonson. As in his earlier work, *The Alchemist* (1610), Jonson's subtle critique of alchemy – here articulated through the persecution and eventual 'vindication' of Mercurie – is also a critique of social values and a corrupt patronage system. In *Mercurie Vindicated*, the target of Jonson's critique is the Jacobean court, which has become infected, as Stanton J. Linden observes in his reading of this entertainment, by 'falseness and artificiality ... materialism and pretension'.[2] But, as Mercurie turns to address the ladies of Queen Anna's retinue, it is the women of the court who are shown to be particularly susceptible to alchemy's considerable charms. The alchemist, he explains, offers 'perpetuity of beauty, (do you hear, ladies?), health, riches, honors, a matter of immortality is nothing. They will calcine you a grave matrone (as it might be a mother o' the maids) and spring up a young virgin out of her ashes, as fresh as a phoenix' (ll.83–87). Mercurie compares Anna's female attendants to the *prima materia* that is killed, washed, 'calcined', reformed, and reborn in the course of the alchemical opus. In this court of would-be alchemists, where courtiers seek transmutations in their identities – translation up the social hierarchy – the women covet eternal youth and virginity, and, thereby, perpetual health, beauty, and honour. In Jonson's satire this feminised opus – a process of 'virginification' – provides a measure both for the absurdity of the alchemical enterprise, and for the self-delusion to which he believes the Jacobean court has descended. Importantly, Jonson's poetic opus invokes the memory of Queen Elizabeth I, who made the very attributes sought by Anna's ladies central to her self-fashioning as an immortal virgin and a Protestant queen.

Alchemy provided an important imaginative and intellectual framework through which Elizabethans saw, interpreted, and transformed their realities. Throughout her reign, alchemists courted Elizabeth, and poets and dramatists drew upon the language and imagery of alchemy in order to write for and about the queen. In different ways, all imagined their queen as a kind of Lady Alchymia, the presiding deity, or muse, of alchemy, in who could be found the twin powers of the Philosopher's Stone and its correlative, the Elixir: unlimited riches and eternal life, wealth, and health. Lady Alchymia is a significant, although largely overlooked aspect of the iconographic arsenal upon which subjects could draw in order to reimagine their Queen and themselves. In this chapter I will examine Queen Elizabeth's representation as this muse and Sapientia (the biblical Wisdom figure), with whom Alchymia is often elided in alchemical literature. By representing Elizabeth in this manner, natural philosophers and alchemists were able to petition the queen with appeals for support of their own experiments and schemes. Often this use of iconography was part of a coercive strategy, motivated by a desire for patronage or protection, or in order to advance a particular political, religious, or intellectual agenda. However, in the writings of alchemists such as Samuel Norton and poets such as John Davies, I will suggest, more subtle meanings are encoded, and the figure of Lady Alchymia is used to interrogate both the nature of the patron/client relationship and the notion, common in alchemical literature, that women possess a unique, privileged, and unsettling knowledge of the secrets of Nature. Further, I will examine what we can recover of Elizabeth's response to her representation as Lady Alchymia, and to her patronage of natural philosophy and occult knowledge. Elizabeth was notoriously evasive in her responses to petitions for favour. I will argue that Elizabeth, in her dealings with alchemists and natural philosophers, adopted what Allison Heisch, in her analysis of the Queen's parliamentary rhetoric, has called a 'technique of evasion'.[3] Instead of realising the dreams of alchemists and poets, Elizabeth frustrates, equivocates, and withholds the material benefits that could transform the lives of her would-be clients. This strategy, I argue, was necessitated by Elizabeth's need to be seen to be, like Johannes Trithemius's vision of Lady Alchymia, a 'chaste prostitute, who has many lovers but disappoints all and grants her favour to none'.[4]

Lady Alchymia: a 'chaste prostitute'

'Alchymya', the muse of alchemy, faces the title page of *The newe jewell of health* (1576), George Baker's edition of the alchemical receipts of Conrad Gesner, which Baker dedicated to Anne Cecil de Vere, Countess of Oxford (1556–1588) (Figure 1).[5] Surrounded by the apparatus of her art, Alchymya stands between the sun and moon, *sol* and *luna*, representing, respectively, the masculine and feminine principles which must be isolated, synthesised, and transmuted in the course of the alchemical opus. *Sol* overlooks the furnace, while *luna* is associated with the alembic: equipment corresponding to the elements of fire and water, and denoting the rapid heating and gentle distillation – processes which, M.E. Warlick notes in her analysis of the portrayal of gender in alchemical art, were correlated with male and female practitioners respectively.[6] A concept fundamental to the alchemical tradition – which reaches back at least as far as third-century CE Alexandria – is this same need to combine masculine and feminine principles in practical work and in the production of knowledge.[7] In *The Smaragdine Table* (or 'Emerald Tablet'), the 'Ten Commandments' of alchemy, first published in an English translation in 1599, the importance of the feminine principle is acknowledged. In this work, attributed to 'Hermes Trismegistus', the mythical founder of alchemy, it is written of the Philosopher's Stone: 'His father is the sun, his mother is the moone, the wind bore it in hir belly. The earth is his nurse.'[8] For this reason, some of the earliest extant alchemical texts were attributed to female 'authors', including 'Mary the Jewess', 'Isis', and 'Cleopatra'.[9] Whether mythical or historical, the attribution of foundational alchemical texts to female authors acknowledged the centrality of the feminine principle within alchemical language, knowledge, and imagery. This tradition continued into the Renaissance period, filtering into English alchemy – 'Mary the Jewess' (alternatively 'Mary the Hebrew' or 'Mary Hebraica') is regularly cited as a source for alchemical recipes, most obviously the *bain marie*, still used in cookery today,[10] and recipes attributed to 'Cleopatra' were published in Thomas Bonham's *The chyrurgians closet* (1630)[11] and Johann Wecker's *Eighteen books of the secrets of art & nature* (1660)[12] – and poetry, perhaps most vividly in the use of the 'chymical wedding' in the alchemical poems of John Donne.[13]

Of course, the invocation of a female muse in alchemical literature did not necessarily translate into reality, and it may even have worked to preclude the involvement of women in the production and ownership of alchemical knowledge.[14] However, there is evidence to suggest that women were integral to the production and transmission of alchemical knowledge throughout the early modern period, serving as both patrons and authors of alchemical texts, and as experimenters and practitioners, working in the laboratory and stillroom.[15] But it is as patrons that women's participation in alchemy is most apparent. Addressing Lady Knowles in his *Letter of Chemistry* (1614), John Thornborough (1551–1641), who was appointed Elizabeth's chaplain-in-ordinary before 1580, invokes 'Lady *Alcumy*' in order to appeal to his female patron:

> Good madame, understanding that you have a desier to spend your howers from greater occasions in distilling waters and extracting tinctures, I thought good to write to your Ladishippe how muche the Lady *Alcumy* rejoyceth. That a Lady of your birth and worth will ... knock at her first and outmost gate that hath long tyme bene forced to hide her hede and flye from rowme to rowme imprisoned in her owne howse by the unlawfull and violent assaults against her chastitie and

honor, of many base and beggarlie cosening fellowes, who have broughte her worthynes allmost into contempt. This Ladye speaketh out of a window to your Ladishipp (for yet she dareth not open her chamber dores) that she hath onelie two children: Th'one a faire daughter named *Distillation*, on whom do waite many handmayds, as *Extractions* of *Tinctures* and *Salts*, drawing oyles by Serpentines, forcing of Sperits by retorts with many other of that kinde: Thother is a faire yong man, of complexion white and red, who in his fulle age and strength is altogether sanguine; having both power of health to cure diseases in men; and of welth to clense and take away corruption in mettalls. The Ladies daughter withall her handmaydes, humblie present their service and are willing to attend your Ladiships command.[16]

The chastity and learning of his patron, Lady Knowles, stands as proof of the integrity of Thornborough's alchemy and his personal honour. Importantly, it is a noble woman who must mediate between 'Lady *Alcumy*' and the male alchemist: the masculine and feminine principles (the 'faire yong man' and 'faire daughter', 'withall her handmaydes') offer 'service' to Ladies Knowles and '*Alcumy*', the latter of whom waits patiently in her 'privie chamber' before moving forward to offer her gifts of 'pleasure, health and profitte' (fol. 76r).

In particular, royal women are targeted as potential patrons, and this association is reflected in and reinforced by the importance accorded to queenship and female sovereignty in alchemical imagery. Personified as the queen and/or empress, the feminine principle features strongly in representations of the final stages of the alchemical opus, the *multiplicatio* and/or *projectio*. She appears, for example, in emblem 28, '*reginae mysteria*' (the 'mysteries of the queen'), of Johann Daniel Mylius's *Philosophia Reformata* (Frankfurt, 1622).[17] In this emblem the queen is shown seated in the philosopher's garden, 'squandering the riches of her endlessly multiplying gold' by handing out gold coins to three beggars, male and female. Although the Stone itself was often represented as a king or as a hermaphrodite child, the dissemination of its gifts – in the form of health and wealth – was frequently represented with reference to the charitable, nurturing characteristics traditionally attributed to women. Thus, it was perhaps inevitable that, as Charles Nicholl has remarked, Queen Elizabeth I figured 'in many alchemists' dreams as the ultimate patron'.[18] Indeed, there are striking parallels between the traditional attributes of Alchymia and the symbolism used in representations of the Virgin Queen, and these correspondences provided a discourse through which alchemists could imagine and approach their 'ultimate patron'.

Chastity, which, as Philippa Berry has noted, was crucial to Elizabeth's representation as an authoritative, but potentially unsettling, bearer and creator of power, meaning, and wisdom, was central in her identification with, and her representation as Sapientia, the biblical Wisdom figure, with whom Lady Alchymia was frequently identified.[19] The Paracelsian distiller John Hester (fl.1576–1593) accomplishes this elision in his autobiographical account of his early career. Hester describes his decision to dedicate himself to alchemical studies in terms of a meeting, 'in my minde', with two muses, the Ladies of 'Mettalles and Mineralles' and 'Hearbes and Spices':

> the one gallant and gorgeous garnished with gold and silver, bedect with jewels sole Ladie and Governesse of all the rich Mines and Mineralles that are in the bowels of the earth: the other sweet and odoriferous, adorned with flowers and hearbes, beautified with delicate spices, sole Lady and Regent of all the pleasant things that grow upon the face of the earth. These I vowed to serve and to honour, even to the losse of life and limbe … divers and sundry their affaires have they imployed mee in, in the which I have faithfully, painfully, and chargeably applied myselfe, and attained by their instructions (to my own destruction almost) manie their hidden secretes aswell in Mettalles and Mineralles, as in Hearbes and Spices.[20]

Using metaphors of romantic seduction and servitude, the young Hester is enticed by a Janus-faced Alchymia, who promises 'hidden secretes' behind the veils of matter. It is a dangerous relationship, in which the adept must remain faithful to a muse who might disdain or even destroy him at any moment. But it is ultimately a rewarding and empowering one, resulting in the acquisition of knowledge and wealth. For his presentation of the twin aspects of Lady Alchymia, Hester draws upon the Wisdom of Proverbs:

> Happy is the man that findeth wisedom, and the man that getteth understanding. For the merchandise of it is better than the merchandise of silver, and the gain thereof than fine gold. She is more precious than rubies: and all the things thou canst desire are not to be compared unto her. Length of days is in her right hand; and in her left hand are riches and honour … She is a tree of life to them that lay hold upon her: and happy is every one that retaineth her.[21]

The alchemical reinterpretation of the Wisdom tradition is perhaps best exemplified in Michael Maier's emblem book, *Atalanta Fugiens* (Oppenheim, 1617). The picture from emblem 26 shows Sapientia standing by the *arbor scientiae* (the 'tree of knowledge', a traditional symbol for the alchemical opus) bearing *sol* and *luna* as its fruits (Figure 2). Sapientia holds two inscribed banderoles which proclaim '*longitudo dierum et sanitas*' (length of days and health) and '*gloria ac divitiae*' (honour and infinite riches). In his discourse on this emblem, Maier explains that Sapientia personifies the whole '*cogitionem Chymiae, cum praxi*', and in the epigram which accompanies this emblem he identifies Sapientia both with the means by which the adept may achieve wisdom (his inspiration, or muse) and with the wisdom itself (the Philosopher's Stone, or 'fruit of the Tree of Life'):

> In human affairs there is no greater wisdom,
> Than that from which arise wealth and health.

> In her right hand she keeps a long life in good health,
> But her left hand conceals overwhelming treasures.
> When somebody approaches her with head and hand,
> She will be for him of the same value as the fruit of the Tree of Life.[22]

True wisdom, Maier asserts, comes from a union of theory ('head') and practice, or experience ('hand'): 'Experience may be considered as the father, the ratio as the mother, and wisdom as their child.'[23]

For English alchemists, inspired by Queen Elizabeth and the 'romance' of her court, Lady Alchymia is a queenly figure, who tantalises her male courtiers with promises of love and favour. Hugh Plat (bap. 1552, d. 1608), who sought patronage from Elizabeth for many years, is unusual in referring to Lady Alchymia by name: '*Amultis amatur Alchimia & tamen virgo est.*'[24] His words echo those of the German astrologer Johannes Trithemius (1462–1516), who described 'Alchemy' as 'a chaste prostitute, who has many lovers but disappoints all and grants her favors to none. She transforms the haughty into fools, the rich into paupers, the philosophers into dolts, and the deceived into loquacious deceivers.'[25] The physician and distiller John French (c.1616–1657) identified this capricious, evasive feminine principle with both Nature and her 'daughter', 'the Mercury of Philosophers': 'Court the Mother, and you winne the Daughter; prevail with Nature, and the fair *Diana* of the Philosophers is at your service.'[26] 'This Art of Alchymie', French concludes, is the 'Queen of Arts' (A3r).[27] Using similar language, Elias Ashmole (1617–1692) identified 'Dame Nature' as the female beloved who is 'woo'd and courted' by 'our Hermetique Philosophers'.[28] The alchemist, gendered male, is a courtier, and his queen or patron is Nature, through whom he seeks the Philosopher's Stone, or '*Diana*' — one of Elizabeth's favourite and most equivocal personae.[29]

When Michael Maier described the dual nature of Lady Alchymia as a coming together of 'head and hand' (*gnosis* and *praxis*), he could equally have been describing Queen Elizabeth as she was conceived by her natural philosophers. But this discourse of courtly love carries with it the fear — perhaps even certainty — that the female beloved would not deliver on her promises. For this reason John Dee (1527–1609) was careful to quote Queen Elizabeth's response to the *Monas Hieroglyphica* (1564),[30] his alchemical cosmology of sovereignty: '[The Queen] ... very gratiously vouchsafed to account herselfe my scholler in my booke ... and said, whereas I had prefixed in the forefront of the book: *Qui non intelligit, aut taceat, aut discat*: if I would disclose unto her the secretes of that booke, she would *discere et facere*.'[31] In so doing, Dee attempts to bind his Queen in ties of mutual obligation: in return for explaining, by oral instruction, the profound secrets occluded within his book, she undertakes to implement those lessons, transforming material reality in the image of Dee's *Monas Hieroglyphica*.

Discere et facere: 1560–1580

'Magic or occult philosophy', Malabika Sarkar has written, 'was a philosophy of power'.[32] Work done by historians of science can help us re-establish the links between natural philosophy and political power, and thus avoid falling into the stereotype of Queen Elizabeth as a passive and gullible victim of the occult.[33] In recent years, attention has rejected the notion of the early modern scientist as a disinterested and isolated discoverer of scientific 'truths' and has instead insisted on the role of the patron in the production of scientific knowledge.[34] In his study of Galileo, for example, Mario Biagioli argues that scientific knowledge is accomplished as a negotiation between (at least) two individuals, both of whom are situated within the codes and expectations of a patron–client relationship.[35] The interdependency of philosophers and monarchs found its authority in Plato's *Republic*, and was reasserted in *The Advancement of Learning* (1605), in which Francis Bacon fashions the new king, James I, in the image of his learned predecessor:

> For although he might be thought partial to his own profession, that said 'then should people and estates be happy, when either kings were philosophers, or philosophers kings', yet so much is verified by experience, that under learned princes and governors there have been ever the best times …[36]

Queen Elizabeth was perceived as just such a 'learned prince', who actively encouraged natural philosophy in all its manifestations. Testimonies to the queen's accomplishment in the sciences came from the herbalist William Turner, who commended her familiarity with 'all partes of Philosophie and good learninge', and Bacon himself, who recalled her 'learning of language [and] of science; modern or ancient; divinity or humanity'.[37] Indeed, Elizabeth was a popular choice of patron for works in all branches of natural philosophy, receiving dedications in Turner's *The First and Second Parts of the Herbal* (1568); Henry Lyte's *A Niewe Herball: Or, Historie of Plantes* (Antwerp, 1578); John Harvey's *An Astrologicall Addition* (1583), which also contained a translation of a work of astrological medicine, the *Iatromathematica*; John Jones's *The Art and Science of Preserving Bodie and Soule* (1590); Maximilian Bonman's translation of Jacques Guillemeau's *The French Chirurgerye* (Dorte, 1597); William Tooker's *Charisma* (London, 1597); and Isaak Caen's publication of a translation of Oswaldus Gebelhover's *The Boock of Phisicke* (Dorte, 1599).[38] Each of these writers adapts his rhetoric to imagine a queen, instead of a king, as the ultimate source and ideal reader of natural philosophical knowledge. In the dedicatory epistle to *A Niewe Herball*, for example, Lyte compares Elizabeth's patronage of medicine to the 'love' a mother shows towards her children: 'a thankful hart towards a natural mother cannot be better testified, then by the love shewed and practised towards her deare children' (2r).[39] Just as a mother protects her own health by caring for that of her children, it is implied, the queen will maintain her position only if she is careful with the lives of her subjects.

But of all the sciences, quasi-sciences, and occult arts, alchemy had to be handled with particular care. For the patron of an alchemist who actually delivered on his or her promises, and who actually discovered the means to multiply gold and/or prolong life, the rewards were unimaginable: alchemy, as Jonson suggests in *Mercurie Vindicated*, promises 'health, Riches, Honours' (l. 153), and gestures towards 'Immortality' – the very powers that set apart and define the monarch. As an ideal, practice, and body of knowledge, therefore, alchemy simultaneously threatened and, if properly controlled (i.e. patronised), affirmed the monarch's pre-eminence. Addressing members of the Elizabethan Privy Counsel in the *Gesta Grayorum* (1594–95), Bacon's advocate of the 'Study of Philosophy' affirms that it is incumbent upon all princes to discover 'all whatsoever is hid and secret in the world'.[40] An important route to this knowledge rests in the establishment of a 'still-house':

> so furnished with mills, instruments, furnaces, and vessels, as may be a palace fit for a philosopher's stone. Thus, when your Excellency shall have added depth of knowledge to the fineness of [your] spirits and greatness of your power, then indeed shall you be a Trismegistus; and then when all other miracles and wonders shall cease, by reason that you shall have discovered their natural causes, yourself shall be left the only miracle and wonder of the world.[41]

The knowledge and power acquired in these stillrooms and laboratories are possessed by the monarch; by sponsoring alchemy, he or she becomes not simply an alchemist but the transcendental sign that is the Philosopher's Stone itself: 'the only miracle and wonder of the world'.

Although there were no alchemists resident within the royal household, the surviving inventories of the queen's New Year's gifts and household wage accounts testify to the presence of physicians, apothecaries, distillers, and perfumers, whose work may well have involved alchemical procedures, operations, and products.[42] The cosmographer and alchemist Richard Eden (c.1520–1576) served as distiller of waters in the royal household under Henry VIII, a position that carried a salary of £40 a year.[43] At least one of the royal stillrooms was housed around the small courtyards to the north side of Hampton Court Palace, where Henry VIII's Great Kitchen was supplemented by a number of subsidiary rooms, including a wine cellar, pantry, buttery, and spicery. The stillrooms were provided with a ready supply of fresh ingredients by flower gardens, orchards, and a herb garden.[44] It is difficult to discern precisely what went on in these buildings. Ralph Rabbards, 'studicus and expert in Alchemicall Artes', evidently felt that the royal stillrooms were not fulfilling their true potential.[45] Addressing Queen Elizabeth in 1599, Rabbards laments her 'manifold fruitlesse still-houses', claiming that if he had spent the past seven years in these 'still-houses', he would now be able to 'promise more of my selfe than I will speake of' (A2r). I will return to the possible reasons for Rabbards's criticisms later in this chapter.

But the potential dangers facing the monarch who encouraged alchemy – in the form of fraud, coining, or, perhaps worse, humiliation – were considerable. 'Fools flock to Princes Courts, for there they are honoured, and fare better then others' (l. 52), Mercurie quips in Jonson's *Mercurie Vindicated*. Until 1689, alchemy, defined as the multiplication of gold and silver, was illegal in England, a felony punishable by death and forfeiture of goods.[46] Only by special dispensation of the monarch could individuals practise the art. In one of the earliest such licences, granted by Henry VI in 1456, it is conceded that the Philosopher's Stone has the potential to bring 'advantages ... to ... the Commonwealth': it is therefore in the interest of monarchs to grant licences to those alchemists who are deemed to be genuinely capable of achieving 'the mother and Empress of medicines ... the Philosopher's Stone and Elixir of Life'.[47] The characterisation of the Stone as a 'mother' or 'empress' was apt. Although patents to practise alchemy were awarded by Edward III (1329), Henry VI (1444 and 1456), and Edward IV (1476), it was a queen, Isabella of France (1295–1358), the consort of Edward II, whose name was connected with a work of chymical medicine (the so-called 'Dietary of Queen Isabel') and with a supposed Elixir of Youth, '*aqua miraculosa cum qua Regina Iezabella septuaginta, decrepita, guttosa et paralitica*'.[48] By the turn of the sixteenth century, alchemy, in both its practical and its esoteric forms, was, as Charles Webster observes, 'an entrenched interest within court circles'.[49] George Ripley (d. c.1490) dedicated *The Compound of Alchymy* (1471), a poetic description of the twelve stages in the alchemical opus, to King Edward IV.[50] Elizabeth's father, Henry VIII, was known to have made experiments in distillation in an attempt to find some relief for his various ailments, and thus received dedications in works by the English alchemist William Blomfild [Blomefield] (fl.1529–1574), including *The Compendiary of the Noble Science of Alchemy*.[51]

Of course there was no guarantee that Elizabeth would respond to unsolicited bids for patronage. Franklin B. Williams's assessment of Queen Elizabeth as the greatest of the 'great patronesses' of Renaissance England now seems somewhat naive.[52] But in the 1560s and '70s there was sufficient optimism among established and would-be alchemists, both native and foreign, as to inspire something of a scramble for patronage. Charles Webster has detailed the measures taken under Queen Elizabeth to harness the talents of 'foreign chemists and mineral masters' on behalf of Britain.[53] These practitioners, skilled in the technology of mining and metallurgy, and in alchemical processes such as refinement and transmutation, were awarded grants for the exploitation of native mineral resources, including salts, iron, copper, tin, lead, and silver, and for the transmutation of gold from the ore which navigators such as Martin Frobisher promised to import.[54] The *Calendar of State Papers* shows that Queen Elizabeth's government employed a number of alchemists, usually on a short-term basis, and that the queen was approached by many more in bids for patronage. Neither the nature of these contracts, nor that of the work undertaken, is specified. Many of these alchemists – 'John Dethicke' and 'John Bulkeley', who was accused of divulging 'various alchemical secrets and practices for diminishing and lessening the coin of the realm by sweating, etc.', for example – are little more than names.[55] Some, however, left literary remains, which provide some insight into the nature of their alchemy. The Venetian alchemist Giovanni Battista Lambi, who performed services for the government in the 1560s,[56] composed works of spiritual alchemy, one of which was translated by 'R.N.E.' and published as *A Revelation of the Secret Spirit* (1623).[57] In 1570 John Peterson of Lubeck wrote a letter to the queen offering his services as an alchemist, together with a brief 'Apollogie to the noble Science of Alcumey'.[58] As proof of his skills, Peterson mentions the existence of three phials, currently in 'the handes of the Senate of Lubick', one containing 'Sol', another containing 'Luna', and a third of 'Mercury'. The three phials to which Peterson alludes presumably were supposed to contain the constituents from which he proposed to concoct the Stone: 'Sol' and 'Luna' represent the opposing principles that the agent 'Mercury' will disintegrate and reintegrate into the 'quintessence'. Like a poem written to display the wit and talent of a young courtier, these alchemical preparations gave the queen some notion of Peterson's abilities, and, consequently, of his potential usefulness to foreign monarchs, or even the 'Senate of Lubick', should she wish to pass over his petition. The conveyor of this letter, Robert Smythe, endorsed Peterson's promise, offering his head should the alchemist fail to 'bringe for the thowsande dollars into [Queen Elizabeth's] coffers without one penny of her charges'. No records are extant to confirm whether or not Peterson was successful in his bid, but subsequent correspondence, on unrelated matters, reveals that Smythe kept his head.

An apparently successful attempt for royal patronage was made by the alchemist Cornelius de Lannoy (Alneto), whose relationship with the queen and her Privy Counsellors is recorded in an extensive correspondence.[59] In a letter dated 7 February 1565, Lannoy offered his services to the queen, claiming to be able to transmute base metals into gold (at a rate of 50,000 marks a year), manufacture precious stones, and distil the elixir of eternal youth. To prove his claim Lannoy was granted a room in Somerset House, where he produced a short alchemical treatise in Latin, *De Conficiendo Divino Elixire, Sive Lapide Philosophio*.[60] The treatise, dated 14 July 1565, features rather commonplace recipes for a number of distilled waters and oils, including '*Primum oleum Secondum oleum, Aqua fortis, Aqua regia, Lac Virginis, menstruum + acqua Mercurialis*'. On the basis of this work Lannoy was granted enough money to establish his laboratory in Somerset House, together with a regular allowance. His first act, however, was to offer a loan of £10,000 to the exiled daughter of King Gustavus I of Sweden, who was lodged nearby. Cecil, who, it seems, had been suspicious of Lannoy's motives from the start, had the alchemist closely observed. In a series of letters written during the final months of 1566 and the beginning of 1567, Lannoy attempted to appease Cecil, promising to carry through 'our great and glorious design'.[61] On 7 March 1566 Armigall Waad wrote to Cecil warning him that Lannoy was planning to escape with the elixir and the irons for casting ingots under the protection of 'a certaine person'.[62] Lannoy was committed to the Tower, and the last known reference to him is an order dated 28 May 1567 demanding his presence at court the following day. In his diary entry for 10 February 1567, Cecil somewhat tersely notes that 'Cornelius de la Noye, an alchemist, wrought in Somerset House and abused many in promising to convert any metal into gold'.[63]

Mary M. Luke finds it 'incredible' that in the case of Cornelius Lannoy 'even Elizabeth's own strong intelligence was momentarily duped'.[64] But there is nothing to link Elizabeth herself to Lannoy. Instead, she insulated herself from any such scandal by using Cecil and/or Walsingham as intermediaries in her dealings with Lannoy and other alchemists. Gesturing towards the 'technique of evasion' that was, I argue, central to the Queen's control of alchemical knowledge, Paul Johnson is more generous and more subtle in his assessment, observing that, although Elizabeth 'constantly saw and patronized those who were pushing forward the frontiers of knowledge', she was equally careful not to allow this intellectual circle to 'overlap the centre of power'.[65] Further, Lannoy's case highlights the importance of fidelity in the patron–alchemist relationship. Even before his imprisonment in the Tower, Lannoy was kept under close surveillance at Somerset House. Offering services to a foreign princess, Lannoy's fidelity to Queen Elizabeth had been fundamentally compromised, and a relationship that had once been advantageous to the Crown suddenly became a threat to national security.

The more sophisticated bids for patronage fashion the Queen as the kind of Lady Alchymia they would wish her to be. Thomas Charnock's (1526–1581) appeal to Elizabeth is shaped by nationalistic rhetoric.[66] A Booke Dedicated unto the Quenes Majestie (c.1565) is a kind of curriculum vitae in which Charnock details his education and accomplishments in alchemy and sketches a scheme through which he undertakes to achieve the Stone on behalf of the Queen.[67] As with Lannoy, Cecil was Elizabeth's intermediary here. Charnock's Booke, an elegant manuscript still bound in its original gold-tooled presentation cover, passed into Cecil's keeping, and we cannot even be certain that it came to Elizabeth's attention. However, throughout the Booke, Charnock makes every effort to fashion the queen as his ideal patron. Like Dee, he presents his text as a work of 'revelation' – what David Meakin, writing of hermetic discourse, calls 'a reveiling, a perpetual dialectic of offering and with-holding' – requiring personal guidance and instruction that will require an ongoing dialogue between himself and his patron, the queen.[68] In the Booke, most of which takes the form of a dialogue, Charnock teases out the correspondences between patronage and alchemy, monarch and alchemist, in order to manoeuvre Queen Elizabeth into a position where she will be obliged – or too scared not – to accept his appeal.

Charnock opens his Booke with a brief history of 'natural philosophy' in England, thereby situating himself within a great national tradition of hermetism and alchemy almost ninety years before Elias Ashmole was to do the same in the 'Prolegomena' to his Theatrum chemicum Britannicum (1652).[69] Alongside bookwork and experimental practice, Charnock claims to have had 'the greatest secret of ye science' revealed to him 'under a most sacred othe' by a 'master'.[70] Charnock thus presents himself as the bearer of an essential key to the art, a keeper of knowledge that cannot be bought, and which places him in a position of potential power over Elizabeth herself. Tying himself closely to the fate of the queen, Charnock promises to produce a medicine (an 'Elixir') that will preserve her health and, consequently, her rule. More immediately, he suggests, Elizabeth can expect a regular source of high-quality gold, the output of which will multiply yearly: at the end of eight years Charnock promises fifty ounces of gold, and after fourteen years, he pledges 350 ounces, valued at £1,050. Indeed, Charnock claims that the wealth presently enjoyed by the queen and her nobility on behalf of the nation came from the work of the early alchemists:

> [The Philosopher's Stone] was wrought secretly in great & ryche monestaries by men given to great soliterines, wch by dayley practis and lounge continuance of tyme ther dyd attayne unto it: where wth they dyd inryche them selves wth habundance of golden jouells and plate, And some bylded chapels, cells, colledges, and hospitalls, and some dyd inryche their poore kyndred.[71]

If Elizabeth is to maintain or augment that wealth, it is implied, she must continue to invest in alchemists such as Charnock. Invoking the distinction between the *aurum nostrum* of the alchemists and the *aurum vulgi* of mere gold-seekers, Charnock warns that the gold currently being sought in foreign lands ('Hispaniola ... Guinea ... [and] the Ilands of Molucca') is beneath 'a princes dignitie':[72] royal patronage must be redirected away from navigation and overseas exploration, and concentrated on English alchemists.

William Blomfild dedicated his final major work to Elizabeth. In it, he uses alchemical discourse as a metaphor not for imperial policy but for religious governance. The *Quintæssens: Or, The Regiment of Lyfe* (c.1574) combines alchemical recipes with a celebration of the queen's spiritual alchemy.[73] In the dedicatory epistle, Blomfild, a former Benedictine friar turned Puritan, asks for royal protection against the 'crewel papistes' who have prevented him from ministering to his parishioners, and against the 'Informers & promoters' who, acting in the queen's name ('who by fals tytils do cal them selves your highness husbondes'), have 'abused' the laws against alchemy, and who 'for thes iiij years have sore malestyd me. And have hindred the worke the which I mynded to Imploy al to gyther & holly to your highnes comoditie'.[74] Implicitly comparing Jesuits to unscrupulous apothecaries who adulterate medicines with poisons, Blomfild proceeds to praise Queen Elizabeth's struggle to 'purify' the country of the 'corrupt' doctrines of Catholicism. Likening Elizabeth to Old Testament heroines whom God tried and tested, Blomfild uses alchemical imagery to argue that through internal rebellion and personal assaults the Queen has been thoroughly 'clensed & purged' and thus blessed by God:

> god of his goodness. from tyme to tyme hath tried you in the surnes [i.e. sourness] of adversitie. And proved you many & sondrye wayes. As he dyd prove ... Judith & chaste susanna & many other prophets & prophetises. Kynges & queens. And by soch tryall he hath found your highness with the reste of his electe. worthy of his

owne selfe. And yet not so contentyd with those good & godly exercises toward your highness to exercise you withal. but also of his fatherly goodness hath by sundry wayes. as by rebellion. clensed & purged you. that you shuld bring forth more frute. (fols 6v–7r)

Blomfild draws upon the rhetoric of spiritual and esoteric alchemy, in which the alchemical opus is imagined as a kind of purgatory. Elizabeth, having been tested in the fires of religious tumult, has emerged as someone 'tried & found acceptable to god' (fol. 4v). Like the true philosophical gold, which brings together the four elements in harmony, she has remained untouched despite being tested in the refining fires of religious and political tumult. Indeed, because she is in a state of spiritual equilibrium, persecution has only purified and further strengthened her resolve, transmuting her into the fifth essence, or 'quintessence', the substance from which the angels are made. Caught in an intermediary state half-way between earth and heaven, Elizabeth is uniquely able to transform the world of material reality without being affected (i.e. corrupted) by it. Using this motif to praise Queen Elizabeth's religious policy and spiritual essence, Blomfild skilfully appropriates this cornerstone of Catholic theology on behalf of a Reformist spiritual alchemy.[75]

Tying his interests closely to those of the queen, and both their interests to the workings of divine Providence, Blomfild presents himself as little more than a conduit, returning to the queen, his 'protectrice', the knowledge that she has conceived, knows, and embodies: 'to soch a singuler princes A moste preciose & singuler Jowel or precios perle, the rather without daunger or parel myght be disclosed' (fol. 4v). In portraying himself as the least worthy and most humble of subjects, Blomfild is thus able to write about the most profound of subjects, the divine mysteries of the Stone. Thus Queen Elizabeth is made to fulfil a role analogous to that of the sonnet beloved: contemplating the divinity represented by the mortal queen, Blomfild is inspired to contemplate the divinity of Christ in so far as his dual nature is represented by the terrestrial Stone. Here, then, the rhetorical trope of the Stone functions in Blomfild's autobiographical defence of himself as a loyal subject, as a follower of the true religion, and as a physician who heals and transmutes out of motives other than financial gain. Moving imperceptibly from spiritual alchemy to practical medicine, Blomfild concludes *Quintæssens* by entrusting the queen with some 'higher secretis', including recipes for potable gold, for the 'quintessence' of 'Saturn', and for a mysterious 'ruby ston', which seems to represent the final stage of the alchemical opus, the *iosis* or *rubedo* (fols 10v–11r). The implication, as with so many alchemical texts, is that Blomfild withholds at least as much as he reveals to the queen. If Elizabeth and her ministers want to know more, it seems, Blomfild must be adequately recompensed for his efforts. There are no extant records to confirm whether or not Blomfild's petition was successful, but it may be that this work, composed towards the end of his turbulent life, was designed not so much to gain income and patronage, as to secure his reputation as a godly and faithful subject.

The final alchemical work dedicated to Queen Elizabeth during the period 1560–1580 is simultaneously the most optimistic and the most equivocal. The *Key of Alchimie* (1577) is an alchemical treatise by Samuel Norton (1548–1621), comprising descriptions of the constituent parts and qualities of the Philosopher's Stone.[76] Norton opens with an address to 'Alchemy' herself, in which a 'princely' Lady Alchymia is implicitly compared to Norton's chosen patron, Queen Elizabeth:

> Alchemy noble Muse, of all most worthy praise
> Which bring'st Dame Nature's secret laws to light
> In Sphaere of princely mind again thyself upraise
> From whence at first thou chose to shine with open light. (fol. 2r)

The dedicatory epistle and 'Preamble' follow. Here, the comparison is made explicit. The reign of Queen Elizabeth, Norton suggests, may have been prophesied in an earlier, unidentified work of alchemy:

> that which I most of all desire to come to pass, is that which he intimates in his 6th Chapter where speaking of the stone to be revealed to the kings of the land it shall be found he saith:
> By the fortune + by the grace
> Of a woman faire of face
> And what know I Oh Queene! Whether it be yr. selfe or noe?
>
> (fol. 13v)[77]

In this visionary passage Queen Elizabeth is accorded both an active and a passive role: by virtue of her patronage (her 'fortune') and her spiritual qualities (her 'grace'), she presides over the discovery of the Stone; and, by virtue of these same characteristics (spiritual purity and wealth), she also symbolises the Stone, which is equally mortal and divine, material and spiritual. But the vision is framed as a question, and as such it poses a direct challenge to the queen. The Stone lies within her grasp, but whether or not she will decide to claim it remains in doubt, and this uncertainty anticipates the more general pessimism that was to characterise the final decade of Elizabeth's reign.

'An Alchymist deuine': the 1590s

If the 1560s and 1570s witnessed a guarded optimism regarding the queen's patronage of aspiring or established alchemists, the 1590s saw a marked change.[78] The single alchemical work dedicated to the queen during this period was Ralph Rabbards's translation of George Ripley's *The Compound of Alchymy* (1591). Significantly, *The Compound* is not a work of practical alchemy but a mystical poem, describing the twelve stages of the opus in what Thomas Lodge would subsequently term '*Ænigmata and Problemes darke*'.[79] And it is also significant that Rabbards, a self-titled 'expert in

Alchemicall Artes' (A1r), makes it clear that he is no longer able to practise alchemy. Incapacitated by 'old age' (A2r), Rabbards explains that he has turned to translation in order to satisfie his continuing interest in alchemy, and he uses the dedicatory epistle to argue for more active royal protection of practising alchemists. His own career, he reflects in terms which echo Blomfild's complaint, was marred by 'many yeares spent unprofitably in a laborinth of law suites, and private contention with men of verie great abilitie, and better friended than my selfe' (A2r). Contemporary alchemists, he claims, continue to suffer the 'venymous darts of the envious + malicious tongs' (A2r) of the ignorant. On behalf of those who continue to practise alchemy, Rabbards calls upon the queen to make good her promise to provide 'protection for the instruction and direction of all students, and lovers of the secret Mysteries of naturall Philosophie' (A2v). But, he implies, Elizabeth has consistently failed to fulfil these promises, and those 'very fewe' who have attained the 'hidden Arte and high Mysterie of making the Philosophers Stone' have been allowed to keep that 'secret to themselves', judging 'the world not worthy of so precious a Jewell' (A2r). Despite his pledge of loyalty to the queen and his offer of service, Rabbards, writing towards the end of his life, seems to be implicitly criticising the queen and those in positions of power who have failed to properly distribute the knowledge and the means to power that the Philosopher's Stone represents.

We can complete this changing perception of Queen Elizabeth's patronage of alchemy by examining her presentation as Lady Alchymia in poetry dating from the final years of her reign. In the opening poem of *Hymnes of Astraea* (1599), for example, John Davies uses alchemical imagery to describe Queen Elizabeth's ability to transmute her country from its present crudity into a Golden Age:

> The Mayde ...
> Hath brought againe the golden dayes,
> And all the world amended.
>
> Rudenesse it selfe she doth refine,
> Euen like an Alchymist diuine,
> Grosse times of Iron turning
> Into the purest forme of gold:
> Not to corrupt, till heauen waxe old,
> And be refin'd with burning.[80]

As in Norton's *Key*, Elizabeth is accorded a prophetic role in transmuting the land. Davies pursues this metaphor in the thirteenth hymn, 'Of her Mind', in which he writes: 'Her cleare sweet *Spirit* is refind / Aboue Humane *Creation*' (Biiijr). Of this poem Stanton J. Linden finds it 'remarkable' that Davies 'should have seen fit to use this much disparaged art at all in the praise of his Queen'.[81] Davies's poem is indeed a marked departure from the satirical treatment alchemy often received in sixteenth-century literature. But Davies was able to use it as a vehicle of praise, it seems, precisely because he no longer believed in alchemy as a material reality. The transformation which Davies imagines Elizabeth effecting is spiritual and cultural, not material. Having reneged on her promise '*discere & facere*', the queen is left with a diminished role. Davies no longer believes that alchemy or his queen can deliver eternal life and unlimited wealth. Instead, the true subject of alchemy, and of the alchemical poetry of Davies and his contemporaries, including George Herbert, John Donne, Henry Vaughan, and Andrew Marvell, lies within: the soul. Thus, in *Nosce Teipsum*, which was published alongside *Hymnes to Astraea* in 1622, Davies uses alchemy to describe the particularly rarefied nature of the human soul and to distinguish its composition from both sense and bodily humours. Condemning those '*Alchimists*' who seek to produce gold, Davies sides with those who identify the human soul as the proper subject of the opus:

> [The Soul] is a spirit …
>
> …
>
> [Not] like those spirits which *Alchimists* do find,
> When they in everything seeke gold, in *vaine*.[82]

For Davies the soul is a kind of Lady Alchymia, vaporising material phenomena into immaterial, conceptual forms: 'she turned/ Bodies to spirits by sublimation strange'.[83]

Conclusion

In a letter to Sir Robert Cecil, dated 1598, Sir John Stanhope writes: 'I have ben redyng Mr Edmonds' letter & yours to her Majestie, the which cam not to my handes tyll vi a clocke, for I was all the afternowne with her Majestie at my booke, and then, thynkynge to rest me, went in agayne with your letter. She was plesed with the filosofer's stone & hath ben all this daye reasonably quyett.'[84] The image of the ageing queen, listening to her correspondence being read aloud, and – as something of an afterthought – declaring herself 'plesed' with 'the filosofer's stone', is at once tender and slightly absurd. This is no longer the Philosopher's Stone which can multiply gold and prolong life: it is a fancy, a whim, a fiction to while away the hours.

But it would be wrong to characterise Elizabeth as fanciful in her patronage of alchemy. 'Princes hearts', Francis Bacon reflected, 'are inscrutable'.[85] Mindful of the potential power – and dangers – of the Philosopher's Stone, were it to prove to be more than a mere fiction, Queen Elizabeth, in her dealings with alchemists, adopted the persona of Lady Alchymia as the muse who promises, engages, and confounds her male courtiers. Precisely by failing to combine understanding and action – by severing the promised transaction between heaven and earth, expectation and realisation, and thereby giving emphasis to alchemy as a spiritual discourse – she negotiated a space for herself within the persona of Lady Alchymia that enabled her to use and defend herself against the alchemists who would use her. In so doing, Elizabeth became Trithemius's supremely powerful and unsettling Lady Alchymia: a 'chaste prostitute, who has many lovers but disappoints all and grants her favors to none'.

Notes

1. Ben Jonson, *Mercurie Vindicated*, in *Ben Jonson*, edited by C.H. Herford, Percy Simpson, and Evelyn Simpson, 11 vols (Oxford: Clarendon Press, 1925–1952), VII (1941), ll. 213–223. All subsequent parenthetical line references to *Mercurie Vindicated* are from this edition.

2. Stanton J. Linden, *Darke Hieroglyphicks: Alchemy in English Literature from Chaucer to the Restoration* (Lexington, KY: University of Kentucky Press, 1996), p. 147.

3. Allison Heisch, 'Queen Elizabeth I: Parliamentary Rhetoric and the Exercise of Power', *Signs* 1 (Autumn 1975), pp. 31–55, p. 40.

4. Johannes Trithemius, *Annales Hirsavgienses*, II (Leiden, 1690), p. 53.

5. Conrad Gesner, *The newe jewell of health wherein is contayned the most excellent secretes of phisicke and philosophie, deuided into fower bookes*, ed. by George Baker (London: Henrie Denham, 1576), sig. Ajr. On the circumstances behind this dedication see 'Two Women Patrons of Chymical Literature', chapter 3 of my unpublished Ph.D. dissertation, 'Women and Alchemy in Early Modern England' (University of Cambridge, 2000), n. pag. The woodcut is a modified version of an illustration from Leonhardt Thurneisser Zum Thurn, *Quinta Essentia* (Münster, 1570), and was used again for the frontispiece of Baker's revised edition of *The newe jewell of health*, published as *The practice of the new and old phisicke* (London: Peter Short, 1599).

6. M.E. Warlick, 'The Domestic Alchemist: Women as Housewives in Alchemical Emblems', *Glasgow Emblem Studies* 3 (Winter 1998), pp. 25–48.

7. On Alexandrian alchemy see John Read, *Prelude to Chemistry: An Outline of Alchemy, Its Literature and Relationships* (London: G. Bell, 1939), pp. 12–45.

8. Roger Bacon et al., *The Mirrour of Alchimy ... with certaine other treatises of the like argument* (London: [Thomas Creede] for Richard Oliue, 1599), pp. 16–17. On the reputation of Hermes Trismegistus and the authority of the *Hermetica* in early modern England see Anthony Grafton, 'Protestant Versus Prophet: Isaac Casaubon on Hermes Trismegistus', *Journal of the Warburg and Courtauld Institutes* 46 (1983), pp. 78–93.

9. On the role of female authors in Alexandrian alchemy see Read, *Prelude to Chemistry*, pp. 18–23.

10. See, for example, Samuel Norton, *Key of Alchymie* (1577), Bodleian Library, Oxford, Ashmole MS 1421, fol. 44r. Norton claims to be quoting from an unspecified work by George Ripley.

11. Thomas Bonham, *The Chyrurgians Closet*, edited by Edward Poeton (London: George Miller, for Edwarde Brewster, 1630), a1r. Poeton dedicates this publication to 'Lady, Francis Countesse of Exceter' (a3r).

12. Johann Jacob Wecker, *Eighteen books of the secrets of art & nature being the summe and substance of naturall philosophy*, ed. by R. Read (London: Simon Miller, 1660), A4v. 'Cleopatra' was popularly identified with the Egyptian queen (69–30 BCE), whose skill in chymistry is documented in Pliny [C. Plinius Secundus], *The historie of the world: commonly called, The natural historie*, translated by by Philemon Holland (London: Adam Islip, 1634), Book 9, p. 257.

13. Among the many studies of alchemy in Donne's poetry see, for example, Roberta

Albrecht, 'Alchemical Augmentation and Primordial Fire in Donne's "The Dissolution"', *Studies in English Literature* 45.1 (Winter 2005), pp. 95–115; Linden, *Darke Hieroglyphicks*, pp. 154–192; and Joseph Anthony Mazzeo, 'Notes on John Donne's Alchemical Imagery', in Mazzeo, *Renaissance and Seventeenth-Century Studies* (London: Routledge and Kegan Paul, 1964), pp. 60–89. On the 'chymical wedding' in alchemical literature and imagery see Lyndy Abraham, *A Dictionary of Alchemical Imagery* (Cambridge: Cambridge University Library, 1996), pp. 35–39, and Charles Nicholl, *The Chemical Theatre* (London: Routledge and Kegan Paul, 1980), pp. 232–236.

14. On this discrepancy between feminine icons and the lives of real women see Marina Warner, *Monuments and Matrons: The Allegory of the Female Form* (London: Weidenfeld & Nicolson, 1985).

15. For examples of this phenomenon see Archer, 'Women and Alchemy in Early Modern England', and Penny Bayer, 'Lady Margaret Clifford's Alchemical Receipt Book and the John Dee Circle', *Ambix* 52.3 (2005), pp. 271–284, and 'Women's Alchemical Literature 1560–1616 in Italy, France, the Swiss Cantons and England, and its Diffusion to 1660', unpublished Ph.D. thesis, University of Warwick, 2003.

16. John Thornborough's *Letter of Chemistry to the right Honourable the Lady Knowles*, an alchemical treatise based on the Pythagorean decad, is British Library, London, MS Sloane 1799, fols 74–104 (I quote from fols 75r–76r). Thornborough, Bishop of Worcester, published an alchemical treatise, *Lithotheorikos* (Oxford: Johannes Lichfield & Jacobus Short, 1621).

17. Cited in Johannes Fabricius, *Alchemy: The Medieval Alchemists and Their Royal Art* (Copenhagen: Rosenkilde and Bagger, 1976), pp. 176–177. The emblems in *Philosophia Reformata* were based, in part, on those in the *Rosarium Philosophorum*, for which see n. 21, below.

18. Nicholl, *The Chemical Theatre*, p. 18.

19. Philippa Berry, *Of Chastity and Power: Elizabethan Literature and the Unmarried Queen* (London: Routledge, 1989). See, in particular, the discussion of John Lyly's *Campaspe*, in which Berry argues that the Queen's chastity enables her to function as 'a type of transcendental sign … the royal agent of a poetic mode of alchemy, which transforms the dross of text and performance to pure gold by stamping it with her image like a new-minted coin'. 'In this conception', Berry adds, 'Elizabeth resembles the biblical Wisdom figure … who signified the possibility of a spiritual transformation of material reality' (Berry, *Of Chastity and Power*, p. 120).

20. John Hester, *The First Parte of the Key of Philosophie* (London: Valentine Simmes, 1596), A7v.

21. Proverbs 3:13–16, 18 (King James version). This passage provided inspiration for material in two influential alchemical texts, the *Rosarium Philosophorum*, in *Alchymia: De alchimia opuscula complura*, vol. 2 of 2 (Frankfurt, 1550), and *Aurora Consurgens*, in *Auriferae artis, quam chemiam vocant … authores* (Basel, 1572), popularly attributed to St Thomas Aquinas.

22. Michael Maier, *Michael Maier's Atalanta Fugiens: Sources of an Alchemical Book of Emblems*, edited and translated by H.M.E. De Jong (London: E.J. Brill, 1969), p. 402. *Atalanta Fugiens* was originally published in Latin.

23. *Atalanta Fugiens*, p. 196.

24. Hugh Plat, *The jewell house of art and nature* (London: Peter Short, 1594), Book 1, p. 85. Plat's services to the nation as an inventor were finally acknowledge by King James I in 1605, when he was awarded a knighthood. Plat's frustration under Elizabeth is perhaps alluded to in his preface to his *Delightes for Ladies to adorne their persons, tables, closets, and distillatories with beauties, banquets, perfumes and waters* (London: Peter Short, 1602), A2r.

25. Trithemius, *Annalium Hirsaugensium*, II, p. 53. Trithemius's description of Lady Alchymia is the inspiration for Chapter 58 of Umberto Eco's *Foucault's Pendulum* (*Il pendolo di Foucault*), trans. William Weaver (London: Secker & Warburg, 1989).

26. John French, *The Art of Distillation* (London: E. Cotes, for Thomas Williams, 1653), sig. A3r.

27. See also the American alchemist George Starkey (1628–1665), writing under his pseudonym 'Eirenaeus Philalethes': 'our *Water* is a most clean Virgin, and is loved by many, but she meets all her Wooers ... Therefore honour ye this Female, the *Sister* and *Wife* of our *King* ... this our *Queen* is clean above measure, whom if you shall behold, you will think you look upon a certain Heavenly Body, for she is indeed the Heaven or the fifth Essence of *Philosophers*' (Eirenaeus Philalethes, *The Fountain of Chymical Philosophy*, in *Three tracts of the great medicine of philosophers for humane and metalline bodies* (London: T. Sowle, 1694), pp. 147–186, pp. 154–155).

28. Elias Ashmole, *Theatrum chemicum Britannicum* (London: J. Grismond for Nathanial Brooke, 1652), B4v.

29. On Elizabeth's identification with Diana see Berry, *Of Chastity and Power.*

30. Dee's *Monas Hieroglyphica* was first published in Antwerp in 1564, and was dedicated to Emperor Maximilian II. On the reception of the *Monas Hieroglyphica*, see the special issue of *Ambix* 52.3 (2005), edited by Stephen Clucas, esp. Peter J. Forshaw, 'The Early Alchemical Reception of John Dee's *Monas Hieroglyphica*', pp. 247–269.

31. John Dee, *Autobiographical Tracts*, edited by James Crossley, in *Chetham Miscellanies*, 1 (1851), p. 19.

32. Malabika Sarkar, 'The Magic of Shakespeare's Sonnets', *Renaissance Studies* 12 (June 1998), pp. 251–260, p. 251.

33. On this stereotype see, for example, Mary M. Luke, who assumes that Elizabeth's interest in astrology and the occult served as a substitute for her lack of emotional intimacy: 'Husbandless and childless, Elizabeth had the inclination and the time for interests which an older, busier matron with family responsibilities might have forsaken' (*Gloriana: The Years of Queen Elizabeth I* (London: Gollancz, 1974), p. 305).

34. See, for example, Melissa Meriam Bullard, 'Marsilio Ficino and the Medici: The Inner Dimensions of Patronage', in *Christianity and the Renaissance: Environments of Religious Imagination in the Quattrocento*, edited by Timothy Venton and John Henderson (Syracuse, NY: Syracuse University Press, 1990), pp. 467–492.

35. Mario Biagioli, 'Galileo's System of Patronage', *History of Science* 28 (1990), pp. 1–62.

36. Francis Bacon, *The Advancement of Learning*, in *The Major Works*, edited by Brian Vickers (Oxford: Oxford University Press, 1996), pp. 154–155.

37. William Turner, *The first and seconde partes of the* herbal (Collen: By [the heirs of] Arnold Birckman, 1568), sig. Aijv. Bacon, *The Advancement of Learning*, in *The Major Works*, ed. Vickers, p. 158.

38. Harvey's edition of the *Iatromathematica* was the only English translation of a Hermetic text to be published during Queen Elizabeth's reign.

39. *A Niewe Herball* was a translation from a French version of Rembert Dodoens's Dutch herbal.

40. Francis Bacon, *The Device for the Gray's Inn Revels*, in *The Major Works*, ed. Vickers, p. 54.

41. Bacon, *The Device for the Gray's Inn Revels*, pp. 53–54.

42. See, for example, the New Year gift rolls in *The Progresses and Public Processions ... of Queen Elizabeth I*, edited by John Nichols, second edition, 3 vols (London: John Nichols, 1823), I, 108–130; II, 65–91, 249–275; III, 1–25, 445–467.

43. See Andrew Hadfield, 'Eden, Richard (c.1520–1576)', in *Oxford Dictionary of National Biography*, ed. H.C.G. Matthew and Brian Harrison (Oxford: Oxford University Press, 2004); online ed., ed. Lawrence Goldman, May 2005, http://www.oxforddnb.com/view/article/8454 (accessed 30 May 2006).

44. June Osbourne, *Hampton Court Palace* (Kingswood: Kaye and Ward, 1984), pp. 46–47.

45. George Ripley, *A Compound of Alchymy*, trans. Ralph Rabbards (London: Thomas Orwin, 1591), A1r.

46. Frank Sherwood Taylor, *The Alchemists* (St Albans: Paladin, 1976), p. 124.

47. Cited in Charles Webster, 'Alchemical and Paracelsian Medicine', in *Health, Medicine and Mortality in the Sixteenth Century*, edited by Webster (Cambridge: Cambridge University Press, 1979), pp. 301–334, pp. 302–303.

48. See W.L. Brackman, 'Queen Isabel's Dietary and its Context', in *Studies on Alchemy, Diet, Medecine [sic] and Prognostication in Middle English* (Brussels: Omirel, 1986). Copies of the 'Dietary', dating from the fifteenth century, are held at the Wellcome Library, Western MSS 397, 404, 408, 411, and 5262.

49. Webster, 'Alchemical and Paracelsian Medicine', p. 307.

50. Like John Dee with Queen Elizabeth, Ripley warned Edward that the secrets contained in *The Compound of Alchymy* could only be understood by personal instruction. See Anthony Gross, 'Ripley, George (d. c.1490)', in *Oxford Dictionary of National Biography*, edited by H.C.G. Matthew and Brian Harrison (Oxford: Oxford University Press, 2004), www.oxforddnb.com/view/article/23663 (accessed 30 May 2006). Ripley's epistle to Edward is printed in Rabbards's translation of *The Compound of Alchymy*, L3r–M2v.

51. On Blomfild see Lawrence M. Principe, 'Blomfild, William (fl. 1529–1574)', in *Oxford Dictionary of National Biography*, edited by H.C.G. Matthew and Brian Harrison (Oxford: Oxford University Press, 2004), www.oxforddnb.com/view/article/53658 (accessed 30 May 2006), R.M. Schuler, 'William Blomfeld, Elizabethan Alchemist', *Ambix* 20 (1972), pp. 75–87, and 'An Alchemical Poem: Authorship and Manuscripts', *The Library*, fifth ser., 28 (1973), pp. 240–242.

52. Franklin B. Williams, 'The Literary Patronesses of Renaissance England', *Notes and Queries* 9 (1964), pp. 364–366, p. 364. B.B. Gamzue, in contrast, concludes that Elizabeth's reputation as a great patron – a 'legend based upon the many adulatory dedications to her – was "cheaply bought"' (B.B. Gamzue, 'Elizabeth and Literary Patronage', *PMLA* 49 (1934), p. 1049).

53. Webster, 'Alchemical and Paracelsian Medicine', p. 303. On foreign scientists and craftsmen in Elizabethan London see Deborah Harkness, '"Strange" Ideas and "English" Knowledge: Natural Science Exchange in Elizabethan London', in *Merchants and Marvels: Commerce and the Representation of Nature in Early Modern Europe*, edited by Pamela H. Smith and Paula Findlen (London: Routledge, 2001), pp. 137–161.

54. On the patronage of craftsmen and engineers in Elizabethan England see Eric H. Ash, *Power, Knowledge, and Expertise in Elizabethan England* (London: The Johns Hopkins University Press, 2004), and 'Queen v. Northumberland, and the Control of Technical Expertise', *History of Science* 39 (2001), pp. 215–240.

55. *CSPD* (1547–1580), pp. 77, 269.

56. *CSPD* (1547–1580), pp. 543, 570–571.

57. John Baptista Lambye, *A Revelation of the secret spirit, declaring the most concealed Alchymie*, trans. R.N.E. (London: John Haviland for Henrie Skelton, 1623). The translator has been identified as Richard Napier, and the publication was dedicated to John Thornborough.

58. *CSPD* (1547–1580), pp. 75, 66.

59. *CSPD* (1547–1580), pp. 249, 256, 273, 275–277, 289, 292; *CSPD* Addenda (1566–1579), p. 10. On Lannoy see Webster, 'Alchemical and Paracelsian Medicine', p. 307.

60. This work was first published in *Secreta Secretorum* (1592), and also appeared in *Theatrum Chemicum*, edited by Lazarus Zetzner, vol. 5 (Strasbourg, 1660), pp. 815–821. An English translation, *Alneto on the Divine Elixir* (1565), exists in a manuscript collection of alchemical works compiled by Thomas Robson (Bodleian Library, Oxford, Ashmole MS 1418). Regarding Lannoy's residency in Somerset House see Raymond Needham and Alexander

Webster, *Somerset House Past and Present* (London: T. Fisher Unwin, 1905), pp. 78–79.

61. Cited in Needham and Webster, *Somerset House Past and Present*, p. 78.

62. Needham and Webster, *Somerset House Past and Present*, p. 78.

63. Needham and Webster, *Somerset House Past and Present*, p. 78.

64. Luke, *Gloriana*, p. 305.

65. Paul Johnson, *Elizabeth I: A Study in Power and Intellect* (London: Weidenfeld & Nicolson, 1974), p. 221.

66. Charnock's uncle, also called Thomas, had practised alchemy and served as confessor to King Henry VII. See Robert M. Schuler, 'Charnock, Thomas (1524x6–1581)', in *Oxford Dictionary of National Biography*, edited by H.C.G. Matthew and Brian Harrison (Oxford: Oxford University Press, 2004), www.oxforddnb.com/view/article/5173 (accessed 30 May 2006).

67. The MS is British Library, London, Lansdowne MS 703. It is discussed in Alan Pritchard, 'Thomas Charnock's Book Dedicated to Queen Elizabeth', *Ambix* 26 (1979), pp. 56–73.

68. David Meakin, *Hermetic Fictions: Alchemy and Irony in the Novel* (Keele: Keele University Press, 1995), p. 30.

69. Ashmole, *Theatrum Chemicum Britannicum*, pp. 8–10.

70. Cited in Pritchard, 'Thomas Charnock's Book Dedicated to Queen Elizabeth', p. 65.

71. Pritchard, 'Thomas Charnock's Book Dedicated to Queen Elizabeth', p. 67.

72. Pritchard, 'Thomas Charnock's Book Dedicated to Queen Elizabeth', p. 70.

73. Blomfild's *Quintæssens* exists in a single, incomplete MS copy, written in the hand of Myles Blomefylde [Blomefield] (1525–1603), an alchemist and priest, and William's probable kinsman. Cambridge University Library, MS Dd. III. 83 (Item 6). All parenthetical references are taken from the MS.

74. Cited in Schuler, 'William Blomfild, Elizabethan Alchemist,' p. 61. Blomfild had been made vicar of the parish of Sts Simon and Jude in Norwich in April 1569, but was forced out, 'by obstinate papistes' (fol. 1r) in less than a year. On the biographical background to the *Quintæssens* see Schuler, pp. 80–85.

75. See, for example, St Catherine of Genoa's fifteenth-century *Treatise on Purgatory*, cited in *The Book of Catholic Quotations*, edited by John Chapin (London: John Calder, 1957), p. 743. On the motif of the spiritual touchstone, see Archer, 'Women and Alchemy in Early Modern England', Chapter 2, pp. xiii–xiv.

76. Bodleian Library, Oxford, Ashmole MS 1421.

77. The text to which Norton refers is, presumably, the *Ordinal of Alchemy* (1477), an alchemical poem by his great-grandfather, Thomas Norton (d. 1513), but the *Ordinal* does not contain such a prophecy. A presentation copy of the *Ordinal* may have been given to Edward IV: see Anthony Gross, 'Norton, Thomas (d. 1513)', in *Oxford Dictionary of National Biography*, edited by H.C.G. Matthew and Brian Harrison (Oxford: Oxford University Press, 2004), www.oxforddnb.com/view/article/20358 (accessed 30 May 2006).

78. On the literary and political contexts of the 1590s see *The Reign of Queen Elizabeth I: Court and Culture in the Last Decade*, edited by John Guy (Cambridge: Cambridge University Press, 1995), and Georgia Brown, *Redefining Elizabethan Literature* (Cambridge: Cambridge University Press, 2004).

79. Thomas Lodge, 'The Anatomie of Alchymie', in *A Critical Edition of Thomas Lodge's A Fig for Momus, 1595*, edited by Wesley Dennis Rae (Ann Arbor: n. pub., n.d.), p. 58.

80. John Davies, *Hymnes of Astraea in acrosticke verse* (London: [by R. Field] for I. S[tandish], 1599), sig. Aijr.

81. Linden, *Darke Hieroglyphicks*, p. 94.

82. John Davies, *Nosce teipsum* (London: Augustine Mathewes for Richard Hawkins, 1622), p. 7.

83. John Davies, *Nosce teipsum*, p. 7.

84. Edmund Lodge, *Illustrations of British history, biography, and manner*, 3 vols (London: G. Nicol, 1791), II, p. 95.

85. Francis Bacon, *The Device for the Gray's Inn Revels* (1594–1595), in *The Major Works*, ed. Vickers, p. 52.

Part II

Virginia and the Virgin: Elizabeth and the New World

4

Elizabeth I: size matters

Deanne Williams

Miniature is one of the refuges of greatness (Gaston Bachelard,
The Poetics of Space)

At first, David Starkey didn't recognise Princess Elizabeth in this portrait (Figure 3).
However, he was immediately struck by her 'painfully thin shoulders, exposed by
the low, square-cut dress, [that suggests] an aching vulnerability'.[1] Inspired by the
smallness of the princess in this portrait, which has been attributed to William
Scrots, Starkey composed *Elizabeth: Apprenticeship* (2000): a book about the queen
when she was little. The portrait, which Starkey believes Elizabeth 'gave to her
father just before his death', provides an emblem for his project, which offers an
alternative to the prevailing vision of Elizabeth as Astraea or Gloriana.[2] Starkey
dismisses the monumental and the magnificent in Elizabethan portraiture, so
central to the work of Dame Frances Yates and Sir Roy Strong, as mere 'apparatus',
all 'flummery' and 'superstructure' (xii).[3] His work reflects the recent interest,
instead, in the Elizabethan aesthetics of the miniature, the diminutive, the trifling,
the fragmentary.[4] Of course the Astraea and Gloriana of Yates and Strong were
a response to the tendency of their Victorian predecessors to diminish Elizabeth,
either by recollecting her as a child or by placing her in undignified settings, as
Nicola J. Watson puts it, 'in disarray or *en déshabillé*'.[5]

Just as each generation refashions Shakespeare, each generation recreates Elizabeth I
in its own image. Yet, as our book title *Goddesses and queens* illustrates, scholars often
pay closer attention to the aspects of magnificence and monumentalism in the portraits
of Elizabeth, reflecting the various agendas of nationalism and feminism. However,
portraits of Elizabeth depict an unresolved tension between size and scale. On the one
hand, they celebrate Elizabeth as Gloriana, while, on the other, they call attention to
the diminutive qualities that led to Elizabeth being dubbed the Fairy Queen. This allows
them to be read either way. As Stephen Orgel comments in 'Gendering the Crown',
an analysis of the competing gendered image systems attached to Elizabeth I, 'the

notorious profligacy of Renaissance symbolic imagery' allows 'its endless adaptability to conflicting, and often diametrically opposed, ideologies'.[6] The dialectic produced by the conflicting imagery of large and small in portraits of Elizabeth provides if not Ariadne's thread itself then at least a provisional 'guide through the labyrinthine ways of Elizabethan art' that Strong himself requests.[7]

As they rework the visual markers of Henrician magnificence, portraits of Elizabeth reflect debates concerning women and power motivated by Protestantism and by the presence of a woman on the throne of England. They illustrate the interactions between the contemporary vogue for limning and the miniature, and the long-established traditions of life-size or large-scale portraiture.[8] They reflect, as well, the ongoing Elizabeth conversation about size crystallised in Marlowe's line, 'infinite riches in a little room'.[9] Whereas Holbein and others represented Henry VIII as great, Elizabethan portraitists represented Elizabeth's power as, instead, a conversation between (as the famous nineteenth-century hymn puts it) great and small.[10] The Bachelard quotation that provides the epigraph to my chapter suggests how this Elizabethan dialogue between great and small actually constitutes a meditation upon the dynamics of Elizabethan power, which wavers, compellingly, between the monumental and the human, the awesome and the pocket-size.

To a certain extent, representations of Elizabeth as great or small reflect simple chronology. Like Starkey, Strong begins his *Portraits of Queen Elizabeth I* (1963) with this 'slip of a girl'.[11] (3). The painting provides the perfect starting point to chart the movement from the diminutive princess portrayed in the Scrots portrait, to the 'visionary figure, towering above her realm of England, a vision of almost cosmic power' in the Ditchley portrait.[12] The Scrots portrait, painted around 1547, when Elizabeth was a teenager, is a conventional early Tudor portrait in the tradition of Holbein. The subject creates a slender triangular shape in the centre of the canvas, with her narrow head and shoulders tapering out into a skirt made stiffly conical by means of a Spanish farthingale (a kind of reinforced petticoat). The bell-shaped sleeves reinforce this elegant visual rhythm. Whether the painting was presented to her father or to her brother, it is consistent with Elizabeth's self-presentation within the family as '*humillima filia*', to use her signatory phrase in letters to her father and to Katherine Parr.[13] At a time when she had been declared illegitimate and was denied her place in the succession, the Latin *humilis* signifies not only the modesty of her appeal but also the lowliness and insignificance of her position. Often frightened for her life, the young Elizabeth described herself as 'altogether nothing' and her accomplishments as 'small work', making apologies for her 'small learning'.[14] Casting herself as small, Elizabeth casts aside her imposing royalty and maximises the impact of her appeal to addressees, such as her brother King Edward VI, whom she thanks for the 'magnitude' of his generosity.

Half a century later, in 1592, Marcus Gheeraerts's Ditchley portrait illustrates the evolution of Elizabethan representation. Here, to quote Strong, 'an individual has been transposed into a symbol' (Figure 4).[15] The Ditchley portrait presents not an elegant, conical, triangle but a square, even squat, pentagon. Elizabeth's dress extends and expands the proportions of her figure to three or four times her width: no longer just starting with the petticoats, expansion is a process that moves from the head up and out. As the upswept hairdo and wired, bejewelled headdress, known as a *palisadoe*, extend Elizabeth's height, the trunk (or demi-cannon) sleeves and immense floor-length hanging sleeves, along with the farthingale, magnify her width. Although her feet are touching Oxfordshire, Elizabeth was international in her taste: as one chronicler recalls, she possessed 'diverse attires, italian, spanyshe and frenshe, as occasion served'.[16] These continental fashions facilitate the portrait's emphatic expression of size: the fan-shaped ruff, a style usually worn by single women, frames the head and expands its circumference.[17]

Yet the overall effect of the portrait is not to make Elizabeth look large, but instead to flicker between the appearance of greatness and the appearance of smallness. Elizabeth's slim and delicate fingers, complete with ringed little finger, clutch a tiny fan. Her waist is minimised by a tight corset and lengthened with an inverted triangular stomacher, setting off the expansive sleeves and skirts. She is bedecked with dozens of diminutive pearls. Note also the tiny little feet that peep out from beneath Elizabeth's skirts. As the painting is saying that Elizabeth is great, it is also depicting her as somewhat overwhelmed. Whereas the famous images of Henry VIII (Figure 5) are all sword and swagger, the Ditchley portrait expresses something very different. It is as if Elizabeth could just float away if she weren't anchored by so much silk and fustian.

The Ditchley portrait enshrines the idea that it is necessary to protect what is little about the queen as well as to celebrate what is great. Elizabeth famously deploys this dialectic between great and small in her Tilbury speech, which plays upon the contrast between her small frame and the qualities of greatness that it contains: 'I know I have the body of a weak and feeble woman, but I have the heart and stomach of a king.'[18] Her writings make frequent reference to the idea of the smallness of woman; as she puts it, 'being a woman by my nature weak, timid, and delicate, as are all women'.[19] She enjoys casting herself in the role of 'maidservant' or 'handmaid' to God.[20] After the defeat of the Armada, Elizabeth expresses thanks that she, as 'the weakest sex hath been so fortified by Thy strongest help that neither my people might find lack by my weakness nor foreigners triumph at my ruin'.[21] An alternative to the commonplace of the 'queen's two bodies', Elizabeth's self-representations as small reflect the evolving idea of a little England, which Elizabeth describes as her 'little flock'. Pope Sixtus comments on the inverse relation between England (and Elizabeth's) size and power when he exclaims, 'She is only a woman, only mistress of half an island, and yet she makes herself feared by Spain, by France, by the Empire, by all'.[22] In the case of Elizabeth, small is not only beautiful, it is also intensely powerful.

Visiting Ditchley, the Oxfordshire estate which Elizabeth's toes are touching, the eighteenth-century antiquarian Thomas Hearne paid homage to this portrait in the Great Hall. He then proceeded to Elizabeth's bedroom, where she stayed when she visited Ditchley, a mark of favour that signified her forgiveness of Sir Henry Lee, its owner, for living openly with his mistress. On the bedroom Hearne writes: 'it is far from being large. The bed is still preserved, in which she lay; low, but decent, and agreeable enough to the humour of this queen, who affected popularity, and tho' proud and imperious, yet would not seem to aim at high things.'[23] In this passage Hearne expresses the characteristically Elizabethan combination of great and small as a tension between elitism and populism, entitlement and diffidence. Hearne's entry into the queen's bedroom constitutes a retrospective performance of the Elizabethan dialectic, according to which queenly power performs itself by moving theatrically between the magnificent and the slight. As Hearne performs the need to penetrate the secret, human places associated with this goddess-like figure, he participates in the portrait's deft use of light and dark, and large and small. He thus engages the terms of Lee's experience itself, with fidelity ultimately overcoming infidelity, just as sunshine follows storms.

Portraits of Elizabeth distinguish themselves not only from the Holbeins of her ancestors but also from the Titians and Van Dycks of her continental contemporaries. Their engagement with contrasts in size and proportion takes its cues from the mannerist tradition, with its rather fantastical (Arnold Hauser calls it 'fictitious') concept of space, which caught on in earnest in Jacobean England.[24] However, Elizabethan portraiture differs from classic mannerism in its interest in size instead of elongation, and in the emphasis upon girth rather than attenuation. A 1565 painting in the collection of Col. C.T. Wingfield presents Elizabeth with elbows bent and shoulders extended: a posture that pushes outside the clean triangular lines of the Princess portrait. In the late 1570s Nicholas Hilliard's attenuated lines use puffed sleeves to extend the horizontal thrust of his figure, creating the characteristically squarish and squat Elizabethan aesthetic. If, on the one hand, the Ditchley portrait depicts Elizabeth as fashion victim, drowned, or dwarfed, by the sheer volume of her dress, it also reveals an enlarged Elizabeth, standing on top of and dominating an England that is overwhelmed, even diminished, by her personality. No wonder Marcus Gheeraerts gives the skies an apocalyptic flavour. England has become a courtier's cape, thrown down over a puddle, for Elizabeth to walk over. This motif of physical domination may be found in images such as the 1589 *Eliza Triumphans*, by William Rogers, in which Elizabeth dominates a landscape with castles and moats and (most importantly) ships. In the Armada portrait, overstuffed bishop sleeves adorned with bows, pearls, and embroidery express sartorially the mastery that the English ships in the background symbolise in naval terms (Figure 6). There are also images of Elizabeth as Europa itself or as the cosmos, with Elizabeth's head topping a string of ever enlarging concentric circles.

The Siena Sieve portrait dramatises the interaction between expansion and diminution (Figure 7).[25] Attributed to Quentin Massys the Younger or Cornelis Ketel, this painting was unknown until 1895, when it was discovered rolled up in the attic of a former Medici palace. It depicts Elizabeth sweeping towards the viewer, its composition looking back upon a tradition of paintings of Aeneas walking away from the burning Troy. The Siena Sieve portrait is one of a group of Sieve portraits produced through the 1580s which draw upon a popular Petrarchan emblem of chastity: a Roman vestal virgin, Tuccia, carries water in a sieve from the Tiber to her temple without spilling a drop. Together, these portraits forge a connection between Elizabeth's virginity and England's military, and specifically naval power. In the case of the Siena Sieve portrait, the painting places Elizabeth within the Virgilian narrative of empire: casting, as Strong puts it, 'Elizabeth as this century's Aeneas'.[26] The pillar to Elizabeth's right depicts scenes from the *Aeneid*, such as Aeneas's ships setting sail from Carthage, that pursue the themes of conquest and expansion raised elsewhere in the portrait: on the globe, England and its industrious ships are flanked by the coasts of Africa and the New World, and Elizabeth appears to be leading the merry troupe of courtiers in a kind of forward procession. As the portrait aligns Elizabeth with Aeneas, the solitary expansionist wanderer, the scenes on the pillar also include images of Virgil's paramour, Dido, Queen of Carthage. They include her first meeting with Aeneas at Juno's temple, their idylls in the cave, and, ultimately, Dido's self-immolation. The painting thus sets up the great Elizabeth, the Virgin Queen, against a Dido diminished by love: Dido the sensualist, Dido the seduced, the Dido who wanted to marry Aeneas, and the Dido who considered herself married to him anyway.

However, the opposition between Elizabeth and Virgil's Dido is complicated by the fact that Elizabeth had a long-standing association with Dido, who was first known, in history and legend, as Elissa. As Dido was invoked as a paradigm of queenship in discussions of Elizabeth, the ancient Elissa became mixed up with Eliza, a short form of Elizabeth's name that Spenser associates with Dido in *The Shepheardes Calender*.[27] This Elissa/Dido belongs to an alternative, non-Virgilian tradition, according to which Dido is (like Aeneas) the founder of an expansionist city-state. When her brother Pygmalion tries to marry her off to Iarbus, the King of Gaetulia, she escapes her home in Tyre with a band of loyal followers, sailing across the Mediterranean to north-east Africa, where she founds Carthage.[28] An early example of colonialist bad faith, Dido pretends to the African inhabitants that she did not wish to establish a major settlement on their land, and requests, humbly, that they sell her only as much land on the beach as a cowhide could enclose. The deal made, Dido proceeds to slice up the cowhide into the smallest and thinnest possible strips, connecting them to enclose a very large piece of land around the port that became Carthage, eventually naming its highest tower Byrsa, in honour of the cowhide. Dido provides a model of female ruled empire that precedes Rome. Carthage grew from a small trading post to a major Mediterranean power. At its height, it controlled much of north-west Africa, southern Spain, Sicily, Sardinia, and Corsica. During the Punic wars, when Carthage was a major obstacle to Roman expansion, Hannibal famously led the Carthaginian army, complete with elephants, across the Alps into Italy.

The Siena Sieve portrait thus invites the viewer to register the difference between Virgil's tragic Dido and the Dido of the earlier tradition, the solitary and mighty ruler who transformed a tiny cowhide into a great empire. As Orgel explains, 'the epic iconography here ingeniously provided the queen with both her heroic ancestor and the prototype of her chastity. The sieve, emblem of the Roman vestals and thus symbolic of Elizabeth's virginity, declares that this Dido will resist the temptations of any modern Aeneas.'[29] The portrait argues that Elizabeth is not the Dido reduced to ashes, painted so small on the pillar, but the other Dido, the founder of the Carthaginian city-state (known for its Alpine-climbing elephants). By identifying Elizabeth with 'this Dido', the portrait presents the imperialist binaries of triumph and defeat, and the erotic and moral distinctions between discernment and profligacy, within the dialectic of great and small. Dido/Elissa's expanding cowhide is invoked by Elizabeth's sieve, covered in tiny holes: an emblem of virginity used as an aid to consolidate power. The Virgilian Dido depicted on the pillar is rendered even smaller, and more static, by contrast to the sweeping Elizabeth, who overwhelms her diminishing train of followers. As it shows the small becoming great, the Siena Sieve portrait celebrates Elizabeth.

The Rainbow portrait moves these questions of size and scale into a religious dimension (Figure 8). As René Graziani argues, the portrait moves between presenting Elizabeth as '*Fidei Defensor*, official champion of the Christian religion' and depicting her 'utter dependence on God'.[30] For Daniel Fischlin, who sees the painting as a response to the Essex rebellion and to anxieties about succession, the portrait's 'conflation of conflicting and ambiguous images represents the struggle to maintain the illusion of autonomy in the face of an approaching political apocalypse beyond Elizabeth's control'.[31] Possibly painted as an altarpiece for an entertainment staged by Sir Robert Cecil in 1602, in which a maid, widow, and wife contend before a shrine to the goddess Astraea, the portrait depicts eyes and ears embroidered gorgeously into Elizabeth's dress, conferring on her the omniscience of a God. In her sixties at the time the portrait was painted, the queen sports an enormous fan-shaped double ruff. With her headdress like gossamer wings, she holds a rainbow in her hands like a child's toy hoop. The dress communicates how Elizabeth's position expands her physical form into that of a deity. At the same time, however, the embroidered eyes recall Elizabeth's complaint: 'we princes, I tell you, are set on stages in the sight and view of all the world duly observed. The eyes of many behold our actions; a spot is soon spied in our garments; a blemish quickly noted in our doings.'[32] The portrait thus depicts Elizabeth deified and apotheosised, as well as the danger of Elizabeth diminished, with her smallest fault easily magnified in the eyes of the court.

With the motto *NON SINE SOLE IRIS* (No rainbow without the sun) the portrait places Elizabeth as the source of this world-enveloping magic: the rainbow possesses associations with peace and divine communion as well as conveying the idea of global dominion, as the ends of the rainbow connect one end of the world with the other. The rainbow alludes, specifically, to the covenant between Noah and God following the flood: the King James Bible reads, 'I do set my bow in a cloud, and it shall be for a token of a covenant between me and the earth' (Genesis 9:13). An image of Elizabeth's covenant with England, this painting also figures Elizabeth, with her crescent-moon-shaped jewel, as Cynthia, goddess of the moon (reminding us how the moon itself waxes and wanes).

Together, the moon and the story of Noah refer to England's naval strengths, underpinning the Protestant history of England's particular covenant with its queen and with its God, with a biblical narrative. Once there was earthly wickedness, with giants walking the earth and humans so corrupt that God repented creation. So God instructed Noah to build a little ark, 300 cubits long, in which to preserve a small selection of living creatures (much smaller than the world itself, of course, but 300 cubits is still about the length of a good-sized cruise ship). The rainbow signals the moment of peace, when the happy few, with their little patch of dry land surrounded by the waters, are given instructions to go forth and multiply. An allegory of the Reformation, of the nascent stages of English exploration and discovery, the painting is also a reminder of the fact that Elizabeth did not herself go forth and multiply, that she did not herself become great with child, or produce any little ones. Although she did not participate in the generational aspects of Noah's covenant with God, she made a little island great. The Rainbow portrait reminds us, in portraits of Elizabeth, to attend to the small as well as to the great, to be aware of what is magnified and to attend to what otherwise goes unseen.

The double vision of Elizabeth as at once great and small constitutes an Elizabethan aesthetic. The paradoxical nature of Marlowe's epigrammatic 'infinite riches in a little room' is consistent with the contradictions inherent in some recent accounts of Elizabethan culture. For Patricia Fumerton, the paradox lies in the interactions between secrecy and disclosure, and public and private; for Jeffrey Knapp it lies in the tension between the country's geographic status as a 'trifle' and its expansionist ambitions; for Julian Yates, it is in the distinctions between the appropriate use of objects, and their misuse.[33] Quintessential Elizabeth forms such as the sonnet and the miniature also express the paradox between great and small. Not merely (to use a favourite Elizabethan term) 'toys', they are instead parts that gesture toward an imposing whole. An individual sonnet takes its place within a sequence that, as the period continues, becomes more expansive and inclusive; the miniature is the alter-ego of the life-size portrait, with its size and scope, and often indicates a personage, or a relationship that is, indeed, larger than life. This dialogue between great and the small, which we may also think of as the constant refocusing of a lens, is illustrated by the famous anecdote in which Sir James Melville, the ambassador of Mary Queen of Scots, is shown Elizabeth's 'little cabinet', where she kept the miniature of Leicester wrapped in paper and marked 'My Lord's Picture'.[34] The miniature, the trinket, the little cabinet all provide ready metaphors for the romantic status of a suitor of Elizabeth, their diminutive size bearing an inverse relationship to the romantic attachment.

Elizabethan and Jacobean portrayals of Elizabeth as the queen of the fairies dramatise the dialectic between great and small in Elizabethan portraiture. In Shakespeare's *A

Midsummer Night's Dream, Titania, Queen of the Fairies, is usually read as a figure for Elizabeth. Certainly her vexed relationships with men, from Oberon to Bottom, and the adoptive, protective role she takes on with the Indian boy invoke certain aspects of the queen's love life. The play's overarching interest in size, with references to acorns and dewberries paired with allusions to circumnavigating the globe, engages the interactions between great and small in Elizabethan portraiture, which qualifies the aching for solidity and centrality that is expressed through greatness with an attention to its opposite, the power of the small.

Shakespeare frequently pairs references to greatness and smallness throughout *A Midsummer Night's Dream*.[35] For example, Puck counters a fairy's claim to 'wander everywhere / Swifter than the moon's sphere' (II.1.6–7) with a collection of references to 'freckles', 'dew-drops', 'pearls' (13–15).[36] Shakespeare often endows the small with a higher value than the great. He figures the transformative qualities of love in terms of the smallness of the fairies, with their jewels and their flowers, and names such as 'Peaseblossom! Cobweb! Moth! and Mustardseed!' (III.1.155) invoking small, delicate things. Their smallness not only contrasts but also counteracts what Titania calls Bottom's 'mortal grossness' (III.1.153). The lovers also make distinctions between great and small. They deploy the Petrarchan registers of celestial and earthly (or beastly), and of black and white, to reinforce rhetorically the differences between Helena and Hermia that occur when one becomes beloved of both Demetrius and Lysander, and the other of neither. Within this context, the idea of their physical difference – that Helena is tall and Hermia small – engages the key dialectic of Elizabethan portraiture. However, as the language of great and small fits into the metaphorical worlds of Petrarchan love, it produces a confusion in representation: the lovers are making distinctions without a difference.[37] Hermia's comment, 'And are you grown so high in his esteem / Because I am so dwarfish and so low?' (III.2.294–5) may magnify slight physical differences between the girls, but she is also creating distance. In the topsy-turvy world of the lovers, the smallness that is elsewhere associated with magic and beauty becomes an insult: 'you minimus, of hindering knot-grass made, / You bead, you acorn' (III.2.329–330).

As the play addresses size matters in relation to the queen of the fairies herself, it translates them into the nascent realm of imperialism. Titania's famous speech about the Indian votaress situates her pregnancy within the context of mercantilism:

> … we have laugh'd to see the sails conceive
> And grow big-bellied with the wanton wind;
> Which she, with pretty and with swimming gait
> Following (her womb then rich with my young squire),
> Would imitate, and sail upon the land
> And fetch me trifles.
>
> (II.1.128–133)

Here the burgeoning sails and the votaress's expanding girth contrast with the trifles the votaress fetches for Titania, trifles that would appear even smaller against her pregnant belly. Here, as the play attaches size to pregnancy (quite literally 'mortal grossness'), it distances the threatening world of female sexuality from Titania, queen of the fairies (who, on the Elizabethan stage, is played by a boy), displacing it instead on to her adult, mortal, great-bellied servant.[38] For Titania as for Elizabeth, pregnancy is something witnessed but never experienced. Yet each is an adoptive mother: Elizabeth to England, and Titania to the Indian boy; in each case, the child is inherited. Titania's loves, moreover, are anything but erotically charged. Her affair with Oberon is tinged with rivalry more than with eros, and her love for Bottom is primarily nurturing, defined by the maternal concern that Bottom is sufficiently fed. As an adoptive or surrogate mother, Titania remains 'virgin', outside the overwhelming physicality of sex and the ensuing magnification and loss of status as an object of sexual desire or conquest. She thus remains for ever small, childlike, and desirable.

Titania's speech associates the Indian votaress with the world of trinkets, trifles, and spices acquired through England's growing trade with the east. Elizabeth was beginning to enjoy, through her navy and her merchants, the experience of expansion that her votaress enjoys in bodily terms. To the east, John Newbery and Ralph Fitch made an overland journey to India in 1583, reaching Goa and the court of the Mogul emperor, Akbar. Newbery disappeared, and Fitch did not return to England until 1591, where his traveller's tales entertained the reading public. Oberon's account of the love flower brings the old Ovidian story of a flower turning purple together with the current language of circumnavigation:

> It fell upon a little western flower,
> Before milk-white, now purple with love's wound:
> And maidens call it 'love-in-idleness' ...
> Fetch me this herb, and be thou here again
> Ere the leviathan can swim a league.
> PUCK: I'll put a girdle round about the earth
> In forty minutes.
>
> (II.1.166–176)

Here the little 'western' flower, a thumbnail-sized herb, is juxtaposed against the 'leviathan', the naval term 'league', and Puck's plan to circle the globe.

Puck's journey around the world for a 'trifle' echoes the labours of Titania's votaress; as their efforts bring together great efforts and large distances with small, highly valued objects, they invoke the discourse of Elizabethan trade, and gesture towards the emerging world of imperialism.

However, the project of empire hadn't happened yet. Henry VIII declared, in the 1533 Act in Restraint of Appeals, that 'This Realm of England is an Empire'.[39] And

Giordano Bruno endowed Elizabeth herself with the powers of Sir Francis Drake when he said that 'If her earthly territory were a true reflection of the width and grandeur of her spirit, this great Amphitrite would bring far horizons within her girdle and enlarge the circumference of her dominion to include not only Britain and Ireland but some new world, as vast as the universal frame'.[40] But the East India Company, formed in 1600, was more of a Jacobean creation: English ships started arriving at the port of Surat in 1608. And to the west, the English settlements in Roanoke failed intermittently through the 1580s, even as Thomas Hariot's *Briefe and True Report of the New Found Land of Virginia* (1588) gamely advertised its merits and potential. When Henry VIII used the term 'empire', he was invoking the Latin *imperium*, with its literal significance of command, order, and mastery, and its historical and humanist associations with ancient Rome. But during Elizabeth's reign the term was translating itself into a mentality of expansion. In the preface to the second edition of *The Principal Navigations, Voyages, Traffiques and Discoveries of the English Nation* (1598), Richard Hakluyt writes in praise of Elizabeth, contrasting her to her predecessors:

> For, which of the kings of this land before Her Majesty, had their banners ever seen in the Caspian Sea? Which of them hath ever dealt with the Emperor of Persia, as her Majesty hath done, and obtained for her merchants large and loving privileges? Who ever found English Consuls and agents at Tripolis in Syria, at Aleppo, at Babylon, at Basra, and which is more, whoever heard of Englishmen at Goa before now?[41]

Hakluyt's words literally put Elizabeth on the map – she is everywhere – and his compendium (a great collection of small treatises) places her representatives all over the globe. As Oberon says, 'we the globe can compass soon / Swifter than the wandering moon' (IV.1.96–7).

Although he takes his inspiration from Spenser's *Faerie Queene*, which represents Elizabeth as Gloriana, Shakespeare relates the queen to the fairy world in *A Midsummer Night's Dream* to an extent that eludes Spenser. *The Merry Wives of Windsor*, written a few years later, starkly dramatises the Elizabethan dialectic between great and small in its closing pageant of punishment. Falstaff, who is represented throughout the Henriad and *The Merry Wives* as 'plump Jack' and 'a globe of sinful continents', is captured and punished by children posing as little fairies, with names such as 'Bead'.[42] His punishment is presided over by the housekeeper Mistress Quickly, who is dressed as the Faerie Queene. Pinching is, of course, a kind of punishment in miniature; fingers take a little piece of flesh and squeeze it together till it is, at least temporarily, smaller. As Falstaff's fat body is assaulted by tiny creatures, they sing a little song:[43]

> Fie on sinful fantasy,
> Fie on lust and luxury!
> Lust is but a bloody fire,

Kindled with unchaste desire,
Fed in heart, whose flames aspire,
As thoughts do blow them, higher and higher.

(V.5.93-98)

Pinching, which is the traditional means by which fairies punish perceived malefactors, is tied to an overarching return to sexual order in *The Merry Wives of Windsor*: Falstaff, his fat body associated with appetitive, 'unchaste desire', even poses as the Fat Woman of Brainford as a strategy of seduction. His great size dominated and contained by the diminutive fairies, Falstaff no longer represents a sexual threat.

Dressed as an Elizabethan queen of the fairies, Shakespeare's Mistress Quickly reinforces the rhetoric of chastity that overlaid the language of courtship as Elizabeth reached her sixties. Here, the Augustinian language of lust as a fire draws attention away from the cheeky decision to cast a servant as the Fairy Queen. Although it is placed within a similarly punitive context in *The Alchemist*, Ben Jonson's treatment of Elizabeth as Fairy Queen is a darkly satiric recollection of the queen. With Subtle, Face, and Dol 'cozening' the deluded and aspirational of London, the play looks back to the devotional aspects of the cult of Elizabeth, as well as poking fun at the meteoric rise of her favourites. Dapper, who requests a tiny 'fly' to help him with his gambling, is persuaded that 'he's o' the only best complexion, / The Queen of Faery loves' (I.2.105-106).[44] Dol (also a pincher), posing as the Queen of Fairy, possesses a name that classifies her as a diminutive plaything, like a puppet: it is also the name for a runt, the smallest pig in a litter. However, Dol is also called 'a Bradamante' by Sir Epicure Mammon, gesturing towards the Ariostan source material of Spenser's Britomart, and to the alternative, masculine and martial, Elizabethan persona. Discussions of Dol thus segue between small and the great: in one instance, Face calls Dol 'my little God's gift' (III.3.49), while he later observes, 'Why this is yet / A kind of modern happiness, to have / Dol Common for a great lady' (IV.1.22-24).

Dol's appearance of greatness fools not only Dapper but also Sir Epicure Mammon, who asserts that there is, in Dol, 'a certain touch, or air, / That sparkles a divinity, beyond / An earthly beauty' (IV.1.64-66). Of course, as no more than the daughter of an Irish costermonger, Dol's greatness is a disguise. This may be Jonson's posthumous insult to the (by then) late Queen Elizabeth, with whom Jonson was never popular. He had written *Cynthia's Revels* in 1601 in the hopes of gaining preferment and patronage: hopes which were dashed as the play's satire of the court, which hit a little too close to home, cast him even further out of Elizabeth's orbit. With Dol, Jonson caricatures the ideology of the Elizabethan prodigal – the idea that one may rise from insignificance to a position of power through courtly preferment – as well as the overarching Elizabethan aesthetic according to which smallness is a quality of greatness.

It is fitting that Shakespeare's final treatment of Elizabeth is not as Fairy Queen, but, instead, in a cameo appearance as a tiny baby at the end of *Henry VIII* or *All Is True*. This switch in size highlights the bewildering yet ultimately instructive changes in perspective produced by the warring projects of magnification and minimisation that define responses to, and representations of, Queen Elizabeth I.

Notes

Different versions of this chapter were presented to the Shakespeare Association of America (in a seminar organised by Susan Frye) and at 'Creating Women', a conference organised by Manuela Scarci and Konrad Eisenbichler at the Centre for Reformation and Renaissance Studies at the University of Toronto, and I would like to thank the organisers and audiences for most helpful feedback. I would also like to express my gratitude to the Social Sciences and Humanities Research Council of Canada for financial support.

1. David Starkey, *Elizabeth: Apprenticeship* (London: Chatto and Windus, 2000), p. x.
2. It may alternatively have been sent as a gift to Elizabeth's half-brother, King Edward VI. Elizabeth writes a letter to Edward accompanying, apparently, a portrait: 'For the face, I grant, I might well blush to offer, but the mind I shall never be ashamed to present ... when you shall look on my picture you will witsafe to think that as you have but the outward shadow of the body before you, so my inward mind wisheth that the body itself were oftener in your presence.' See Leah S. Marcus, Janel Mueller, and Mary Beth Rose, eds, *Elizabeth I: Collected Works* (Chicago: University of Chicago Press, 2000).
3. See Frances Yates, *Astraea: The Imperial Theme in the Sixteenth Century* (London: Routledge and Kegan Paul, 1975), and Roy Strong, *Portraits of Queen Elizabeth I* (Oxford: Clarendon Press, 1963); *The Cult of Elizabeth: Elizabethan Portraiture and Pageantry* (London: Thames and Hudson, 1977) and *Gloriana: The Portraits of Queen Elizabeth* (London: Thames and Hudson, 1987).
4. See, for example, Patricia Fumerton, *Cultural Aesthetics: Renaissance Literature and the Practice of Social Ornament* (Chicago: University of Chicago Press, 1991); Jeffrey Knapp, *An Empire Nowhere: England, America and Literature from Utopia to The Tempest* (Berkeley: University of California Press, 1992); Julian Yates, *Error, Misuse, Failure: Object Lessons from the English Renaissance* (Minneapolis: University of Minnesota Press, 2003).
5. See Nicola J. Watson, 'Gloriana Victoriana: Victoria and the Cultural Memory of Elizabeth I', in *Remaking Queen Victoria*, edited by Margaret Homans and Adrienne Munich (Cambridge: Cambridge University Press, 1997), pp. 70–104, p. 85. See also the discussion of Victorian portraits of Elizabeth in Michael Dobson and Nicola J. Watson, *England's Elizabeth: An Afterlife in Fame and Fantasy* (Oxford: Oxford University Press, 2002), chapter 4. Augustus Leopold Egg's *Queen Elizabeth Discovers She Is No Longer Young* (1848) has the queen looking away, mortified, from the mirror held up to her by a not-so-well-meaning member of her youthful entourage, and David Wilkie Wynfield's *Incident in the Life of Elizabeth* (1875) makes this point less subtly by figuring her as, quite simply, bald.
6. Stephen Orgel, 'Gendering the Crown', in *Subject and Object in Renaissance Culture*, edited by Margreta de Grazia, Maureen Quilligan, and Peter Stallybrass (Cambridge: Cambridge University Press, 1996), pp. 133–165, p. 155.
7. See Strong, *Portraits of Queen Elizabeth I*, p. 60.
8. Elizabethan artists such as Nicholas Hilliard and Isaac Oliver worked in both media.
9. See Christopher Marlowe, *The Jew of Malta*, I.1.37, in *The Complete Works of Christopher Marlowe: The Jew of Malta*, vol. 4, edited by Roma Gill (Oxford: Clarendon Press, 1995).
10. Although the hymn was composed by the nineteenth-century Irish poet Mrs Cecil Francis Alexander, it was based on a seventeenth-century melody.
11. See Strong, *Portraits of Queen Elizabeth I*, p. 3.

12. See Strong, *Portraits of Queen Elizabeth I*, p. 3.

13. See Marcus et al., *Elizabeth I: Collected Works*, p. 25.

14. Marcus et al., *Elizabeth I: Collected Works*, pp. 170, 320, and 411.

15. Strong, *Portraits of Queen Elizabeth I*, p. 15.

16. See Kervyn de Lettenhove, *Relations politiques des pays-bas et de l'Angleterre sous la regne de Philippe II* (Brussels: Royal Academy of Sciences, Letters and Fine Art of Belgium, 1890), pp. ix and 336, and, for discussion, Strong, *Portraits*, p. 20.

17. This particular squarish kind of farthingale was known as a French farthingale: its shape is different from the tapering, funnel-shaped Spanish farthingale which was introduced by Catherine of Aragon.

18. See Marcus et al., *Elizabeth I: Collected Works*, p. 326.

19. See Marcus et al., *Elizabeth I: Collected Works*, p. 157.

20. For 'maidservant' see Marcus et al., *Elizabeth I: Collected Works*, pp. 146, 156; for 'handmaid' see *Elizabeth I: Collected Works*, pp. 136, 140, 142, 143, 154, 158, 311, 317, 411.

21. See Marcus et al., *Elizabeth I: Collected Works*, p. 424.

22. See J.E. Neale, *Queen Elizabeth I* (London: Cape, 1938), p. 284.

23. *Reliquae Hernianae: The Remains of Thomas Hearne, M.A. of Edmund Hall, Being Extracts from his MS Diaries*, edited by Philip Bliss, 3 vols (London, 1869), II, p. 71.

24. See Arnold Hauser, *Mannerism: The Crisis of the Renaissance and the Origin of Modern Art* (Cambridge, MA: Harvard University Press, 1965).

25. For further discussion of this portrait see my 'Dido Queen of England', *English Literary History* 73 (2006), pp. 31–59.

26. See Strong, *Gloriana*, p. 99.

27. See Edmund Spenser's November Eclogue in *The Shepheardes Calender* (London: Hugh Singleton, 1579).

28. See Truedell S. Brown, ed., *Timaeus of Tauromenium* (Berkeley: University of California Press, 1958) and Justin, *Epitome of Philippic History of Pompeius Trogus*, trans. J.C. Yardley (Oxford: Clarendon Press, 1997). For further discussion of the Dido tradition see Marilynn Desmond, *Reading Dido: Gender, Textuality and the Medieval Aeneid* (Minneapolis: University of Minnesota Press, 1994).

29. See 'Shakespeare and the Cannibals', in *Cannibals, Witches, and Divorce: Estranging the Renaissance*, edited by Marjorie Garber (Baltimore: Johns Hopkins University Press, 1987), pp. 40–66, p. 62.

30. René Graziani, '"The Rainbow Portrait" of Queen Elizabeth I and its Religious Symbolism', *Journal of the Warburg and Courtauld Institute* 35 (1972), pp. 247–259 at p. 255 and 259.

31. Daniel Fischlin, 'Political Allegory, Absolutist Ideology, and the "Rainbow Portrait" of Queen Elizabeth I', *Renaissance Quarterly* 50 (1997), pp. 175–206 at p. 204.

32. See Marcus et al., *Elizabeth I: Collected Works*, p. 167.

33. See note 4.

34. This anecdote is discussed in Fumerton, *Cultural Aesthetics*, and is the jumping-off point for her earlier article, '"Secret" Arts: Elizabethan Miniatures and Sonnets', *Representations* 15 (1986), pp. 57–97.

35. The Lion's 'smallest monstrous mouse' in the Pyramus and Thisbe masque renders Petrarchan opposites as nonsense. See *A Midsummer Night's Dream*, edited by Harold Brooks (London: Routledge, 1979), V.1.215.

36. For another example of this connection between the moon and small things see III.1.191.

37. On the metaphorical world of Petrarch see Roland Greene's *Unrequited Conquests: Love and Empire in the Colonial Americas* (Chicago: University of Chicago Press, 1999).

38. On the threatening aspects of the maternal body see Patricia Parker, *Literary Fat Ladies:*

Rhetoric, Gender, Property (London: Methuen, 1987).

39.   24 Henry VIII, c.12. 1533 in *English Historical Documents*, edited by Charles H. Williams, 12 vols (London and Edinburgh: Eyre and Spottiswoode, 1967), V (1485–1558), p. 738. The complete phrase, from the 1533 Act in Restraint of Appeals, is 'This realm of England is an Empire … governed by one supreme head and king, having the dignity and royal estate of the imperial crown of the same'.

40.   Giordano Bruno, *La Cena de la Ceneri* (1584), discussed in Frances Yates, *Giordano Bruno and the Hermetic Tradition* (Chicago: University of Chicago Press, 1964), p. 289.

41.   Richard Hakluyt, *Voyages and Discoveries: The Principal Navigations, Voyages, Traffiques and Discoveries of the English Nation*, edited by Jack Beeching (London: Penguin, 1972) p. 34.

42.   William Shakespeare, *The Merry Wives of Windsor*, edited by Giorgio Melchiori (London: Routledge, 1999). *The Riverside Shakespeare*, edited by G. Blakemore Evans (Boston: Houghton Mifflin, 1997).

43.   Shakespeare, *The Merry Wives of Windsor*, ed. Melchiori.

44.   Ben Jonson, *Five Plays*, edited by G.A. Wilkes (Oxford: Oxford University Press, 1981).

5

'And in their midst a sun': Petrarch's *Triumphs* and the Elizabethan icon

HEATHER CAMPBELL

Prominent among the personae adopted by Elizabeth I in her self-presentation is Petrarch's Laura, the unattainable love-focus of the *Canzoniere* and the central figure in the *Triumphs*.[1] It is easy to blur these two Lauras into one another, and indeed at various points in her life Elizabeth gained political capital from identification with each of them. In both the pageantry and the portraiture, however, it is with the Laura of the *Triumphs*, and specifically with the Laura of the Triumph of Chastity, that Elizabeth is consistently identified. The evocation of the *Triumphs* was calculated to appeal particularly to the older generation of courtiers, whose primary interest was in issues of succession and nation-building, and whose support she emphatically needed. As the lady of the sonnets she would figure as the transcendent chaste beauty, certainly, but the vocabulary of desire implied by the text would have been limiting and, especially in the early years, potentially damaging to her political credibility. Her identification with the powerful victor from the Triumph of Chastity might include the lady of the sonnets by extension, but it placed primary emphasis on the imperial dimension, with its quasi-masculine implications of power. The vocabulary of victory and the evocation of Rome supported her position as monarch, neutralising the problems inherent in her gender at the same time as the Laura image exploited both the mystical power of virginity and her potential as a chaste object of desire. Thus the popularity of the *Triumphs* in sixteenth-century England provided a crucial element in the creation of the Elizabethan icon. It offered a vocabulary and a cluster of associations through which Elizabeth could be presented to her own subjects and to other European political figures as the Virgin Queen, but in a context resonant of military victory and masculine royal authority.

The *Triumphs* is a quasi-allegorical poem in six parts. The first section, the Triumph of Love, establishes the poem as a dream vision in which the poet-dreamer sees a vision of Cupid in Roman imperial triumphal procession, and becomes part of the train of captives himself when he encounters Laura for the first time. In the Triumph of Chastity, Laura defeats Love in single combat and takes him captive, then proceeds in victory procession to the temple at Linturno. In the third triumph, Death engages with Laura and captures her earthly self but not her spirit. Subsequent sections show Fame in triumph over Death, Time over Fame, and Eternity over Time. It is not much read now but, judging from the proliferation of manuscripts and editions, the *Triumphs* enjoyed extraordinary popularity from its first appearance just after Petrarch's death in 1374 well into the sixteenth century and beyond, outstripping the *Canzoniere* on almost all counts. According to Ernest Hatch Wilkins's apparently exhaustive study,[2] the fourteenth and fifteenth centuries produced eighty-five manuscripts of the *Triumphs* alone and seventy-nine of the *Triumphs* and *Canzoniere* together.[3] Whereas the effects of the *Canzoniere* in England were primarily literary, in that other poets imitated and experimented with the sonnet form and adopted the poet-lover persona, the effects of the *Triumphs* were also political, aesthetic, and philosophical. A handful of poets did produce imitations of it early in the sixteenth century, and it reappears here and there in the work of major poets up to the Civil War.[4] Much broader, however, is the contribution the poem made to civic and religious celebrations, and to the systems of signs that permitted such celebrations to carry meaning. By the middle of the sixteenth century, the *Triumphs* and its illustrations were so firmly established, so pervasively familiar throughout Europe, that they had become part of the furniture not only of literary endeavour but of the visual arts, and of the world of civic and religious celebration as well.

It was inevitable that, among the many editions of both the *Triumphs* and the *Canzoniere* that issued from the Italian presses during the sixteenth century, a substantial number made their way to England. In fact, we know of three copies of the *Triumphs* that existed at the court of Henry VIII: two in his library at the Palace of Westminster, one in Italian and one a Castilian translation,[5] and an elaborately bound copy of the Venetian edition of 1544, with Velutello's notes and introduction, which was the personal possession of Queen Catherine Parr.[6] In a letter dated April 1530, Bishop Bonner reminds Cromwell that he had promised to lend him his copy of the *Triumphs* and asks also for a copy of *Il Cortegiano*, to help him become 'a good Italyoun'.[7] Like Lord Morley, who was the first to translate the whole of the *Triumphs* into English, Cromwell belonged to a group with a particular interest in Italian literature and culture, so it is possible that more than one copy of the *Triumphs* was in circulation among them. Lord Morley's translation of the *Triumphs* was completed during the reign of Henry VIII and presented to the king in manuscript, although it was not printed until much later.[8] Morley's inspiration to translate the *Triumphs* also attests to its popularity: he had discovered that Francis I of France owned a copy which had been translated for him by a groom of his chamber, and which he

> always caryed with hym for his pastime to loke upon, and [was] as much esteemed by hym as the richest Diamonde he had: whiche sayde booke, when I saw the coppye of it, I thought in my mynde, how I beynge an Englyshe man, myghte do as well as the Frenche man, dyd translate this sayde worke into our maternall tounge.[9]

Much later, Morley made the rather surprising decision to have his translation printed,[10] and to present it to Henry FitzAlan, Lord Maltravers, the eldest son of the Earl of Arundel. Morley refers to King Henry's reception of his gift in his dedicatory letter to Maltravers, noting that the King 'toke … the worke verye thankfullye, merveylynge muche how I could do it'.[11] Kenneth R. Bartlett suggests a date between May and July 1554 for the printing,[12] and makes an engaging argument for an association between the decision to print the translation and dedicate it to Maltravers with the 1554 plot to marry (then Princess) Elizabeth to Maltravers. Bartlett notes that Parker's interest in the marriage stemmed from his deep interest in maintaining an English succession free from foreign involvement. The marriage plot came to naught, but the decision to print the translation made a major contribution to its visibility in the English courtly culture of the second half of the century, and to its availability as a contributor to the Elizabethan icon.

In addition to Morley's full translation, several partial translations were made in England before the end of the century. Early in her reign, or perhaps before it, Elizabeth translated the first ninety lines of the Triumph of Eternity.[13] The translation is laborious and precise, which suggests that it may have been a schoolroom exercise. The 1580s saw several translations: in the middle of the decade, Mary Sidney made an excellent rendering of the first two capitoli of the Triumph of Death, maintaining the difficult terza rima,[14] and in 1585 Sir Edward Dyer made a short partial translation of the same triumph.[15] Meanwhile in Scotland, where Mary Queen of Scots owned a copy, William Fowler produced the second full translation of the poem.[16] Clearly then, the Triumphs was still current in England as late as the 1580s. In fact all the indications are that it was more than current, it was established to the point of easy familiarity: in 1570 Roger Ascham complained in The Scholemaster that Englishmen were guilty of holding 'in more reverence, the triumphes of Petrarche, than the Genesis of Moses'.[17]

The poem's unusual position in the world of Renaissance English letters helped to make it an appropriate source of reference for Elizabeth. Petrarch's initial reputation in Europe was that of the great Latin poet, humanist and philosopher. The Triumphs seems to have provided a bridge between the classical respectability of his Latin works and the dramatically modern and innovative Canzoniere. Like the Canzoniere, the Triumphs was in the vernacular, but the subject matter brought it closer to Petrarch's philosophical writings than to his literary experimentation. The first fully annotated version of the poem,[18] which effectively set the standard for its interpretation, reads it as an allegory of the progress of a man's soul. Bonner's bracketing of it with Il Cortegiano, an equally respectable and established text, supports this view, as do the imitations and translations. The innovative Petrarchists, the young courtiers, tended to leave the poem alone: Wyatt ignores it completely, and Surrey mines it only for a poem that is closer in spirit to the sonnets than to the rest of the Triumphs.[19] For Morley, on the other hand, it was a natural choice: himself elderly and part of the establishment, he would have considered translating the sonnets to be a task for a younger man, while the Triumphs was wholly appropriate to his senior position.[20]

The illustrative tradition which accompanies the poem seems to have developed simply in response to Petrarch's choice of the Roman triumph as an organising motif. The illustrators were called on to provide their own versions of the spectacle, and did so with rich and imaginative detail. Departure from the content of the poem is already in evidence in the 1488 edition of Bernardino da Novara,[21] in which each woodcut shows a triumphal procession with cart and triumphator, although Petrarch describes only one chariot (in the Triumph of Love). After this, the illustrations of the *Triumphs* became a tradition in their own right and passed beyond the world of book illustration into almost every field of artistic endeavour: they are found in paintings, frescos and tapestries, on *cassoni*, on birth plates and other ceramics, and in manuscript illuminations of psalters and prayer books.[22] A particularly fine set of the *Triumphs* tapestries, still preserved at Hampton Court Palace and in the Victoria and Albert Museum, was purchased from the estate of the Bishop of Durham by Cardinal Wolsey in 1522 or 1523. They are of Flemish origin, and similar to several sets found at courts throughout Europe. They are very large – about 15 by 23 ft each – and very finely worked, with an immense amount of detail.[23] The purchase caused quite a stir, and provided material for John Skelton's pointed criticism of Wolsey's worldliness in *Colin Clout*.[24] Like the rest of the illustrations, the tapestries emphasise the spectacular, which is almost entirely absent from Petrarch's poem. In the poem, Death, who is represented as an old woman rather than the more usual Grim Reaper figure, has neither a procession nor a real victory; Time is represented by Phoebus, but his chariot is not a triumphal car, it is the sun; and the Triumph of Eternity, a vision of the New Jerusalem, contains neither procession nor triumphator. In fact, the *Triumphs* is not a very visual poem at all, and would be very difficult to illustrate with any accuracy. By the middle of the sixteenth century, illustrations of the *Triumphs* were at least as familiar a part of the cultural background as the poem was. It would have been common enough, among the educated and/or wealthy, to have seen versions of the illustrations without having read the poem. This dual tradition, the illustrations and the poem itself, is apparent in the iconography that surrounds Elizabeth. The pageants and some of the early woodcuts and illustrations appear to draw as much from the illustrative tradition as from the poem, whereas the portraits refer directly and specifically to the poem in its Italian original.

The tradition of civic celebration that precedes Elizabethan entries and progresses owes much to the central presence of both the Roman victory procession and Petrarch's poem in processions at home and across Europe. The triumph as a symbol of victory had begun to be revived in Italy in the early part of the fourteenth century. For example, Roy Strong notes that as early as 1326, Castruccio Castracane entered Lucca in a version of an imperial triumph, standing in a chariot and driving prisoners before him.[25] About the time of the circulation of the *Triumphs* and the appearance of the first illustrations, triumphal entries were rapidly becoming essential to the expression of power, first of all for the rulers of the Italian city states and before very long throughout Europe. Processions became more and more elaborate, and the allegorical figures introduced by Petrarch's poem began to appear with increasing regularity.[26] The influence of Petrarch may be clearly seen, for example, in the entry of Duke Borso d'Este into Reggio in 1453, a very elaborate affair involving several triumphal cars and representations of St Prospero, various cherubim and angels, Justice, Julius Caesar, and the seven Virtues. The wedding of Lucrezia Borgia to Alfonso d'Este in Rome in 1501 was graced by several triumphal processions, including one representing Petrarch's triumph of Scipio Africanus. And the entry of Louis XII into Milan included an elaborately decorated triumphal arch and a chariot containing the seat of Victory supported by the figures of Prudence, Fortitude, and Renown.[27] By the mid sixteenth century the triumph as a vehicle for the celebration of power had become firmly established throughout Europe, and the importance of Petrarch's *Triumphs* is still apparent. For example, the entry of Henri II into Rouen in 1550 included a full-scale imperial triumph, beginning with a chariot piled high with trophies in which the figure of Death appears bound at the feet of Fame. Later in the procession came a car drawn by unicorns bearing Vesta, the goddess of Religion, supported by Royal Majesty, Virtuous Victory, Reverence, and Fear. Vesta held aloft a model of a church, so that this car represented the reunion of the Catholic Church under Henri.[28]

In England the Italian influence was marked in all forms of court celebration throughout the sixteenth century including the royal entries, all kinds of civic processions, and the allegorical masques presented to Queen Elizabeth during the royal progresses.[29] Indeed, the triumph lies behind both the royal processions and the masques and pageants which attended them, to such an extent that the word 'triumph' came into general use to mean a wide variety of royal celebrations and pageants.[30] The presence of the *Triumphs* in the ceremonial tradition helped to provide a route through which the difficulties of the royal entry might be negotiated for that most anomalous of entrants, the Queen Regnant. The royal entry is traditionally an expression of military as well as monarchical power. The new king enters the city on horseback, and the trappings are those of victory and strength in war. The Queen Consort rides into the city in a litter, and the symbolic elements of her procession support her role as the chaste wife of the king who can be depended on to maintain the integrity of the royal line. Both Elizabeth and her sister Mary before her chose to enter the city in a litter, but both wore royal cloth of gold to indicate their position as reigning monarchs.[31] For Elizabeth the presence of a powerful female victor in Petrarch's poem provided a pattern for a victory procession that both communicated the special power of virginity and introduced Elizabeth to the nation as reigning monarch.

In the Triumph of Chastity the Roman triumph is employed as a structural principle rather than a motif. The first half of the *capitolo* describes the initial engagement between Love and Laura. She moves against him attended by sixteen virtues arranged foursquare about her, and Cupid is unable to withstand the radiance of the sight. At the numerical centre of the poem, she rescues his victims and wrests from him the symbols of victory: 'Mille e mille famose e care salme / tòrre gli vidi e scuotergli di mano / mille vittoriose e chiare palme' (ll. 94–96) ('Thousands of victims, famed and dear, from him / She rescued; and a thousand shining palms / Of victory she wrested from his hands').[32] The second half of the *capitolo* describes the triumphal procession to the temple at Linturno, where Scipio himself joins the triumph, and where Laura deposits her spoils and her laurel crown. Once again the procession is precisely arranged to emphasise the central position occupied by Laura. In his numerological analysis of triumphs as an art form and a form of entertainment, Alastair Fowler cites the Triumph of Chastity as a particularly precise example of the triumphal form in literature, 'in which the procession not only is symmetrical but even finesses the sovereign centre'. He suggests that the square number sixteen — the number of virtues accompanying Laura against Love, and the number of participants in the triumphal procession — symbolises virtue because of its geometrical rectitude, and he finds Laura's central position in the procession, like the centrality of the moment of victory in the structure of the poem, 'makes [her] a divine representative and solar surrogate'.[33] The centre in any procession or masque was essential to the expression of royal power, because it exploited connections with other mystical centres: when the triumphator is placed in the centre of the procession he or she is placed in synchrony with, for example, the Tree of Knowledge, the Temple of Jerusalem, the Sun. In identifying herself with this Laura, then, Elizabeth exploits not only the mystical power of virginity implied by the nature of the victory of Laura over Cupid but also the masculine and royal associations of the symbolic centre.

The notion of the triumphal entry is evoked early in Elizabeth's coronation procession by the structure erected across Gracechurch Street, which resembled a triumphal arch with battlements and three gates. Over the main gate were three platforms showing, in ascending order, Henry VII with Elizabeth of York, Henry VIII and Anne Boleyn, and Elizabeth herself. The whole structure was decorated with red and white roses, to indicate the uniting of the houses of York and Lancaster. This is not an uncomplicated set of references, as Susan Frye points out,[34] but it does have the effect of accessing the memory of a war for the succession, so that Elizabeth here may figure, on one level at least, as a victor and bringer of peace. In Cornhill a still masque or tableau introduced allegorical figures: Pure Religion was shown trampling Superstition underfoot; Love of Subjects treading on Adulation and Bribery; Wisdom treading on Folly and Vainglory; and Justice treading on Rebellion. There is a particular echo here of the illustrations of the *Triumphs*, which frequently show the victorious trampling on the captive, and perhaps also of the Vesta chariot in Henri II's procession only nine years earlier.

The most strongly Petrarchan of the Coronation pageants, however, is the one in Cheapside, on the Little Conduit by St Peter's Church.[35] Two hills were made to represent two Commonwealths, one flourishing, the other in decay. From between them came a figure representing Time leading his daughter Truth. The scene establishes a context in which Elizabeth is to be presented with a copy of the Bible in English, here entitled *Verbum Veritatis*. Elizabeth entered enthusiastically into the pageant. Mulcaster records that when the subject of the pageant was identified for her as she approached, she cried out, 'And Tyme hath brought me hether',[36] implicitly drawing herself into the play in the role of Truth. She accepted the Bible and 'as soon as she had received the book, kissed it and with both hands held up the same, and so laid it on her breast, with great thanks to the city therefore'.[37] Elizabeth's political purpose here was exactly the same as Henri's had been – only the Church is different. She goes a step further in method, however, by joining in the dialogue and the action of the pageant. She does not merely accept the triumph of Truth: she becomes it, just as later she becomes Astraea, Deborah, Diana, and Laura. Frances Yates suggests that, in its echo of the Petrarchan triumph, the Little Conduit pageant provides a possible association of the *Triumphs* with religious politics:

> Protestant propagandists, collecting criticisms of the Papacy, enrolled both Dante and Petrarch on their side as having, at some time or another, ventured to call the Pope the Whore of Babylon ... Thus Puritan associations were tinging the Elizabethan image of Petrarch, and his poem, the *Triumphs*, already fashionable in England, became more fashionable still ... [Elizabethans perceived] ... a reformed and anti-papal Petrarch who teaches rejection of earthly love and worldliness, is against religious persecution, and is associated with apocalyptic visions.[38]

Iconographical identifications of Elizabeth with the Laura of the *Triumphs* appear as early as the first decade of her reign, suggesting that the image was already established or becoming so. In 1594 an edition of Anthony Munday's *Zelauto* was published which includes a woodcut of Elizabeth in a Triumph of Fame very similar in style to the early *Triumphs* woodcuts. Roy Strong identifies the costume and the profile as belonging to the 1560s and points out two drawings that were made from it, one in 1580 and the other between 1560 and 1570, so that the woodcut must have been in circulation quite early in Elizabeth's reign, and may well belong to the earliest stages of Elizabeth's identification with Laura.[39] She is here portrayed not as Fame – neither, of course, was Laura – but as the principal beneficiary of the lady's efforts, so that the identification with Laura is preserved. Elizabeth rides in the triumphal car, which is drawn by horses, and Fama rides perched on the front, winged and bearing an elaborate trumpet.

Between 1579 and 1580 a number of portraits appear showing Elizabeth holding a sieve, one of her favourite emblematic devices. The sieve represents Tuccia, the Vestal Virgin who brought water from the Tiber in a sieve to prove her virginity and who is prominent in Laura's procession in *The Triumph of Chastity*:

> Fra l'altre la vestal vergine pia.
> Che baldanzosamante corse al Tibro.
> e per purgarsi d'ogni fama ria.
>   porto del fiume al tempio acqua col cribro.

(ll. 148–151)

Among the others was the vestal maid.
Who that she might be free of ill report.
Sped boldly to the Tiber, and from thence.
Brought water to her temple in a sieve.

(p. 45)

The 1579 Sieve portrait by George Gower shows the queen elaborately ruffed and gowned with the sieve in her left hand and the royal arms behind her left shoulder (Figure 9).[40] Below the arms is a quotation from Petrarch's Triumph of Love: 'Stancho riposo e riposato affano' (IV.145) ('Weary I rest, and having rested I am troubled'), one of a long series of Petrarchan conceits that attend the triumphal entry of Cupid. In his 1525 edition of the poem Vellutello glosses this line as referring to lovers' foolish hopes and dreams,[41] although in this context it could also be applied to the stresses of rulership. Behind her right shoulder is a globe with the motto 'Tutto vedo e molto mancha' ('I see everything and much is lacking') which I would suggest refers to the developing empire.

The 1580 Sieve portraits press the allegory further (Figure 7).[42] The costume here is no less imperial but much more severe. Elizabeth is dressed in black with a white mantle; a double rope of pearls, the jewel which represents chastity, is around her neck, and a large pearl drop is suspended from her brooch. There are pearls in her hair and headdress and about her waist, but she is much less bejewelled than in most of her portraits, perhaps in order to emphasise the symbolic significance of the pearls. Behind her right shoulder is a pillar set with medallions depicting the story of Dido and Aeneas, and the globe replaces the royal arms behind her left shoulder. Critics generally agree that the narrative on the pillars is intended to link Elizabeth with Aeneas,[43] which makes sense in terms both of his renown as a builder of empires and also of his mythical position as ancestor of the English royal line, and which is underscored by the imperial diadem at the base of the pillar. The presence of Dido, however, a queen who in Virgil's narrative lost her realm for an adulterous passion, is a potentially troublesome element. The quotation directs us back to Petrarch's poem, via the Triumph of Love. Dido is not actually mentioned in the first triumph, although we might have expected to find her in Cupid's train of captives; however the prominent sieve refers us to the Triumph of Chastity where she appears twice, and on both occasions the narrator explicitly rejects Virgil's version of her story of seduction by Aeneas. In both references she appears as an example of constancy in married love, initially in implied consolation for the plight of the poet-lover: 'e veggio ad un lacciuol Giunone e Dido, / ch'amor pio del suo sposo a morte spinse, / non quel d'Enea, com'è 'l publico grido, / non mi debb'io doler s'altri mi vinse' (ll. 10–13) ('And if in a single snare Juno may fall, / And Dido, she whom love for her own spouse / (Not – as they say – for Aeneas) drove to her death, / I should not grieve if I be overcome') (p. 39), and then as a prominent member of the cohort that supports Laura as she moves against Cupid:

poi vidi, fra le donne pellegrine,
quella che per lo suo diletto e fido.
sposo, non per Enea, volse ire al fine.
    Taccia il vulgo ignorante! Io dico Dido,
cui studio d'onestate a morte spinse,
non vano amor come è il publico grido.

(ll. 154–159)

And there I saw, 'mid those of other lands,
Her who for a belov'd and faithful spouse.
(Not for Aeneas) willed to meet her end.
    Let ignorance be still! I speak of her,
Dido, whom honour led to death, and not.
An empty love, as is the public cry.

(p. 45)

Here she is in company with the most famously chaste women of Scripture and classical mythology: Penelope, Lucretia, Virginia, Judith, Hersilia and the Sabines, and most particularly Tuccia. The references to Petrarch's poem in the portrait, then, privilege the alternative story of Dido, still very much current in sixteenth-century England. According to this legend, surviving primarily in accounts by Justinius and Timaeus, Dido, a princess of Tyre, flees to North Africa after her husband Sychaeus is slain by her brother Pygmalion. She purchases a piece of land from Iarbas, a local chieftain, and on it founds the great city of Carthage.[44] When the city prospers, Iarbas presses her to marry him, and to escape the marriage she constructs a funeral pyre and stabs herself before her people.[45] Until Virgil's version turned her story into one of adulterous passion, Dido had figured as the great builder of Carthage, and as a model of female chastity, loyalty, and constancy, and this reading of her person was still very much present in sixteenth-century discourse.[46] I would suggest, then, that a layered interpretation of the medallions is appropriate, one which gathers together a constellation of references to empire building, lineage, constancy, loyalty, and chastity.

    In the 1580 portrait the globe behind the queen's left shoulder has been lowered to make room for a representation of a cloister and a procession of courtiers with a maid of honour.[47] The association with the *Triumphs* is once again underscored by the quotation from the Triumph of Love located directly below the pillar and below the queen's right hand, suggesting that she has the power of Love firmly under control. The juxtaposition of the courtiers and the globe indicates the important relationship between Elizabeth's power at home and her power abroad; and the spatial relationship between the figures is balanced so that the initial impression is of a version of a triumphal procession, with the pillar forming part of the triumphal arch and the procession stretching out behind the triumphator. Thus, this intriguing portrait may also on one level be read as a visual replication of the Triumph of Chastity.

The link between Elizabeth's iconography and the *Triumphs* is similarly direct in the familiar Ermine portrait (1585) (Figure 10). Here Elizabeth is portrayed as elaborately costumed, again in black and white, with a profusion of jewels. At least two-thirds of them are pearls, once again emphasising chastity. The imperial theme is represented by the Sword of Justice lying close to her left hand and the olive branch of Peace in her right, while on her left sleeve is an ermine wearing a golden crown-shaped collar. The ermine is a very old symbol for chastity, but the collar links it directly to the *Triumphs*.[48] The opening of the Triumph of Death shows Laura returning from Linturno, still in procession and surrounded by her cohort of the chaste and constant.

> Era la lor vittoriosa insegna.
> in campo verde un candido ermellino,
> ch'oro fino e topazi al collo tegna.
>
> Non uman veramente, ma divino.
> lor andare era, e lor sante parole:
> beato s'è qual nasce a tal destino.
> Stelle chiare pareano, in mezzo un sole.
> che tutte ornava e non togliea lor vista.
> di rose incoronate e di viole.
>
> (ll. 19–27)

> The banner of their victory displayed.
> An ermine white upon a field of green,
> Wearing a chain of topaz and of gold.
>
> Not human, rather to be called divine,
> Were both their bearing and their holy words:
> Blessed is one born for such destiny!
> With violets and roses they were decked;
> Bright stars they seemed, and in their midst a sun.
> Adorned them all, and made them brighter still.
>
> (p. 54)

The presence of the ermine, then, identifies Elizabeth with the moment in the poem at which Laura is imaged as the sun, that most potent symbol of male monarchy. The Sun, at the centre of the Ptolemaic universe, designates the monarch as God's vicegerent on earth, existing in relation to the nation in the place held by God in relation to all creation.[49]

The very profusion of the jewellery suggests a further association with Petrarch's poem. Leonard Forster links this device in portraiture to Petrarchan hyperbole, as exemplified in Sonnet 263:

Gentillezza di sangue e l'altre care.
Cose tra noi, perle e robini et oro,
Quasi vil soma, egualmente dispregi.
L'alta belta, ch'al mondo non ha pare,
Noia t'e, se non quanto il bel tesoro.
Di castita par ch'ella adorni e fregi.

The pride of birth, with all that here we deem.
Most precious, gems and gold's resplendent grace,
Abject alike in thy regard appear:
Nay, even thine own unrivall'd beauties beam.
No charm to thee – save as their circling blaze.
Clasps fitly that chaste soul, which still thou hold'st most dear.

The device is also, as Forster points out, used elsewhere in portraiture, particularly in the well-known portrait thought to be of Diane de Poitiers, in which a lady sits before a mirror trying jewels against her naked breast. The implication here is that, however beautiful and rare the jewels, the lady surpasses them.[50] In the Ermine portrait, though, the sheer number of jewels is overwhelming. I would suggest here a device similar to the extended enumeration which establishes the processions of Love, Fame, and Time in the *Triumphs*. The figure is decked with jewel upon jewel, pearl upon pearl, but the viewer understands that the queen surpasses them all, both physically and symbolically. In a visual equivalent of the inexpressibility *topos*, the profusion of jewels restates the impossibility of representing either her beauty or her virtue.

The triumph motif is also employed in a pair of engravings dating from around 1589, and in the well-known Procession picture of approximately 1600. By this time the link with Petrarch's Laura is so firmly established that allusions to it need be far less explicit. The first engraving, designed by William Rogers to commemorate the defeat of the Armada, is emblematic in style.[51] It is entitled *Eliza Triumphans*, an expression by this time commonplace, and shows Elizabeth as Peace, bearing an olive branch. Mounted on an obelisk on either side of her are Victory and Plenty each offering her a crown: the crown of Victory is a laurel wreath, providing an associative link with both Laura and the Roman imperial triumph. The second engraving is a development of Rogers's *Eliza Triumphans*, dating from a little later.[52] The similarities in pose and costume are close, but instead of Victory and Plenty the obelisks each contain three niches, which house representations of six of the seven Virtues. The seventh Virtue is of course represented by Elizabeth herself, so that the grouping as a whole recalls the company in which Laura moves against Love in the Triumph of Chastity.

The picture entitled *Queen Elizabeth I in Procession to Blackfriars*, attributed to Robert Peake, depends to some extent for its effect on the familiarity of Elizabeth's identification with Laura the triumphator (Figure 11). The figure here is of a very young queen, derived from Hilliard's 'mask of youth', which was much in use at the end of Elizabeth's reign as part of the *semper eadem* fiction. She is dressed in white and proceeds in a precisely structured triumphal procession, seated in a chariot with an elaborate floral canopy carried above her. She is preceded by a double column of courtiers in order of rank, and by her Master of the Horse. Immediately following walk a young couple in white, a group of six ladies-in-waiting and three grooms, one of them pushing the triumphal chair. The beginning and the end of the procession have been lost by the picture's having been cut away at the sides and the top. The structure of the procession remains clear, however, with powerful emphasis on the central position of the monarch.[53]

In one of the posthumous portraits of Elizabeth, dated between 1608 and 1610, she is shown in a contemplative pose with two shadowy figures behind her: Time and Death (Figure 12).[54] Two cherubim hover above her, holding a crown between them in their left hands while one of them holds a sceptre in his right. Above the crown floats a laurel wreath, and it appears that all these trappings of earthly power and glory are being taken away by the cherubs. On the table by her right elbow, beneath the figure of Time, lies a broken hourglass, and behind her left shoulder, beside the figure of Death, is another hourglass, whole but with all the sands collected in the bottom. In her left hand she holds the Book of Common Prayer, with her thumb marking the place at she which she has paused in her reading. The face is modelled on the death mask, rather than the mask of youth much used in portraits in her later years, and there is a lambent glow to the skin and to the silver of her gown and the ermine trim to her robe, while the figures of Time and Death are in deep shadow behind her, and the cherubim with the crowns appear to be receding into the distance beyond her head. The messengers of God remove the symbols of earthly achievement and power, but the Prayer Book remains, not only present but in use, indicating the eternal truth which is manifested in Protestant Christian practice. A similar implication is found in an engraving by Frances Delaram, from about 1617–1619, in which the queen is depicted as receiving a crown consisting of the moon, the sun and the stars (Figure 13).[55] The apocalyptic imagery in the engraving and the implication of triumph in the portrait also suggest that, like Laura, after her death Elizabeth has become a part of the vision of the New Jerusalem in The Triumph of Eternity.

An intriguing acknowledgement of Elizabeth's identification with the Laura of the *Triumphs* may be seen in Ralegh's first dedicatory sonnet to *The Faerie Queene*, in which he describes the soul of Petrarch weeping at having been surpassed in poetic achievement by Spenser.[56] Ralegh's verse is in itself a miniature of the *Triumphs*. His title, 'A Vision vpon this conceipt of the *Faery Queene*', and the opening phrase 'Methought I saw' establish the sonnet as a dream vision, like the *Triumphs*. The moment of the vision occurs somewhere between the Triumph of Fame and the Triumph of Time: the dreamer sees the grave of Laura and describes the vision in terms of its place in the triumph sequence:

> Me thought I saw the graue where *Laura* lay,
> Within that Temple, where the vestal flame.
> Was wont to burne, and passing by that way,
> To see that buried dust of liuing fame,
> Whose tombe fair loue, and fairer virtue kept,
> All suddenly I saw the Fairy Queene:

The order of the triumphs has been precisely maintained. Laura, herself representing the triumph of Chastity whose victory is over Love, is required to succumb to Death: thus her grave contains both 'fair Loue', her captive, and 'fairer virtue', herself as captor. The victory of death is limited, however. In *The Triumph of Death* Laura reminds Death that she has power only over her body: '– In costor no hai tu ragione alcuna / ed in me poca; sola in questa spoglia' (ll.49–50) ('Thou hast no power over those with me' – ... And little over me save for my body') (p. 55).

Therefore in Ralegh's sonnet the 'vestal flame' of Laura's chaste spirit still burns in the temple, and Laura herself has become the 'dust of liuing fame' the triumph of Fame which defeats Death. Ralegh's central image here echoes Petrarch's description of Laura's spirit at the moment of her death: 'non come fiamma che per forza è spenta, / ma che per se medesma si consume, /se n'andò in pace l'anima content' (ll. 160–162) ('Not like a flame that is forcibly quenched, / But like to one that doth itself consume, / Her soul, contented, went its way in peace') (p. 59). The echo suggests that Ralegh is familiar with Petrarch's original and expects his readers to know it too. Morley's translation of these lines is fuzzy:

> Eche one dyd beholde that moste swete face.
> How preciouse it was, how full of grace,
> Not dyssolved with no violent payne,
> But passynge awaye with an easy vayn,
>
> (Carnicelli, p. 122)

He has added two lines and dropped one, leaving out the image of the flame altogether in a very vague translation of 'per forza è spenta'.

The action of the sonnet involves a triumphal battle similar to the one described in the Triumph of Time, in which Time is represented by Phoebus. Spenser triumphs over Petrarch, and hence Gloriana defeats Laura, as the latter's attendants are drawn into the former's retinue:

> All suddenly I saw the Fairy Queene:
> At whose approach the soule of Petrarcke wept,
> And from henceforth those graces were not seene:
> For they this Queene attended, in whose steed.
> Obliuion laid him downe on Laura's herse.

Gloriana usurps Laura's fame – her victory over death – and consigns her to oblivion which, in the *Triumphs*, is the domain of Time:

> a' suoi corsier radoppadiato era l'orzo;
> e la reina di ch'io sopra dissi,
> d'alcun de' suoi già volea far divorzo.
>   Udi' dir, non so a chi, ma 'l detto scrissi:
> In questi umani, a dir proprio, ligustri,
> di cieca oblivion che scuri abissi!
>
> (ll. 97–102)

> His coursers now he fed more copiously,
> Striving to separate her followers.
> From queenly Fame, of whom I have had my say.
> And then I heard a voice, and, listening, wrote:
> 'What dark abyss of blind oblivion.
> Awaits these slight and tender human flowers.'
>
> (p. 99)

Once again, Morley's translation is loose and inaccurate, and he misses the intention of Time to usurp Fame's retinue. Ralegh's lines echo Petrarch's original very closely and include a wordplay on *la reina*, who in the *Triumphs* is, of course, Fame. Spenser's Virgin Queen, then, becomes the queen of queens in her defeat of Laura as Fame. It is Gloriana and a better poet who consign Laura to oblivion; nor is Petrarch able to save her, even though in the Triumph of Time Phoebus the triumphator is particularly envious of those whose fame is protected by poets and historians, 'ché per se stessi son levati a volo, / uscendo for de la comune gabbia' (ll. 92–93) ('For they, escaping from the common cage, / Had mounted upward, into soaring flight') (p. 99).

For the commendatory verse to be effective on the public and private levels at which such compliments work, Ralegh must have composed it in the confidence that Spenser and other readers would recognise the references without difficulty, and indeed they would have done. From the earliest years of Elizabeth's reign the Laura of the Triumphs has been such an increasingly familiar and fundamental element in the Elizabethan icon that it provided a rich ground for admirers such as Ralegh to mine for multilayered compliments. The possibility of separating virginity from the more feminine virtue of chastity, with its potentially problematic associations with the sister virtues of obedience and silence,[57] and of invoking the power of virginity in terms of military victory allowed Elizabeth to negotiate some of the more treacherous terrain of gender and opened up the possibility for the later outpourings of Petrarchan adulation in a context that still maintained her position of monarchical power. More than almost any other iconic figure, Laura the triumphator has helped to inscribe Elizabeth in the public consciousness as a victor, a ruler, and a monument to virtue, constancy and divinely ordained authority.

Notes

The Faculty of Arts at York University, Canada, provided financial assistance and the York University Faculty Association awarded me a release-time fellowship, both of which were of great assistance in the completion of this essay. I am particularly grateful to the members of my writing group, Elizabeth Cohen, Joan Gibson, Agnes Juhasz-Ormsby, and Margaret Reeves, for their valuable comments and suggestions.

1. The earliest full discussion of Elizabeth's various images is E.C. Wilson, *England's Eliza* (Cambridge, MA: Harvard University Press, 1939). Frances A. Yates, *Astraea: The Imperial Theme in the Sixteenth Century* (London: Routledge and Kegan Paul, 1975), and Roy C. Strong, *The Cult of Elizabeth: Elizabethan Portraiture and Pageantry* (London: Thames and Hudson, 1977), were the first scholars to define the cult of virginity as the product of a conscious stratagem on the queen's part. Further discussions of the Elizabethan icon in its various forms include David Moore Bergeron, *English Civic Pageantry, 1558–1642* (London: Edward Arnold, 1971); Jean Wilson, *Entertainments for Queen Elizabeth I* (Woodbridge: Boydell and Brewer, 1980); Louis Adrian Montrose, '"Shaping Fantasies": Figurations of Gender and Power in Elizabethan Culture', *Representations* 2 (1983), pp. 61–94; Roy C. Strong, *Gloriana: The Portraits of Queen Elizabeth I* (London: Thames and Hudson, 1987); Philippa Berry, *Of Chastity and Power: Elizabethan Literature and the Unmarried Queen* (London: Routledge, 1989); John King, 'Queen Elizabeth I: Representations of the Virgin Queen', *Renaissance Quarterly* 43 (1990), pp. 30–74; Susan Frye, *Elizabeth I: The Competition for Representation* (Oxford: Oxford University Press, 1993); Helen Hackett, *Virgin Mother, Maiden Queen: Elizabeth I and the Cult of the Virgin Mary* (London: Macmillan, 1995); Roy C. Strong, *The Tudor and Stuart Monarchy: Pageantry, Painting, Iconography, Vol. II: Elizabethan* (Woodbridge: Boydell Press, 1995), pp. 9–54; Diane Purkiss, 'The Queen on Stage: Marlowe's *Dido, Queen of Carthage* and the Representation of Elizabeth I', in *A Woman Scorn'd: Responses to the Dido Myth*, edited by Michael Burden (London: Faber and Faber, 1998); Louis Adrian Montrose, 'Idols of the Queen: Policy, Gender, and the Picturing of Elizabeth I', *Representations* 68 (1999), pp. 108–161; Susan Doran, 'Virginity, Divinity and Power: The Portraits of Elizabeth I', in *The Myth of Elizabeth*, edited by Susan Doran and Thomas S. Freeman (Basingstoke: Palgrave Macmillan, 2003); and Matthew Woodcock, 'The Fairy Queen Figure in Elizabethan Entertainments', *Elizabeth I: Always Her Own Free Woman*, edited by Carole Levin, Jo Eldridge Carney, and Debra Barrett-Graves (Aldershot: Ashgate, 2003), pp. 97–115.

2. Ernest Hatch Wilkins, *The Making of the 'Canzoniere' and Other Petrarchan Studies* (Rome: Edizioni di storia e letteratura, 1951).

3. For fuller discussions of the editions and translations see 'The *Quattrocento* Editions of the "Canzoniere" and the "Trionfi"' and 'The Separate Quattrocento Editions of the triumphs', in Wilkins, *Making*, pp. 379–401 and pp. 403–406; and D.D. Carnicelli, ed., *Lord Morley's Tryumphes of Fraunces Petrarcke: The First English Translation of the Trionfi*, "Introduction" (Cambridge, MA: Harvard University Press, 1971), pp. 29–37.

4. The earliest and closest imitation in English is Thomas More's *Nyne Pageantes* written in 1502. The 'pageants' are nine stanzas which More wrote to accompany a set of tapestries of his own design, and they bear a closer relationship to the pictorial tradition than to the poem. For detailed surveys of imitations of the Triumphs in English Renaissance

literature see Carnicelli, *Tryumphes*, pp. 47–49; Ivy Mumford, 'Petrarchism in Early Tudor England', *Italian Studies* 19 (1964), pp. 56–63; Robert Coogan, 'Petrarch's *Trionfi* and the English Renaissance', *Studies in Philology* 67 (1970), pp. 306–327; Stephen Minta, *Petrarch and Petrarchism: The English and French Traditions* (Manchester: Manchester University Press, 1980).

5. James P. Carley, ed., *The Libraries of King Henry VIII* (London: The British Library, 2000), p. 110.

6. James P. Carley, *The Books of King Henry VIII and His Wives* (London: The British Library, 2004) p. 142.

7. Mumford, 'Petrarchism', p. 60.

8. Carnicelli, *Tryumphes*, Introduction, p. 10.

9. Henry Parker, Lord Morley, 'Epistle' in Carnicelli, *Tryumphes*, p. 78.

10. This is the only text that Morley, a prolific translator and author, chose to have printed. James P. Carley, 'The Writings of Henry Parker, Lord Morley', in *'Triumphs of English': Henry Parker, Lord Morley, Translator to the Tudor Court. New Essays in Interpretation*, edited by Marie Axton and James P. Carley (London: The British Library, 2000), pp. 27–68, p. 53.

11. Parker, 'Epistle', p. 78.

12. Kenneth R. Bartlett, 'The Occasion of Lord Morley's Translation of the *Trionfi*: The Triumph of Chastity over Politics', *Petrarch's Triumphs: Allegory and Spectacle*, edited by Konrad Eisenbichler and Amilcare A. Ianucci (University of Toronto Italian Studies, 1990), 4, pp. 325–334. Carley, 'Writings', pp. 53–54, is sceptical of Bartlett's interpretation, pointing out that it is equally possible that the text was presented to Maltravers in manuscript, and that the decision to print was taken by the Arundel family.

13. Leicester Bradner, ed., *The Poems of Queen Elizabeth I* (Providence: Brown University Press, 1964), pp. 13–16.

14. Frances Young, *Mary Sidney, Countess of Pembroke* (London: Nutt Press, 1912), Appendix A.

15. A.B. Grosart, ed., *The Writings in Verse and Prose of Sir Edward Dyer*, 4 vols (St George's, Blackburn, printed for private circulation, 1870–1876). The translation forms part of *The Prayse of Nothing*.

16. Henry W. Meikle, ed., *The Works of William Fowler* (Edinburgh and London: The Scottish Texts Society: 1914–1940), I, pp. 13–134.

17. Carnicelli, *Tryumphes*, p. 54.

18. Published in 1475, with a long introduction and extensive notes by Bernardo da Pietro Lapini da Montalcino, known as 'Glicino' or 'Illicino', and generally known as the Illicino edition. Wilkins, *Making*, p. 405; Carnicelli, *Tryumphes*, pp. 28–29.

19. 'Suche waiwarde waies hath love' is a translation of *The Triumph of Love*, III.151–187. See Carnicelli, *Tryumphes*, p. 54 and note.

20. For useful and detailed discussions of Morley's work and his place in the Tudor court see Carnicelli, *Tryumphes*, pp. 9–19, and Axton and Carley, eds, *'Triumphs of English'*.

21. Wilkins, *Making*, p. 406; Carnicelli, *Tryumphes*, p. 29.

22. For fuller discussions of the illustrative tradition see Esther Nyholm, 'A Comparison of the Petrarchan Configuration of the *Trionfi* and their Interpretation in Renaissance Art', and Barbara Dodge, 'Petrarch and the Arts', in *Allegory*, eds Eisenbichler and Iannuci, pp. 235–258 and pp. 177–182.

23. H.C. Marillier, *The Tapestries at Hampton Court Palace* (London: Her Majesty's Stationery Office, 1931).

24. John Skelton, *The Complete English Poems*, edited by John Scattergood (New Haven: Yale University Press 1983), pp. 246–278.

25. Roy C. Strong, *Art and Power: Renaissance Festivals, 1450–1650* (Los Angeles: University of California Press, 1984), pp. 44–45.

26. Strong, *Art and Power*, pp. 46–48.

27. Strong, *Art and Power*, pp. 45–47.

28. For a full description of this procession see Victor E. Graham, 'The Entry of Henry II into Rouen in 1550: A Petrarchan Triumph', in *Allegory*, eds Eisenbichler and Ianucci, pp, pp. 403–413.

29. See Enid Welsford, *The Court Masque: A Study in the Relationship Between Poetry and the Revels* (New York: Russell and Russell 1927), pp. 81–85; Alexandra Johnson, 'English Civic Ceremony', in *Allegory*, eds Eisenbichler and Ianucci, pp. 395–402; Strong, *Art and Power*, pp. 44–48.

30. As, for example, in Shakespeare's *A Midsummer Night's Dream*, Theseus promises Hippolyta: 'I will wed thee in another key, / With pomp, with triumph, and with revelling' (William Shakespeare, *A Midsummer Night's Dream*, edited by Harold Brooks (London: Methuen, 1979), I.1.18–19).

31. Germaine Warkentin, 'Introduction', in *The Queen's Majesty's Passage & Related Documents*, edited by Germaine Warkentin (Toronto: Centre for Reformation and Renaissance Studies, 2004), pp. 31–32.

32. Quotations from the original Italian are taken from Francesco Petrarca, *Triumphi*, edited by Marco Ariani (Milan: U. Mursia editore S.p.A., 1988). The translation is in Ernest Hatch Wilkins, trans., *The Triumphs of Petrarch* (Chicago: University of Chicago Press, 1962).

33. Alastair Fowler, *Triumphal Forms: Structural Patterns in Elizabethan Poetry* (Cambridge: Cambridge University Press, 1970), pp. 27–33.

34. Frye, *Elizabeth I*, p. 33.

35. For a detailed and illuminating discussion of the pageant see Warkentin, 'Introduction', *Passage*, pp. 58–65.

36. Warkentin, *Passage*, p. 85.

37. Warkentin, *Passage*, p. 98.

38. Yates, *Astraea*, p. 113.

39. Roy C. Strong, *Portraits of Queen Elizabeth I* (Oxford: Clarendon Press, 1963), p. 102.

40. This portrait was bequeathed to the Folger Shakespeare Library by Francis T. Plimpton in 1997.

41. Strong, *Portraits*, p. 66.

42. There are two versions of the 1580 Sieve portrait. The best known, and the one under discussion here, is the one currently owned by the Pinacoteca Nationale da Siena, also known as the Siena portrait. The other is a variant, presently owned by His Grace the Duke of Hamilton and Brandon and held at the Palace of Holyroodhouse.

43. See particularly Strong *Portraits*, p. 66, and *Gloriana*, pp. 101–103; Yates, *Astraea*, p. 115; Doran, 'Virginity', p. 187.

44. In most versions of the legend she cleverly tricks Iarbus into selling her a much larger piece of land than he intended: he offers her the amount of land that can be covered by an ox hide, and she cuts the hide into narrow strips to circle a substantial area. For this reason she was also considered an example of circumspection in statecraft.

45. Diane Purkiss, in a discussion of three instances of Elizabeth's identification with Dido, also notes the connection with the *Triumphs*. She finds that in this instance the pillar privileges the Virgilian version of Dido's story, but that 'it can also be read as an instance of how "historical" or "chaste" Dido shaped readings of Virgilian Dido'. See Purkiss, 'Queen on Stage', pp. 156–158.

46. The emphasis on constancy accords with the choice of black for Elizabeth's gown, since black was widely understood to be the colour that represented constancy.

47. The procession does not appear in the variant portrait. It is not known in what order the portraits were painted.

48. Frances Yates was the first scholar to note the association between the ermine in the portrait and Laura's banner in the Triumph of Death. See Yates, *Astraea*, pp. 112–120.

49. This is an image she exploits elsewhere as, for example, in the Rainbow portrait, in which she is depicted holding a rainbow in her right hand, with the motto 'Non sine sole iris'.

50. Leonard R. Forster, *The Icy Fire: Five Studies in European Petrarchism* (Cambridge: Cambridge University Press, 1969), pp. 134–135. The translation Forster offers here is from *The Sonnets, Triumphs and Other Poems of Petrarch, translated by various hands* (London: George Bell, 1883), p. 226.

51. The copy in the British Library is accompanied by a set of celebratory verses, BL C.121.9.6.(14). Strong, *Portraits*, pp. 111–112.

52. Strong, *Portraits*, p. 111.

53. For a very detailed analysis of this picture see Strong, *Cult*, pp. 17–46.

54. The painting is owned by Lord Methuen and held at Corsham Court.

55. Strong, *Portraits*, pp. 154–155.

56. Sir Walter Ralegh, 'A Vision vpon this conceipt of the Faery Qveene', in Edmund Spenser, *The Faerie Queene*, edited by A.C. Hamilton (London: Longman, 1977), p. 476.

57. On the gendering of the virtues see Joan Gibson, 'The Logic of Chastity: Women, Sex, and the History of Philosophy in the Early Modern Period', in *Hypatia: A Journal of Feminist Philosophy* 21 (2006), pp. 1–19.

6

'Nature without labor': Virgin Queen
and virgin land in Sir Walter Ralegh's
*The Discoverie of the Large, Rich and
Bewtiful Empyre of Guiana*[1]

HELEN J. BURGESS

The name of the one who disappeared must have gotten inscribed
somewhere else. (Jacques Derrida, *Specters of Marx*)[2]

Sir Walter Ralegh's *The Discoverie of the Large, Rich and Bewtiful Empyre of Guiana*[3] was
first published in 1595, following his exploratory voyage to the Orinoco Basin in 1594
in search of the legendary 'El Dorado', or City of Gold, reported by early (and, as it
turned out, unreliable) Spanish explorers. Ralegh's *Discoverie* was an attempt to persuade
Elizabeth I and her nobles to invest money in a second trip to Guiana. Ultimately, it was
unsuccessful; Elizabeth refused to put up her money, and Ralegh's mission to conquer
and 'protect' Guiana from Spain was deferred until his second disastrous journey under
the reign of James I. However, the Guiana narrative, as a historical document, also
allows us insight into a peculiar relationship – between Elizabeth the 'Virgin Queen'
of England, and her virtual counterpart, Guiana, the 'virgin land' Ralegh proposes
to conquer in her name. Ralegh's Guiana is presented to Elizabeth as a body – more
specifically, as a woman's (virginal) body. Thus, he claims,

> Guiana is a Country that hath yet her Maidenhead, never sacked, turned, nor
> wrought, the face of the earth hath not been torn, nor the virtue and salt of the
> soil spent by manurance, the graves have not been opened for gold, the mines not
> broken with sledges, nor their Images pulled down out of their temples. It hath
> never been entered by an army of strength, and never conquered or possessed by
> any Christian Prince.[4]

Given Elizabeth's own status as the 'Virgin Queen', a peculiar mirroring was unfolding in the narrative of the *Discoverie*.

In this chapter I want to untangle some of the relationships between Elizabeth's body and the virgin body of Guiana in terms of a kind of virtuality, especially as it pertains to the narration and virtualisation of resources. In the *Discoverie* narrative Ralegh creates a 'virtual narrative space' for Elizabeth through which she can experience the voyage with Ralegh. This space is tied inextricably with the body – Elizabeth's body, Ralegh's body, and the body of 'Guiana' – as a focal point for intensities of desire and intensifications of wealth and subjection. Ralegh's document presents us with a prime example of the way in which (female) bodies are coded as landscapes for exploration and exploitation, while at the same time romanticised as being in some way ultimately inaccessible – a virgin space, inviolate.

I believe that these bodies, abstracted, virtualised, and reincorporated in the Guiana narrative, stand in for a larger anxiety about the state of England's natural resources – timber and food crops, in particular – and Elizabeth's desperate need to find an edge over the Spanish. At the same time they also say something about a search for an abstraction of desire – gold – which closely mirrors Ralegh's desire for power and privilege in the Elizabethan court. According to Elizabeth Grosz, 'the body is a surface to be inscribed, written on, which can be segmented, dissolved into flows, or seen as a part (or parts) of a larger ensemble or machine, when it is connected to other organs, flows, and intensities'.[5] In the case of the Guiana narrative, the body of Elizabeth, as a Virgin Queen and the source of power and wealth, is mapped on to the body of Guiana, a 'virgin land' that is nevertheless endlessly productive. These bodies enter into commerce with each other through the abstract medium of gold, creating a virtual equivalency between the body of a woman and the body of the country. As a supposedly truthful account prepared for a faraway monarch, the Guiana narrative is tasked with finding a way to create a space in which Elizabeth can apprehend the distant land of Guiana; thus Elizabeth's body is 'written on to' the landscape of Guiana in the written text of Ralegh's narrative. But the Guiana narrative is a writing not only of Elizabeth's body but also of many others: the suffering bodies of the sailors, travelling starving through a productive landscape, the desiring bodies of the Spaniards, figured as cruel rapists charged with 'eating out' the native towns, and the body of Ralegh himself, desiring power, desiring resources, and, ultimately, desiring Elizabeth as the signifier of England's wealth. This, finally, is Grosz's 'larger ensemble or machine': a connector of landscape, gold, bodies, and desire, drawn together and circulated in the narrative of Ralegh's Guiana voyage.

The queen protectress

As critics have noted, Elizabeth maintained her virtue and power in part through her successful manipulation of a virgin mystique. Louis Montrose cites the most famous portrait of Elizabeth, the Ditchley portrait in which Elizabeth stands on a cartographic map of England (Figure 4), as a representation simultaneously of maternal protection and virgin impregnability: '[t]his representation of Queen Elizabeth as standing upon her land and sheltering it under her skirts suggests a mystical identification of the inviolate female body of the monarch *with* the unbreached body of her land, at the same time that it affirms her distinctive role as the motherly protectress of her people'.[6] This image of wise management of her people can also be extended to her power over (in the case of the painting, literally over) the natural features of the landscape. Fumbling for a metaphor to explain Elizabeth's greatness to the Guianans, Ralegh describes her in terms of the landscape he sees around him: 'I made them understand that I was the servant of a Queene, who was the great *Casique* of the north, and a virgin, and had more *Casiqui* under her then there were trees in their Iland.'[7] Here power is explicitly related to power over resources, in this case trees – a commodity fast becoming scarce in Elizabethan England.

Ralegh's income from the material resources of England was directly dependent on his favour with Elizabeth. His tenure under Elizabeth's reign had yielded a substantial number of incomes based on the material wealth of England and Ireland. In 1583 he had been granted a monopoly in 'the farm of wines', charging vintners £1 a year for the right to retail wine.[8] This was followed by the monopoly licence to export woollen broadcloths, in 1584; that year Thomas Morgan, an agent for Mary Queen of Scots, informed her by letter that 'Master Rawley is the Queen's dear minion, who daily groweth in credit'.[9] Most significantly, in 1585 he was appointed Lord Warden of the Stanneries, a political position in which he negotiated profits on tin mining in Cornwall and Devon on behalf of the queen.

Ralegh was also able to capitalise on a key shortage in timber. Deforestation and fuel scarcity were a problem becoming increasingly widespread – in some places, desperate – in sixteenth-century Europe. Carolyn Merchant's studies show that, in particular, forests were under pressure by the need for vast supplies of fuel for iron smelting.[10] In addition to new building construction, slow-growing oak was used extensively in various capacities in the production of beer and wine, soap, and glass.[11] Indeed, the very stability of an Elizabethan England capable of sustaining and protecting itself as an independent nation (in other words, maintaining a strong economy and a stronger military) was dependent on trees. Merchant points out that 'the industry most dependent on wood and most critical to sixteenth-century commercial expansion and national supremacy was shipbuilding'.[12] Pitch, too, was needed for caulking ships. In 1586–1587, in a period of scarce fuel supplies due to rapid deforestation, and with permission and letters patent from Elizabeth, Ralegh joined other aristocrats in setting up a 'plantation' in Munster, Ireland, in what amounted to a land-grab on behalf of English settlers. This plantation, which would be lost in 1598, included a large amount of forested land, which was quickly sent to sawmills built on the property and used as fuel in iron production. Brewing practices required oak casks, a need also capitalised on by Ralegh. With the timber from the Irish properties, he set up a profitable business exporting wood for wine and hogshead staves.[13]

Ralegh's ongoing competition for access to resources, especially timber, manifested itself as a continuing need to be in good stead with the queen. This need, as Shannon Miller notes, was a motivating reason to conduct the journey to Guiana: Ralegh's secret marriage, to Bess Throckmorton in 1592, had caused his fall from Elizabeth's good graces. Miller suggests that 'Raleigh's expedition to Guiana can be read as ... a gift of extreme wealth to regain Queen Elizabeth's now elusive affections'.[14] Indeed, in her characterisation of Ralegh's position as a 'fall from grace', Miller's choice of words suggests a possible metaphor that ties in neatly with the Guiana narrative: Ralegh's desire to return to a land of Eden 'before the fall' — a virgin land in which to apprehend once again his Virgin Queen.

In fact what is happening is a cascade of displacements, in which bodies, resources, and gold are continually deferred from one term to the next in the desire for power and wealth. Ralegh's need to maintain his material wealth is tied up with his professed desire for proximity to the queen, who often imposed temporary banishments from court (notably, of her favourites Hatton, Ralegh, and Essex) as a sign of her disfavour; thus, desire for the 'body' of England was tied in with the body of the queen. When his privileged position was cut off, the promise of Guiana's gold seemed like a good way to get Ralegh back into Elizabeth's good graces, and return him to the court from his imposed exile. His characterisation of Guiana as a virgin land suggests a direct flow of desire: the desire for the resources of England (tin, timber, wool) displaced on to desire for Elizabeth's body, which in turn was displaced on to the virgin body of Guiana.

Nature without labour

For Ralegh, Elizabeth's virginity and the virginity of Guiana are linked as an image of wise management and sustainability of resources. Elizabeth, he argues, governs her people so well she can send them out to protect other countries from less wise management; in his interactions with the people of Guiana, he claims on behalf of his queen a superiority in managing resources – the 'resource', in this case, being Guiana's virgin body. His chief competitors the Spaniards, on the other hand, are represented as cruel rapists of Guiana and its people, purposely 'planted there to eat out & wast those that were natural of the place'.[15] In this competition for resources, Ralegh represents Elizabeth as a saviour and protector from Spanish rule: he reports that he has told the Guianans 'that she was an enemy to the Castellani in respect of their tyrannie and oppression, and that she delivered all such nations about her, as were by them oppressed, and having freed all the coast of the northern world had sent me to free them also'.[16] This offer of protection for the virgin body of the land of Guiana even extends to the individual bodies of village women. Ralegh reports that, despite the extreme provocation of nakedness, the women of Guiana remain untouched by the hands of the sailors:

I protest before the majestic of the living God, that I neither know nor beleeve, that any of our companie one or other, by violence or otherwise, ever knew any of their women, and yet we saw many hundreds, and had many in our power, and of those very yoong, and excellently favored which came among us without deceit, stark naked.[17]

This stands in contrast to his reports of the Spaniards, who according to the villagers 'tooke from them both their wives, and daughters daily, and used them for satisfying of their owne lusts, especially such as they tooke in this maner by strength'.[18] Here, again, women's bodies are both metaphorically equated with the 'virgin' body of the land, and rated along with food and resources: 'I suffred not anie man to take from anie of the nations so much as a *Pina*, or a *Potato* roote, without giving them contentment, nor any man so much as to offer to touch any of their wives or daughters.'[19] Rape is figured as both a sexual and an environmental conquest of the imaginary virgin body of Guiana; abstinence the marker of a wise monarch.

Ralegh's characterisation of Guiana as virgin is, of course, a fiction, and one which contains the seeds of its own exploitation. These 'virgin' tropes may help justify Ralegh's presence in Guiana, but they also provide the justification for her projected conquest. Despite Ralegh's protestation that he comes to protect the land from the marauding Spaniards, the land is already figured as a body implicitly ripe for plunder. A virgin, after all, for Ralegh, is a resource, a woman who has not been possessed; even virgin Queen Elizabeth, the exception to this rule, can maintain her power only by representing herself as a 'Prince'. Indeed, Elizabeth's management of herself and her country belies her image of virgin purity and care: the queen is a represented as a virgin who uses her resources wisely, but ironically the very reason Ralegh is in Guiana is to extend its resources to a country already beginning to suffer, among other things, the effects of deforestation and excess 'manurance'.[20] England, even governed by a Virgin Queen, is not a sustainable ecology.

Guiana, on the other hand, is described as self-sustaining, a projection of an endless cornucopia of possible wealth in the form of gold and resources which do not require cultivation:

[the people of Orinoco] never eate of anie thing that is set or sowen, and as at home they use neither planting nor other manurance, so when they com abroad they refuse to feede of ought, but of that which nature without labor bringeth foorth. They use the tops of Palmitos for bread, and kil Deere, fish and porks for the rest of their sustenance, they have also manie sorts of fruits that grow in the woods, and great varietie of birds and foule.[21]

This idea of 'nature without labor' suggests that nature is productive without the intervening hand of human husbandry: a return to an age of plenty before the fall. Later Ralegh describes the upriver country again in terms of a naturally occurring bounty:

we beheld plaines of twenty miles in length, the grasse short and greene, and in divers parts groves of trees by themselves, as if they had been by all the art and labour in the world so made of purpose: and stil as we rowed, the Deere came downe feeding by the waters side, as if they had beene used to a keepers call.[22]

This passage even more explicitly stages Guiana as a kind of compliant landscape; it is so naturally productive that it looks cultivated.

Ralegh's description of Guiana as being virgin in the sense of 'unfarmed' was in fact false, or at least (if we are to be generous) farming activity was not obvious to him. It is possible that the husbandry of the Orinoco tribes people was not evident to English eyes because it lacked the intensified farming practices of Europe: enclosed farming areas, tilled and regularly rotated fields, and the marlpits (clay) and muckheaps (manure) of soil fertiliser. However, this is a generous interpretation, given Ralegh's description of 'art and labour in the world' combining to create 'natural' pastures. Citing Denevan, Whitehead notes that

The lower Orinoco was heavily settled by native people and their own active management of landscape which, anthropology is only just beginning to appreciate, would have been reflected in the practices of maintaining coppices, burning off savannah grasses and a husbandry of fauna, especially deer ... Such native activity has been denied or ignored, in both colonial and anthropological rhetoric, through the ideas of 'wilderness' and the 'natural' landscape, which erases signs of human intervention and so render such regions fit for colonial possession and development.[23]

It is also possible, however, that Ralegh's European models of cultivation blinded him to alternative forms of husbandry. Along with the lack of enclosure, by then the primary marker of farming (and more generally property) in England, the Orinoco Indians' use of raw vegetable sources and the encouragement of wild fauna such as tortugas (turtles) would have seemed alien to a European accustomed to highly regulated single-crop sections of landscape.

All this discussion of 'nature without labor' and 'art and labour in the world' is suggestive of the body of Guiana as an endless productive cornucopia, an Eden or Golden Age, implicitly gendered as a woman of great fertility (the country of Guiana is referred to as 'she'). And yet at the same time Guiana is a country that 'hath yet her Maydenhood', as if the untouched countryside is fertile precisely because it has not been cultivated.'Nature without labor' becomes an implicit trope of virginity: like the popular notion of the 'Golden Age', in which one does not need to work the land in order for it to produce abundant resources, sexual (colonial) conquest is not required in order for Guiana to be endlessly productive. This paradoxical formulation is reconciled through the formulation of a fertile virgin who is able to produce wealth without 'husbandry'.

In terms of the court and Elizabeth, this brings up some interesting questions. Was Elizabeth herself 'nature without labor', despite being a woman cultivated in the territories of the European aristocracy? Certainly the parallel could be drawn that Elizabeth was the ultimate purveyor of wealth, while maintaining her power through her unmarried status. As the arbiter of England's resources, including the parcelling out of monopolies and livings from English tin and woollens, and Irish timber, Elizabeth produces wealth. But at the same time Elizabeth is, like England and its resources, very much the product of labour, not nature. Through the careful maintenance of her image as queen, through wardrobe, the annual progresses, and censorship of official portraits, Elizabeth laboured to retain her monarchy, most especially as a potentially marriageable asset. Elizabeth's management of her subjects, in turn, became husbandry of the country as she distributed land and the income from natural resources. In practical terms, Elizabeth's power manifests itself most often in her ability to parcel out, rather than 'protect': timber monopolies, letters of patent, and gifts of gold and ships.

Ironically, the rich resources accounted by Raleigh are belied by his descriptions of the privations experienced his own men and the inhabitants of the Spanish garrisons already there. Despite his later descriptions of the existence of Indian fermented drinks, he reports that the Spaniards had 'beene many years without wine', and traded eagerly with Ralegh for 'lynnen … and such other thinges as they wanted'.[24]

Ralegh's men also suffered increasingly from the environment and their inability to find fresh water and their need to carry food with them. Sailing up the Orinoco, he reports that

> we caried 100 persons and their victuals for a moneth in the same, being al driven to lie in the raine and wether, in the open aire, in the burning sunne, & upon the hard bords, and to dresse our meat, and to carry al manner of furniture in them, wherewith they were so pestred and unsavery, that what with victuals being most fish, with the weete clothes of so many men thruste together and the heate of the sunne, I will undertake there was never any prison in England, that coulde be founde more unsavory and lothsome, especially to my selfe, who had for many yeares before beene dieted and cared for in a sort farre differing.[25]

Indeed Ralegh's account of the richness of Guiana and the privations of his sailors sometimes becomes quite inexplicable. On one journey he describes, two of his ships 'had spent all their provisions, so as we were brought into despaire and discomfort',[26] such that only a conviction that their destination was ahead kept them going. And yet in the next sentence Ralegh reports of the 'divers sorts of fruits good to eate, flowers and trees of that varietie as were sufficient to make ten volumes of herbals, we releeved our selves manie times with the fruits of the countrey, and somtimes with foule and fish'. He notes the abundance of birds, 'without which, having little or no bread and lesse drink, but onely the thick and troubled water of the river, we had been in a very hard case'.[27]

Ralegh's true problem was one not of resources but of local knowledge and value. While he claims to have seen an abundant land not requiring cultivation, his men were constantly moving between starvation and overeating according to whether or not they were in a native settlement – i.e. whether they were being given food by the region's inhabitants. Ralegh's chief index of plentiful food seems to be bread, a cultivated and manufactured product, rather than the rich meats and plant foods which surrounded them often. This suggests not so much an inability to forage in 'nature' as a system which privileges foods with the value-added operation of labour performed on them. On the return to the port of Morequito, Ralegh describes the arrival of Topiawari's people 'loden with somewhat, as if it had beene a great market or faire in England: and our hungrie companies clustered thicke and threefold among their baskets, everyone laying hand on what he liked'.[28] While celebrating the discovery of a land of abundant food, Ralegh is unable to accept the simple notion of having to forage for food, rather than be presented with it by someone labouring to cultivate it.

The quest for gold

Ralegh's quest for unending bounty does not begin or end with food and trees. The riches of Guiana, as described in the *Discoverie*, hinge on two sources of potential wealth: natural resources and gold. Gold, as a signifier of exchange running through the narrative, is representative of the potential hard currency that can be used to buy ships and arms to fight the Spaniards, but also a way of establishing 'equivalence' in the narrative, to give an evaluative benchmark (i.e. so much gold = so much buying power) for Ralegh's audience – i.e. potential backers – back home. It is interesting, if unsurprising, to note that neither the Spanish nor the English have compunctions about 'protecting' the gold on behalf of the native Indians. But although gold is an abstraction, in the *Discoverie* it is again built upon a more general notion of wealth as naturally abundant. Ralegh includes a translation of an early (and apocryphal) Spanish description of 'the court and magnificence of Guayanacapa, auncestor to the Emperour of Guiana' which explicitly links the bountiful resources of the kingdom with the plentiful existence of their virtual equivalent, gold:

> He had in his wardroppe hollow statues of golde which seemed giants, and the figures in proportion and bignes of all the beastes, birdes, trees and hearbes, that the earth bringeth forth: and of all the fishes that the sea or waters of his kingdome breedeth ... Finally there was nothing in his countrey, whereof hee had not the counterfeat in gold.[29]

In the journey itself, food and gold also come together as related terms. Ralegh describes an incident in which they come upon canoes laden with bread, which are abandoned hurriedly by their occupants (some evidently Spanish). After giving chase unsuccessfully, the sailors return to the canoes, and Ralegh reports that 'nothing on the earth could have been more welcome to us next unto gold, then the great store of very excellent bread which we found in these Canoas'.[30] Given that the canoe occupants included a gold assayer, the bread ironically becomes some sort of 'consolation prize' for the loss of potential information about the whereabouts of the gold. But if one follows through with the idea of bread as a preferable food because it is cultivated and civilised, it is also logical that it would quickly come to be equated with the ultimate marker of economic sophistication: gold, the object of desire. Gold thus comes to occupy a double space in the text: Ralegh's thesis is that Guiana will endlessly produce gold, if they find out where it is, but at the same time it must be fought over, stripped from the ground, and abstracted into currency to be returned to England. The virgin land must 'naturally' produce gold, but it is expected that the gold will have to be laboured over in order to be extracted.

Beyond a potential product of a virgin land, gold also has a gendered value system for Ralegh. He reports of the 'very cruell and bloodthirsty'[31] Amazons not only as warrior women but also as figures in the gold economy of Guiana:

> These *Amazones* have likewise great store of these plates of golde, which they recover by exchange chiefly for a kinde of greene stones, which the Spaniards call *Piedras Hijadas*, and we use for spleene stones, and for the disease of the stone we also esteeme them: of these I saw divers in *Guiana*, and commonly every king or *Casique* hath one, which their wives for the most part weare, and they esteeme them as great jewels.[32]

In a discussion of the *Discoverie* as anthropological text, Neil Whitehead argues that this exchange of gold for the Amazonian 'greene stones' has its basis in Guianan cultural myth. In Cuba and the Hispaniola Islands, notes Whitehead, the Guianan myth-cycle of the Amazons includes an episode in which Guayahona, the 'first ancestor', kidnaps a group of women and abandons them on the island of Matinino, returning with '*guanin* and *takua*' (alloyed gold and carved stone tokens). Whitehead suggests that 'In this context Matinino, the "island of women-without-men," represents the site of these exchanges, just as the land of the Amazons is the source of the "spleen-stones" [*takua*] of Ralegh's account'.[33] He goes on to summarise Goeje's argument that 'the *takua* are representative of the water, nature and woman, and the *caracoli* [gold] are representative of the sun, culture and man'.[34] The figure of the *takua* (possibly nephrite jade) as a feminine currency opposed to masculine gold suggests something about the relative valuation of a woman's body – the *takua* being 'magic stones' associated with the Amazons, but also esteemed as spiritual objects for healing, rather than fully exchangeable currency. Ralegh's description of the routine exchange of the 'feminine' *takua* for 'masculine' gold suggests that, in order for a woman to circulate, she must enter into the gold economy, not the *takua* economy, thence becoming masculinised in the process. In short, female 'nature' can be bought and sold with male gold.

Into this system of female token and male gold comes the paradoxical figure of Elizabeth as a woman's head stamped on to a gold coin. Ralegh reports that 'I gave among them manye more peeces of Golde then I receaved of the new money of 20. shillings with her Majesties picture to weare, with promise that they would become her servants thenceforth'.[35] Shannon Miller notes that through this introduction of iconic Elizabethan coinage 'Elizabeth becomes an exchangeable, substitutable object';[36] but perhaps more accurately she becomes an emblem of the twinned and incompatible desires of the English for a virgin land that is endlessly productive of natural resources while at the same time being within the economic trading zone of gold. In his descriptions of Guianan modes of exchange, Ralegh reveals some of the confusion in the text between the virgin as *naturally* productive and the virgin as potentially exploitable through a *process* of coining and abstraction. On the one hand, he is trying to convince Elizabeth of the country as a place of 'nature without labor'. But on the other hand, he has to describe to her an already established economy based on the exchange of gold and tokens. This paradox leads to the constant tensions in the text, between the quest for gold (a metal associated with masculinity which must be extracted and alloyed, i.e. laboured upon) and the establishing of the metaphor of the virgin land as a naturally abundant feminine landscape.

Unfortunately for Ralegh, despite his descriptions of the circulation of currency that must surely suggest the presence of mines and ores, his trip does not yield the hoped-for plates of gold. Still languishing out of favour after his failure to return with enough gold to justify the expense of the trip, and desperate to redeem himself (or at least to get back to the profitable intrigues of the court), he resorts to narrative speculation, reporting not only his own observations but second-hand accounts from his Spanish counterparts and from local villagers anxious to please him. However, the way in which he chooses to narrate Guiana's worth for future exploration depends on a sleight-of-hand (or possibly 'making the best of a bad situation'), suggesting that in the absence of gold Guiana should still be colonised as a valuable source of replacement for England's own dwindling resources. In addition to gold (for which 'it is in effect nedeles to remember other commodities for trade'),[37] thus, Guiana is depicted as a source of plentiful food and leisure activities: 'It hath so many plaines, cleare rivers, abundance of Phesants, Partridges, Quailes, Rayles, Cranes, Herons, and all other fowle: Deare of all sortes, Porkes, Hares, Lyons, Tygers, Leopards, and divers other sortes of beastes, either for chace, or foode.'[38] This is a land not for protecting, like a virgin, but for *using up* in the manner of the landed wealth of England – blood sport, and plentiful meats of the kind reserved for the richest of English nobles.

Ralegh's *Discoverie* is, in this way, not an adventurer's account of a strange land but a catalogue of resources available for English plunder. His description of the fabled riches of El Dorado, and his wayside descriptions of vast stands of timber, pitch, and stone (all used to justify his trip when no gold is found) are a manifesto for colonisation, or at least exploitation. But, if his representation of Elizabeth to the Guianans hides the immediate English need for resources, then his representation of Guiana to the English court is also less than accurate. In between his descriptions of trees which 'have alwaies fruite either ripe or green, and most of them both blossomes, leaves, ripe fruite, & green at one time',[39] and the wondrous 'thousands of *Tortugas* eggs, which are very wholsome meat, and greatly restoring',[40] we find that Ralegh's boats are rotten and his crew sick and starving. Thus Ralegh subtly shifts his characterisation of Guiana, from an endlessly productive virgin land to a virgin land which must be exploited (raped) in order to produce the resources the English require.

Virtual bodies

In Ralegh's narrative we are offered many 'bodies' to consider as figures of potential wealth and exploitation. Bodies are sites of contestation; they are also virtual spaces, in which battles for power and resources take place (think of the jockeying for proximity to the queen's body which took place so frequently in the English court). However, if these bodies are virtual spaces, what about the resources they seem to represent? Might they be 'virtual' as well? The suffering bodies of Ralegh's sailors would suggest this is the case. The fact that Ralegh's sailors are starving suggests that resources are hard to find, hard to prepare and above all not endless but exhaustible. Ralegh's lists of food sources, pitch, and timber, resources for which England is so desperate, are thus not so much signs of the endless productivity of Guiana as they are signs of England's need to believe that such inexhaustible wealth exists – wealth which England must plunder in order to survive.

The bodies of the suffering sailors thus point to another (virtual) body that is never mentioned – that of England. And since battles for resources are refigured as contested bodies, England's internal contestations for resources are rewritten as the battle for Elizabeth's body. Elizabeth's manipulation of her own body ranges from her assertion of hidden masculinity and thus autonomy (her 'man's heart in a woman's body') to her careful control over official portraits, which continue to represent her as desirable even as an old woman. Elizabeth is engaged in a battle with her subjects over her own body: suitors vie for access and favours, Elizabeth woos Parliament and her people for money, and her adventurers woo her with gifts from strange lands; marriage contracts are negotiated but never consummated. However, if this battle for Elizabeth's body is representative of the contestation for England's resources, ultimately power over her body is not enough. England is an unsustainable ecology; the site of contestation must thus be displaced on to *another* body. This highlights the virtuality of the body as a sign for the competition for resources: the (equally virtual) resources are always someplace else. Guiana, in this case, is that other virtual body, both connected to and a result of the displacement of power from Elizabeth. The environmental rape of England by its aristocracy, displaced on to the (sexual) courtship of Elizabeth by her courtiers, becomes the projected exploitation of Guiana by the English; Elizabeth can maintain her status as a wise virgin only through the environmental and sexual rape of another virgin land.

Both economies and ecologies, of course, are unsustainable. Despite Ralegh's projection of Guiana as a colony 'protected' from its enemies, the virgin body of Guiana cannot be preserved except at the expense of another body – that of England, already deforested, refigured in terms of the suffering bodies of Ralegh's sailors. Conversely, England's Virgin Queen requires new territories to maintain her status as a wise distributor of resources; thus, Guiana's virgin body must be conquered and stripped, in order to feed England. In neither case are these economies 'sustainable' – each is reliant upon the 'rape' of the other to maintain its virgin body. Ralegh understands this, and can appeal only to Elizabeth's sense of pride by comparing her with the fierce fabled Amazon women, who conquer land (and men) in order to take resources and reproduce themselves without husbands. Confusing a local tribe with the fabled Amazons, he reports:

> Upon the river of Caroli, are the Canuri, which are governed by a woman (who is inheritrix of that province), who came farre off to see our nation, and asked mee divers questions of her Majesty, beeing much delighted with the discourse of her Majesties greatnes, and wondring at such reports as we truely made of her highnes many vertues.[41]

Ralegh finally argues that Elizabeth must prove herself greater than these – as a Virgin Queen, the source of all bounty: 'And where the south border of *Guiana* reacheth to the Dominion and Empire of the *Amazones*, those women shall heereby heare the name of a virgin, which is not onely able to defend her owne territories and her neighbors, but also to invade and conquere so great Empires and so farre removed'.[42] Bestowed the title '*Ezrabeta Cassipuna Aquerewana*, ... the great princesse or greatest commaunder',[43] Elizabeth finally becomes Queen of the Amazons – queen of a land of (vanishing) resources, Virgin Queen of a plundered ecology.

Virtual ecologies

The Discoverie of Guiana is in many ways an example of an early virtual reality. Elizabeth never physically apprehends Guiana except through Ralegh's text and the few pieces of plunder he brings back; instead, she travels there through stories and images, related by her faithful soldier to the inhabitants of this distant land. Ralegh reports that 'I shewed them her majesties picture which they so admired and honored, as it had beene easie to have brought them Idolatrous thereof'.[44] In this moment, a supremely mediated moment in which an image of a body comes to stand in for a queen, Elizabeth is transported virtually to the Orinoco delta, imagining herself a Queen of infinite resources.

The chief quality, I think, of the act of virtualisation, is the abstraction of a 'reality' from its underlying material necessities. Indeed, the virtual realities we see today are valued precisely because they do not have 'real' effects: computer game avatars can be reborn, virtual surgery does not penetrate the boundaries of the body, virtual sex is 'safe'. Jacques Derrida notes that it is in the act of virtualisation that we are left with a kind of ghost, or remainder:

> It obliges us more than ever to think the virtualization of space and time, the possibility of virtual events whose movement and speed prohibit us more than ever … from opposing presence to its representation, 'real time' to 'deferred time', effectivity to its simulacrum, the living to the non-living, in short, the living to the living-dead of its ghosts.[45]

But one could argue that Ralegh's narrative has also effected the virtualisation of resources. Elizabeth is given a catalogue of Guiana's riches, displacing and deferring England's desire for timber, pitch, and minerals on to another ecology. The creation of the narrative is a moment of pure virtualisation, in which a Virgin Queen stands in for a virgin land, even while Guiana stands in for, as Derrida puts it, 'the monetary specter, value, money or its fiduciary sign, gold'.[46] Elizabeth's body, stamped on a coin of gold, haunts the narrative of Guiana, a reminder that resources can be plundered in the name of a Virgin Queen just as easily as they can be protected.

Ralegh's tale of Guiana is thus ultimately a story about an ecological crisis in England. But it is also a marker of the virtualisation and abstraction that happens in attempting to represent new resources in such a way that they can be both protected and exploited. This abstraction is reflected in many ways as a series of paradoxes: sailors starving in the land of plenty, landscapes 'cultivated' by nature, a feminine figure stamped on masculine gold. And finally, it is reflected in the paradoxical figure of the endlessly productive virgin: a fond imagining on Ralegh's part of the power of Elizabeth to produce endless favours and rewards, and a New World dream of limitless resources in a time of scarcity.

Notes

1. Many kind thanks are due Robert Markley for early comments on this chapter.
2. Jacques Derrida, *Specters of Marx: The State of the Debt, the Work of Mourning, and the New International* (London and New York: Routledge, 1994), p. 5.
3. Sir Walter Ralegh, *The Discoverie of the Large, Rich and Bewtiful Empyre of Guiana*, ed. Neil L. Whitehead (Norman, OK: University of Oklahoma Press, 1997).
4. Ralegh, *Discoverie*, p. 196.
5. Elizabeth Grosz, *Volatile Bodies: Toward a Corporeal Feminism* (Bloomington and Indianapolis: Indiana University Press, 1994), p. 121.
6. Louis Montrose, 'The Work of Gender in the Discourse of Discovery', in *New World Encounters* (Berkeley: University of California Press, 1993), p. 190.
7. Ralegh, *Discoverie*, p. 134.
8. Raleigh Trevelyan, *Sir Walter Raleigh* (New York: Henry Holt and Co., 2002), p. 55.
9. Trevelyan, *Sir Walter Raleigh*, p. 77.
10. Carolyn Merchant, *The Death of Nature: Women, Ecology and the Scientific Revolution* (San Francisco: HarperCollins, 1983), p. 64.

11. Merchant, *The Death of Nature*, p. 65.

12. Merchant, *The Death of Nature*, p. 65.

13. Trevelyan, *Sir Walter Raleigh*, p. 142.

14. Shannon Miller, *Invested with Meaning: The Raleigh Circle in the New World* (Philadelphia: University of Pennsylvania Press, 1998), p. 153.

15. Ralegh, *Discoverie*, p. 134.

16. Ralegh, *Discoverie*, p. 134.

17. Ralegh, *Discoverie*, p. 165.

18. Ralegh, *Discoverie*, p. 165.

19. Ralegh, *Discoverie*, p. 165.

20. Ralegh, *Discoverie*, p. 159.'Manurance' in this context implies the European practice of intensified land cultivation through the use of fertiliser, enclosure, and crop and stock rotation. For a discussion of the environmental effects of cultivation on topsoil and vegetation during this period see Merchant, *The Death of Nature*, pp. 46–50.

21. Ralegh, *Discoverie*, p. 159.

22. Ralegh, *Discoverie*, p. 163.

23. Neil Whitehead, 'Introduction', in Sir Walter Ralegh, *The Discoverie of the Large, Rich and Bewtiful Empyre of Guiana* (Norman, OK: University of Oklahoma Press, 1997), p. 5.

24. Ralegh, *Discoverie*, p. 132.

25. Ralegh, *Discoverie*, p. 135.

26. Ralegh, *Discoverie*, p. 161.

27. Ralegh, *Discoverie*, p. 161.

28. Ralegh, *Discoverie*, p. 181.

29. Ralegh, *Discoverie*, p. 137.

30. Ralegh, *Discoverie*, pp. 163–164.

31. Ralegh, *Discoverie*, p. 146.

32. Ralegh, *Discoverie*, p. 146.

33. Neil Whitehead, 'The *Discoverie* as Ethnological Text', in Sir Walter Ralegh, *The Discoverie of the Large, Rich and Bewtiful Empyre of Guiana* (Norman, OK: University of Oklahoma Press, 1997), p. 90.

34. *Ibid.*, p. 88.

35. Ralegh, *Discoverie*, pp. 185–186.

36. Miller, *Invested with Meaning*, p. 177.

37. Ralegh, *Discoverie*, p. 195.

38. Ralegh, *Discoverie*, p. 195.

39. Ralegh, *Discoverie*, p. 179.

40. Ralegh, *Discoverie*, p. 167.

41. Ralegh, *Discoverie*, p. 192.

42. Ralegh, *Discoverie*, p. 123.

43. Ralegh, *Discoverie*, p. 134.

44. Ralegh, *Discoverie*, p. 134.

45. Derrida, *Specters of Marx*, p. 169.

46. Derrida, *Specters of Marx*, p. 42.

Part III

The Old World and the New: classical precedents

7

The dark side of the moon:
Semiramis and Titania

LISA HOPKINS

The accession of first Mary Tudor and then her younger sister Elizabeth to the throne of England brought with it iconographic and mythopoeic problems as well as political ones. The only previous women who had attempted to rule England in their own right, the twelfth-century Empress Matilda and the nine days' queen Lady Jane Grey, offered such unfortunate precedents that neither could be used for this purpose, and the mythical Queen Cordelia, though much drawn on by apologists for Elizabeth's reign, was hardly more helpful, because she had met such an unhappy end. As has been much discussed,[1] the abolition of Catholicism had to some extent made it possible to cannibalise some of the iconography of the Virgin Mary for use in representations of Elizabeth, but this could only be hinted at. As a result, it was the classical world which tended to be most extensively plundered for modes of imaging and figuring the queen. However, though the classical world certainly afforded many memorable female rulers, most notably Cleopatra, Dido, and Semiramis, these too presented difficulties because all these queens were as notorious for the extravagance of their love lives as famous for the fact of their rule. Nevertheless, the association with Elizabeth stuck and prospered, particularly in the case of Semiramis, and my aim here is to explore some of the reasons and ways for this,[2] and some of the tensions it generated, with particular reference to a group of texts, starting with Spenser's *The Faerie Queene* and Robert Greene's *The Scottish History of James the Fourth*, moving through the anonymous *Locrine* and Shakespeare's *Titus Andronicus* and A *Midsummer Night's Dream*, and culminating in Thomas Dekker's *The Whore of Babylon*, which associate Semiramis with fairy lore (although the Empress of Babylon in *The Whore of Babylon* is never named, I shall suggest that the strong association between Semiramis and Titania invites us to read Dekker's Empress as a Semiramis figure). This connection, I shall argue, allows a figure ostensibly associated with praise of Elizabeth to activate some of the darker aspects of her reign, most notably her wars in Ireland, which I shall suggest form a crucial subtext of *A Midsummer Night's Dream*'s allusions to Semiramis.

Semiramis provided a particularly problematic precedent, because her story included so many elements and encompassed such extremes. She was said variously to be the epitome of valour and discretion and a woman crazed with lust, whose passions allegedly extended even to bulls and horses; to have been transformed into a dove;[3] to have dressed as a man; to have built the walls of Babylon, 'constructed from brick baked with sulphur and iron',[4] which were sometimes counted as one of the seven wonders of the world;[5] to have slept with her own son; to have invented castration;[6] and to have been responsible for the Babylonian captivity of the Jews.[7] Because of the alleged infatuation for a bull, she was sometimes coupled with Pasiphaë or Lais,[8] other emblems of female lust, but equally she was frequently presented as a nonpareil,[9] and figured positively in medieval royal entries.

Despite this instability in her role, references to her are frequent in writing of the earlier part of Elizabeth's reign. Richard Rainolde, in 'An Oracion historicall, howe Semiramis came to bee Queene of Babilon' (part of his textbook *The Foundation of Rhetoric*, 1563), gives perhaps the period's standard account of her career:

> Semiramis wife to Ninus the firste, feared the tender age of her sonne, wherupon the thought that those mightie nacions and kyngdomes, would not obaie so young and weake a Prince. Wherfore, she kept her sonne from the gouernmente: and moste of all she fered, that thei would not obaie a woman, forthwith she fained her self, to be the soonne of Ninus, and bicause she would not be knowen to bee a woman, this Quene inuented a newe kinde of tire, the whiche all the Babilonians that were men, vsed by her commaundement. By this straunge disguised tire and apparell, she not knowen to bee a woman, ruled as a man, for the space of twoo and fourtie yeres: she did mareuilous actes, for she enlarged the mightie kyngdome of Babilon, and builded thesame citee. Many other regions subdued, and valiauntlie ouerthrowen, she entered India, to the whiche neuer Prince came, sauing Alexander the greate: she passed not onely men in vertue, counsaill, and valiaunt stomacke, but also the famous counsailours of Assiria, might not contende with her in Maiestie, pollicie, and roialnes, For, at what tyme as thei knewe her a woman, thei enuied not her state, but mareuiled at her wisedome, pollicie, and moderacion of life, at the last she desiryng the vnnaturall lust, and loue of her soonne Ninus, was murthered of hym.[10]

Rainolde makes no mention of the alleged passion for a horse, which would indeed have been a highly risky strategy for him because the work is dedicated to 'My Lorde Robert Dudley, Master of the Queenes Maiesties Horse', so he cannot afford even the faintest suggestion of slandering a potential Elizabeth-figure (let alone horses!). In his account Semiramis achieves what even Marlowe's all-conquering Tamburlaine does not, the conquest of India, which makes her a particularly appropriate model for Elizabeth and the growing empire over which she hoped to preside. In short, Rainolde's Semiramis had a generally distinguished career slightly tarnished by its end.

So spectacular was that end, however, that often that emphasis is reversed. Thus Anthony Munday speaks of how '*Semiramis*, honored and extolled for her noblenesse of minde, and vertue in her deedes: by looue brought her name into eternall infamie',[11] and in Book I, canto 5 of *The Faerie Queene*, not published until 1590 but certainly circulating in manuscript before that, Semiramis is listed as the first of the 'Proud wemen, vaine, forgetfull of their yoke' whom Duessa and Night see when they visit hell.[12] Marlowe, who appears to have read *The Faerie Queene* in manuscript and to borrow from it in his *Tamburlaine the Great* (acted in 1587 though also not published until 1590), also mentions Semiramis but, typically, sounds a note of far less moral indignation than Spenser, when Orcanes speaks of how

> So from Arabia Desert, and the bounds
> Of that sweet land whose brave metropolis
> Re-edified the fair Semiramis,
> Came forty thousand warlike foot and horse,
> Since last we number'd to your majesty.[13]

Though Marlowe does not condemn Semiramis, however, he equally does not take her seriously. Tamburlaine himself declares,

> Now in the place, where fair Semiramis,
> Courted by kings and peers of Asia,
> Hath trod the measures, do my soldiers march.
>
> (V.1.73–75)

Tamburlaine the Great, first performed in the year England expected the imminent arrival of the Spanish Armada (although that was in fact delayed until the following year), is above all interested in military power, and might therefore have been expected to admire this even when embodied in a female. But for Marlowe, Semiramis is not primarily a leader but a builder and a dancer. I have argued elsewhere that Marlowe seems to be generally scathing about queens,[14] and this seems to be another instance of the phenomenon, but it is notable that he is merely dismissive rather than actually denigratory.

The poet William Warner, author of *Albion's England*, who may have been the 'Warner' whom Thomas Kyd named as a friend of Marlowe's, also speaks of Semiramis in admiring rather than shocked tones:

Staurobates at his homecoming found his country invaded by that armipotent *Virago Semiramis*, whom (which never happened her elsewhere) he encountered, wounded, and lastly chased her mighty troops from out his territories, wholly delivering himself in a short time of the *Assyrians*.[15]

Ralegh, another probable acquaintance of Marlowe, praised her in his *History of the*

World. Nashe, who was certainly a friend of Marlowe, is more overtly comic when he writes that '*We read that* Semiramis *was in loue with a Horse, but for a Gentlewoman to bee in loue with an Asse is such a tricke as neuer was*',[16] and says of Hero in the parody of the Hero and Leander story in *Lenten Stuff*: 'Down she ran in her loose nightgown, and her hair about her ears' ('even as Semiramis ran out with her lie-pot in her hand, and her black dangling tresses about her shoulders with her ivory comb ensnarled in them, when she heard that Babylon was taken').[17] Again, however, there is no moral outrage here, merely an urbanely comic tone.

What Nashe does do, however, is, like Marlowe, belittle Semiramis by the simple tactic of insisting on her gender. As a woman, she has long hair and an ivory comb, and these trappings of femininity trivialise her. This brings us to the heart of the representation of both Semiramis and Elizabeth. Like her fellow queens of exotic lands Cleopatra, who puts her own clothes on Antony and wears his, and Dido, who dressed Aeneas in what her husband Sychaeus had worn, Semiramis is associated with undermining men's independence and masculinity (in her case literally, since she is supposed to have invented castration). In turn (again like Cleopatra, and as Elizabeth herself was alleged to do at Tilbury),[18] she herself crossdresses as a means (perhaps *the* means) of asserting her authority as a ruler. The ease with which Nashe can demean her by reference to her clothes shows the riskiness of this strategy and the precariousness of both queens' positions. To put it crudely, Semiramis can be either vilified or sillified — and both are equally effective.

Presumably the story of a warrior queen looked rather different in the wake of Elizabeth's appearance in armour at Tilbury in 1588, and it is certainly notable that a number of works certainly written after that date are not at all troubled by either the lewder or the more frivolous aspects of the story of Semiramis and do regard her primarily as a military figure. Thus Robert Greene's *The Scottish History of James the Fourth*, almost certainly written in 1590, makes no mention of either sexuality or comedy in its reference to Semiramis, when Oberon speaks of how

> Semiramis, the proud Assyrian queen,
> When Ninus died, did levy in her wars
> Three millions of footmen to the fight,
> Five hundred thousand horse, of armèd chars
> A hundred thousand more; yet in her pride
> Was hurt and conquered by Stabrobates.
> Then what is pomp?[19]

Here Semiramis functions just as a male figure might, as an emblem of military greatness brought low. Even more positively, Lodowick Lloyd, in 'A Dittie to the tune of Welshe Sydanen, made to the Queenes maj. Eliz. by Lodov. Lloyd', writes of how 'Though Afrike spredd Zenobias name; all Asia range Semiramis fame',[20] while still later Barnabe Barnes calls Caterina Sforza a Semiramis in *The Devil's Charter* (1607).[21]

Most notably, in the anonymous *Locrine* (printed in 1595 in a revised form although probably first written before 1586), Semiramis is not only a successful military figure but closely paralleled with Elizabeth, when Humber says:

> For we'll receive them at the lances points,
> And massacre their bodies with our blades:
> Yea though they were in number infinite,
> More then the mighty *Babylonian* Queen,
> *Semiramis* the ruler of [the] West,
> Brought 'gainst the Emperour of the *Scythians*[22]

The phrase 'the ruler of the West' here – by no means an obvious description of an Assyrian queen – may recall Shakespeare's description in *A Midsummer Night's Dream* of Elizabeth as 'a fair vestal thronèd by the west',[23] and in the last lines of *Locrine* Elizabeth is openly referred to, in Atey's

> And as a woman was the onely cause
> That civil discord was then stirred up,
> So let us pray for that renowned maid,
> That eight and thirty years the Scepter sway'd
> In quiet peace and sweet felicitie,
> And every wight that seekes her graces smart,
> Would that this sword were pierced in his heart.

The reference in *Locrine* is particularly interesting because the version of the play published in 1595 contains material which seems close to Shakespeare (it might also be worth noting that Trompart, whose name is borrowed for the clown in *Locrine*, is mentioned in Book V of *The Faerie Queene* [V.3.17], which I shall be suggesting as a source for *A Midsummer Night's Dream*).[24]

Strumbo in *Locrine* concludes his report of events with a tragicomic song:

> And that which greeues me most,
> My louing wife,
> (O cruell strife!)
> The wicked flames did roast.
> And therefore, captaine crust,
> We will continuallie crie,
> Except you seeke a remedie
> Our houses to reedifie
> Which now are burnt to dust.

$$(\text{II.4.67–75})$$

Both the mixture of tragic content and jigging verse and the specific rhythmical pattern here are strongly reminiscent of *A Midsummer Night's Dream*:

> But stay, O spite!
> But mark, poor knight,
> What dreadful dole is here?
> Eyes, do you see?
> How can it be?
> O dainty duck, O dear!
>
> (V.1.265–270)

The parallel with *Dream* is suggestive because Semiramis is implicitly alluded to in that play's reference to the tomb of Ninus, her husband.[25] She may also be evoked in *Dream*'s many references to doves: her emblem, with which she was often associated in medieval royal entries, was a dove,[26] and in *Dream* we have Bottom saying 'I will roar you as gently as any sucking dove' (I.2.77), Lysander asking 'Who will not change a raven for a dove?' (II.2.120), and Thisbe crying 'What, dead, my dove?' (V.1.317). It is a neat irony that Pyrrhus is played by Bottom, who had been partially transformed to an ass, and that Semiramis was reputed to lust after animals, an idea which Thisbe may glance at when she praises Pyramus as being 'As true as truest horse that yet would never tire' (III.1.89) in the line before she says that she will meet him 'at Ninny's tomb'. It is also, of course, noteworthy that *A Midsummer Night's Dream* features Theseus, whose most famous exploit had been to destroy the Minotaur which was the alleged offspring of Pasiphaë's unnatural coupling with a bull.

Moreover, another play with strong linguistic and allusional connections with *Dream* also mentions Semiramis. This is *Titus Andronicus*, in which Aaron says of Tamora, 'this queen, / This goddess, this Semiramis, this nymph',[27] and in which the Clown enters bearing doves, traditional symbol of Semiramis (though they might, of course, also have many other meanings). Like *Dream*, *Titus Andronicus* is heavily indebted to Ovid: Lavinia uses the *Metamorphosis* to tell her story (IV.1.42), Jonathan Bate relates Marcus's comparison of Lavinia to a conduit (II.3.30) to the description of Pyramus in Golding's Ovid, and Martius says of the dead Bassianus,

> So pale did shine the moon on Pyramus
> When he by night lay bathed in maiden blood.
>
> (II.2.231–232)

In both plays there is the image of a man associated with or embodied as a threatening snake: Hermia dreams that a snake ate her heart while Lysander looked on and smiled (II.2.148–149), while Aaron refers to

> My fleece of woolly hair that now uncurls

> Even as an adder when she doth unroll
> To do some fatal execution
>
> (II.2.34–6)

Perhaps most suggestively, the names of Tamora's two sons, Chiron and Demetrius, both relate to *Dream*. Chiron was a centaur, as is recalled by Titus's words,

> Come, come, be everyone officious
> To make this banquet, which I wish may prove
> More stern and bloody than the Centaurs' feast.
>
> (V.3.201–203)

Demetrius is the name of one of the two lovers in *Dream*, and the rivalry between Chiron and Demetrius in *Titus Andronicus* parallels that between Demetrius and Lysander in *A Midsummer Night's Dream*. Hunting scenes are prominent in both plays; indeed Robert S. Miola implies a further link between the imaginative worlds of the two plays when he argues that 'The dichotomy between Rome and the forest so crucial to this play descends directly from the Ovidian dichotomy between Athens, civilized home of Philomela, and the wild woods in Thrace, scene of the rape'.[28] *Titus Andronicus*, too, glances at the iconography of Elizabeth: Heather James points to '*Titus Andronicus*' sustained abuse of classical models favored by the Tudors. His critique of Elizabethan political iconography begins with the figure of Lavinia and ends with Tamora, who parodies the guises that Queen Elizabeth appropriated from Vergil – Dido, Astraea, and the *Venus armata*.'[29] This may well suggest that the submerged references to Semiramis in *A Midsummer Night's Dream* are no accident but a sustained and ironic glance at the use of Semiramis in Elizabeth's iconography and indeed at the mythmaking process that surrounded the queen in general.

A Midsummer Night's Dream is certainly a complex and multi-faceted play, not least because of the ambiguities and multivalency of the fairy queen tradition on which it draws. As Matthew Woodcock points out, the Fairy Queen *topos* has a long and rather troubled history. Woodcock traces its origins to the 1570s:

> the ambiguity surrounding the exact 'meaning' or signification of the fairy queen in the Woodstock entertainment of 1575 establishes the foundations for the more problematic – potentially negative – representations of Elizabeth as the fairy queen during the 1590s.

Woodcock compares the way in which the fairy queen motif functioned at Woodstock to its use in a second, rather more celebrated entertainment of the same year, that held by the Earl of Leicester at Kenilworth, where 'the queen refused to play the part of the fairy queen …, preferring instead a narrative that allowed her to unequivocally assert and display her sovereign authority'.[30] Woodcock also discusses the use of the fairy queen figure in Sir Henry Lee's entertainment for the queen at Ditchley in 1592, three years before the probable date of *A Midsummer Night's Dream*. Most famously, of course, the figure of the Fairy Queen formed the central plank of the iconographical programme of Edmund Spenser's epic of that name.[31]

As Elizabeth's unwillingness to play the role allotted to her at Kenilworth suggests, and as Woodcock's analysis of the uses of the motif confirms, the figure of the Fairy Queen was one which was not necessarily always perceived as flattering to the actual queen. Even Spenser, whose interests were so closely bound up with achieving a tone of unequivocally fulsome panegyric, struggled with it, since he was essentially unable to find anything very much for the fairy queen to *do*. Shakespeare, who was rarely unequivocal about anything, may have been more deliberately playing with the tensions and ambiguities inherent in the figure. Louis Montrose has influentially argued that *A Midsummer Night's Dream* is more an attack on the values and image of the Tudor queen than a celebration of them, and Elizabeth would certainly have been less than happy about sentiments such as

> But earthlier happy is the rose distill'd
> Than that which, withering on the virgin thorn,
> Grows, lives, and dies, in single blessedness.
>
> (I.1.76–78)

Particularly troubling to the queen's agendas might have been the fact that fairy lore of the kind found in *A Midsummer Night's Dream* was often associated with Catholicism, something that might be particularly pertinent because, as Richard Wilson observes of the love-in-idleness passage,

> Oberon's inset has been tied to the Elvetham Entertainment, which, Philippa Berry has shown, certainly celebrated the Armada's defeat. So, when the 'arm'd' god misfires on the 'little western flower', 'love's wound' might signify the stigmata of England's Catholic community, penalised for its innocent part in an international conspiracy.[32]

'Mary, fary, fary, Mary' went the old rhyme associating the Virgin Mary with the fairy legends, and, although Alison Shell in her forthcoming book notes that 'fairy lore was used by Protestants for a number of imaginative purposes, negative and positive',[33] nevertheless Pamela Allen Brown remarks that in the late sixteenth century 'Rome and Faerie may have seemed plausibly contiguous realms. In *Daemonologie* (1597), James associated Rome and Fairyland',[34] and Reginald Scot declared in *The Discoverie of Witchcraft* (1584) that 'Divers writers report, that in Germanie, since Luthers time, spirits and divels have not personallie appeared, as in times past they were wont to doo … but now that the work of GOD hath appeared, those sights, spirits, and mockeries of images are ceased'.[35] Regina Buccola points out that 'Published writings and court documents from the late sixteenth century make it clear that connections were made between fairy belief and Catholicism by religious reformers even in Spenser's day'.[36] In some sense, therefore, to write a play centring on fairies innately had the potential to articulate a perspective directly opposed to that which dictated the policy of the queen and her ministers. Moreover, *A Midsummer Night's Dream* is heavily dependent on the idea of flower-magic, and, as Alison Shell points out, 'flowers have often been the inspiration for Catholic-inspired imaginative nomenclature'. Particularly notable is *Dream*'s mention of the hawthorn brake as a setting (III.1.4), since Shell observes that '[t]he hawthorn often occurs as a lone bush, called in Ireland "Monument bushes" or "Mass bushes", and reputed to have marked the places where Mass was said in penal times ... the tree has traditionally been associated with both fairies and Catholics'.[37] Another possible connection between the play and Catholicism arises from the fact that the author of the 1590 pamphlet *Tarltons Newes out of Purgatorie* (who was possibly Thomas Nashe)[38] gave his name as 'Robin Goodfellow'; since Purgatory was an exclusively Roman Catholic concept, there may be a suggestion here that the Robin Goodfellow figure is perceived as linked to Catholicism, while Regina Buccola points out that 'There is a decidely Catholic savor, that sounds remarkably like the Catholic sisterhood, to Theseus's menacing order that the intractable Hemia adopt a life of chastity if she continues to defy her father's wish that she marry Demetrius'.[39]

Further evidence that *A Midsummer Night's Dream* could be read as reflecting on Catholicism, and doing so in the context of Elizabeth's iconography, can be found in Dekker's *The Whore of Babylon* (1607),[40] whose *Dramatis personae* includes '*Titania* the Fairie Queene: vnder whom is figured our late Queen *Elizabeth*' and 'Th'Empresse of *Babylon*: vnder whom is figured *Rome*'.[41] The Empress of Babylon is never named, but Semiramis's strong association with both Babylon and the Titania / Oberon story may well make her implicitly a Semiramis figure. The play is also notable for its numerous references to the two creatures most closely associated with Semiramis, doves and bulls. The Prologue promises that its project is to 'lay the Dragon at a Dove's soft feet';[42] Florimell advises Titania 'Be, as the serpent, wise, then, though a dove' (I.2.214); the Third King vows that 'here I'll lurk / And in a dovelike shape raven upon doves' (I.2.297–298); Titania compares corrupted churchmen to 'doves / That have eat carrion' (III.1.128–129), while Truth says 'in mine eyes / Doves sit, not sparrows' (III.3.8–9); and Time tells Truth to 'sit like a dove / Upon the horseman's helm' (V.3.19–20). As for bulls, the play repeatedly exploits the standard play on papal bulls when the Third King hopes for 'Whole herds of bulls loaden with hallowed curses' (I.2.287), when Elfiron defies mad bulls (II.1.16), and when Time refers to 'a bull that roars / To fright allegiance from true subjects' bosoms' (IV.1.21–22) – a metaphor with which Plain Dealing subsequently plays. The Empress also recalls Semiramis in the confusion over whether the kings are her lovers, her sons, or both, and she, like Semiramis, is ultimately defeated when these sons turn against her, with the Second King threatening her with having 'thrust / A ring into thy nostrils!' (V.6.152–153). There seems little doubt, then, whom we are meant to see lying behind the figure of 'That mannish woman-devil, / That lustful bloody Queen of Babylon' (V.2.4–5).

The Empress certainly exemplifies the double-edgedness of the figure of Semiramis when used in conjunction with Elizabeth. Dekker clearly remembers Shakespeare in this play: the Empress complains of 'The Fairie Queene' because, owing to her actions,

> Five summers have scarce drawn their glimmering nights
> Through the moon's silver bow since the crownd heads
> Of that adored beast on which we ride
> Were struck and wounded.
>
> (I.1.53–56)

The measuring of time by a bow-like moon, while a common enough *topos*, seems more particularly reminiscent of *A Midsummer Night's Dream*. The Empress also speaks of a spider (I.1.75) and adders (I.1.89) in connection with the fairy queen, echoing the fairies' lullaby. Meanwhile, Titania herself demands,

> How many plots were laid to bar us hence,
> Even from our cradle! but our innocence,
> Your wisdom, Fairie Peers, and above all
> That Arm that cannot let a white soul fall
> Hath held us up and lifted us thus high
> Even when the arrows did most thickly fly
> Of that bad woman, Babylon's proud Queen.
>
> (I.2.3–9)

Babylon's proud queen clearly suggests Semiramis, at whose husband Ninus' tomb Pyramus and Thisbe plan to meet in *A Midsummer Night's Dream*; the idea of the arrows which quasi-miraculously miss the Fairy Queen looks like another nod to *Dream*, where Cupid's arrow fails to hit the 'fair vestal thronèd by the west' (and where Titania too lies in a cradle). Finally, Florimell speaks of 'our rounds' (I.2.24), and Fideli uses another image familiar from *Dream*: 'He swears the winds have got the sails with child, / With such big bellies' (V.2.16–17). The Empress too echoes this language with her.

> let our galleons feel even childbirth pangs
> Till their great bellies be delivered
> On the soft Fairie shores.
>
> (IV.4.123–125)

In short, *The Whore of Babylon* looks very like a direct reflection on Shakespeare's play which reframes its apparently fairytale events within an explicit and insistent religio-political context.

I want, in particular, to suggest that *The Whore of Babylon* can be used to help us home in on the specific area of discontent that lies at the heart of what I am suggesting is *Dream*'s critique of the image created by the queen's iconography. I think it is of considerable interest that in Dekker's play Ireland is cast as Elizabeth's unruly foster-child, squabbled over by the Fairy Queen and the Empress just as the changeling child is by the fairy king and queen in *A Midsummer Night's Dream*, and is described in terms strongly reminiscent of the earlier play:

> The darts he shoots are his; the winged messenger
> That runs on all the errands of the gods
> Teaches him swiftness: he'll outstrip the winds.
> This child of yours is by adoption
> Our mother's now; her blessing he receives.
> And though, as men did in the golden age,
> He live i'th'open fields, hiding his head
> In dampish caves and woods.
>
> (I.2.151–158)

Ireland is a surprising and apparently previously unnoticed subtext of *A Midsummer Night's Dream*. It is most strongly associated with the character of Puck, unsurprisingly since Puck seems clearly to be derived from the malign Irish spirit known as the Pooka.[43]

Puck introduces himself by announcing that

> Over hill, over dale,
>   Thorough bush, thorough briar,
> Over park, over pale,
>   Thorough flood, thorough fire,
> I do wander every where,
> Swifter than the moon's sphere;
> And I serve the Fairy Queen,
> To dew her orbs upon the green.
> The cowslips tall her pensioners be,
> In their gold coats spots you see.
>
> (II.1.1–10)

The word 'pale' here points us straight in the direction of the area around Dublin, known as the Pale; the mention of the Fairy Queen so soon afterwards reminds us of Spenser, who wrote his incomplete epic in Ireland, and so too indeed may the choice of the name Puck, since Thomas Herron points out that Spenser 'add[s] a "Pouke" to the local list of horrors in his "Epithalamion"', and suggests that he may have done so in honour of Castlepook Cave, near his home.[44] The reference to 'Pensioners' — the gentlemen pensioners were Elizabeth's ceremonial guard — and their uniforms takes us out of the fairy world to remind us of the realities of the Elizabethan military machine. And Ireland continues to be evoked in the play when Puck declares that

> I'll follow you: I'll lead you about a round!
> Through bog, through bush, through brake, through briar.
>
> (III.1.101–102)

Bogs were arguably the most notorious feature of the Irish landscape; Puck's self-proclaimed association with them here thus strongly hints at an Irish subtext for the play, while the injunction in the fairies' song that snakes should be banished (II.2.9–10) also seems to point in the same direction. Indeed the wood can be seen as the Other of Athens in much the same way as the dystopic Ireland lay threateningly just offshore from the self-proclaimed orderliness of England. Not for nothing, I think, does the play direct our gaze so insistently westwards in its references to 'a fair vestal thronèd by the west' (II.1.158) and 'a little western flower' (II.1.166): one might indeed say that 'This green plot shall be our stage' (III.1.3).

In particular there are a number of elements of *A Midsummer Night's Dream* which may owe something to one of the most famous accounts of sixteenth-century Ireland, Edmund Spenser's *A View of the Present State of Ireland*. Shakespeare certainly seems to have read this at some stage, since the reference in *Hamlet* to the Irish habit of swearing on swords is so close to Spenser's observation that 'So doe the Irish at this day, when they goe to any battayle, say certayne prayers or charmes to ther swordes, making a crosse therwith upon the earth',[45] while Edmund's dismissal of astrology in *King Lear* might seem to echo the assertion in *View* that 'it is the manner of men, that when they are fallen into any absurdity, or theyre actions succeede not as they would, they are ready alwayes to impute the blame therof unto the heavens, so as to excuse their own folly and imperfections' (*View* Part I, p. 2). (One might also note the similarity between Caliban's resolve at the end of *The Tempest* to 'be wise hereafter / And seek for grace'[46] and Irenius' declaration that after a defeat the Irish 'creepe a little perhaps, and sewe for grace' (*View* Part I, p. 8).)

In *A Midsummer Night's Dream*, there is a clear parallel between the lawlessness of the wood and the Ireland described by Irenius in *View*:

> ther are many wide countries in Ireland, in which the lawes of England were never established, nor any acknowledgement of subjection made: and also even in those which are subdued and seme to acknowledg subjection, yet the same Brehon law is privily practised amongst them selves, by reason that dwelling as they do, whole nations and septs of the Irish together, without any Englishman amongst them, they may do what they list, and compound or altogether conceale amongst them

selves ther owne crimes, of which no notice can be had by them which would and
might amend the same, by the rule of the lawes of England. (*View* Part I, p. 4)

Ireland is a country at odds with the 'more sharpe restraints' (*View* Part I, p. 15) of
English law just as the wood is with 'the sharp Athenian law' (*MND*, I.1.162). Notably,
too, Spenser describes the unruliness of the Irish in specifically equine terms when
he has Irenius say,

> so were this people at first well handled, and wisely brought to acknowledg
> allegiance to the King of England: but being straight left unto them selves, and
> ther owne inordinate life and manners, they eftsones forgot what before they were
> taught, and so sone as they were out of sight by them selves, shooke of their bridles,
> and began to colt anew, more licentiously than before. (*View* Part I, p. 5)

In this context, one might perhaps want to look in a new light at both the ass's head
which Puck inflicts on Bottom and also Puck's self-description as one who makes
Oberon smile 'When I a fat and bean-fed horse beguile, / Neighing in likeness of a filly
foal' (*MND*, II.1.45–46). In this context the glorious English queen, empress of all she
surveys, might well begin to look like Semiramis indeed, with the image of power she
seeks to project besmirched and tainted by the intrusion of equine passions.

In contrast to the supposed freedoms of Ireland and the wood, Spenser's English
believe in a strict form of patriarchy, just as Shakespeare's Athenians do: Eudoxus
asks

> doth not the act of the parent, in any lawfull grant or conveyance, bind his heires
> forever therunto? Sith then the ancestors of thes that now live yeilded them
> selves their subjects and liege men, shall it not ty their children to the same
> subjection? (*View* Part I, p. 5)

Along similar lines, Theseus declares that Egeus should be as a god to his daughter
(I.1.47). Spenser himself explicitly uses the difference between the Athenians and their
Others to figure that between the English and the Irish when he has Irenius say,

> he that would transfer the lawes of the Lacedemonians to the people of Athens
> should find a great absurdity and inconvenience: for those lawes of Lacedemon were
> devised by Licurgus, as most proper and best agreeing with that people, whom he
> knew to be inclined altogether to warrs, and therfore wholy traynned them up even
> from ther cradles in armes and military exercises, clean contrary to the institution
> of Solon, who, in his lawes to the Athenians labored by all means to temper ther
> warlike courages with swete delights of learning and sciences, so that as much
> as the one excelled in arms, the other exceded in knowledg: the like regard and
> moderation ought to be had in tempering and managing of this stubburn nation of

the Irish, to bring them from their delight of licensious barbarisme unto the love of goodnesse and civillity. (Part I, p. 8)

Since Oxford was often compared with Athens – the Swiss visitor Paul Hentzner, for instance, calls Oxford 'the famed Athens of England'[47] – it might be of particular interest that Annabel Patterson suggests relating *A Midsummer Night's Dream* 'to the abortive Oxfordshire rising of November 1596',[48] and that the play seems to allude to Oxfordshire in that the fairy queen motif had appeared also in the Ditchley entertainment of 1592 (usually attributed to Richard Eedes, a figure in whom Shakespeare is likely to have taken an interest, since he was commended by Meres in *Palladis Tamia* and since his now lost Latin play *Caesar Interfectus* was on the same theme as *Julius Caesar* and is sometimes suggested as a source for it).[49] Such parallels suggestively invite us to read Shakespeare's Athens in openly English terms.

While Athens is clearly identified with the civic, Spenser specifically associates Ireland with wood-lore when he has Irenius speak of a time when

England was very like to Irland, as nowe it standes: for it was, I tould you, annoyed greatly with robbers and outlawes, which trobled the whole realme, every corner havinge in it a Robyn Hoode, that kept all woodes, and spoiled all passengers and inhabitants, as Irland nowe haith. (*View* Part III, p. 21)

(In *Dream*, the Robin Hood legends seem to be directly glanced at in the exchange between Quince and Bottom, 'At the Duke's oak we meet./ Enough: hold, or cut bow-strings' [I.2.103–104]. It is therefore not surprising that the experiences of the Athenians in the woods come so close to what Spenser says of the experiences of the English in Ireland: certainly Demetrius and Lysander, chasing each other in vain, come close to Irenius' declaration that the Irishman

is a flying enimye, hidynge himself in woodes and bogges, from whence he will not draw forth, but into some straight passage or perilous forde where he knowes the armye most needes passe; there will he lye in wait, and, if hee finde advantage owte that still flyeth, and folow him that cann hardlye be found, were vaine and bootlesse. (Part II, p. 23)

One could too compare what Irenius says about the degeneration of the English in Ireland (Part II, p. 20) with the worsening behaviour of the Athenians in the wood, and the possible 'doubling' of Oberon and Theseus. Spenser's *Shepheardes Calender* certainly contributed to the imaginary of *A Midsummer Night's Dream*;[50] perhaps *A View of the Present State of Ireland* did too.

There also seem to be traces in the play of some recollections of another Irish-influenced Spenserian text, Book V of *The Faerie Queene*. There, Radigund is an Amazon queen, and the fight between her and Britomart might parallel that between Hermia and Helena, while that between her and Artegall is similar to that between Theseus and Hippolyta. There is also much reference to the moon, which is both a general symbol of Elizabeth and one used with particular emphasis in *A Midsummer Night's Dream*. It is evoked in the description of Radigund's shield:

> And on her shoulder hung her shield, bedeckt.
> Vppon the bosse with stones, that shined wide,
> As the faire Moone in her most full aspect,
> That to the Moone it mote be like in each respect.[51]

And it recurs again when Artegall unlaces Radigund's helmet and sees her face,

> Which in the rudenesse of that euill plight,
> Bewrayd the signes of feature excellent:
> Like as the Moone in foggie winters night,
> Doth seeme to be her selfe, though darkned be her light.
>
> (V.5.12)

Additionally, the priests of Isis 'wore rich Mitres shaped like the Moone' (V.7.3); Talus watches Britomart 'Like to a Spaniell wayting carefully' (V.6.26), while Helena calls herself Demetrius's spaniel (II.1.203); and, if one concurs with A.C. Hamilton in construing the crocodile of Britomart's dream as a serpent lover (V.7.16), it might well seem close to the suggestively phallic-seeming serpent of Hermia's dream. The two texts also share the same pun: Demetrius complains that he is 'wood within this wood' (II.1.192), while the Pagan in *The Faerie Queene* raves

> like to a Lyon wood,
> Which being wounded of the huntsmans hand.
> Can not come neare him in the couert wood.
>
> (V.3.35)

Moreover, *The Faerie Queene* contains a reference to a character whose fate, Louis Montrose has persuasively argued,[52] is proleptically glanced at in *A Midsummer Night's Dream*, Hippolytus:

> Like as the cursed sonne of *Theseus*,
>> That following his chace in dewy morne,
>> To fly his stepdames loues outrageous,
>> Of his owne steedes was all to peeces torne,
>> And his faire limbs left in the woods forlorne;
>> That for his sake *Diana* did lament,
>> And all the wooddy Nymphes did wayle and mourne.

> So was this Souldan rapt and all to rent,
> That of his shape appear'd no little moniment.
>
> (V.8.43)

Another suggestive parallel comes between Shakespeare's reference to how 'earthlier happy is the rose distill'd / Than that which, withering on the virgin thorn' (I.1.76–7) and Spenser's

> Like as a tender Rose in open plaine,
> That with vntimely drought nigh withered was,
> And hung the head, soone as few drops of raine.
> Thereon distill, and deaw her daintie face,
> Gins to looke vp, and with fresh wonted grace.
> Dispreds the glorie of her leaues gay.
>
> (V.12.13)

Here, too, the words 'distill' and 'withered' occur in close collocation. Finally, both texts draw to a close with a scene of hunting, with the noise of Theseus's dogs echoing that of the Blatant beast, and with a return to fairyland. Shakespeare, it seems, is recalling both Spenser and Ireland on multiple levels in the creation of his wood.

A Midsummer Night's Dream, then, takes a place which seems full of danger and which is figured as Irish and as inhabited by beings associated with Catholicism, the two greatest fears of the Elizabethan establishment – and it presents that place as entirely benevolent and therapeutic in its effects. Particularly suggestive is the contast between the stereotypical insult that Ireland was a country where things were 'soon ripe, soon rotten' and Lysander's remark that 'Things growing are not ripe until their season' (II.2.116), which looks almost like a direct rebuttal. In *A Midsummer Night's Dream*, a complex network of ideas associated with the figure of Semiramis is used to critique rather than celebrate the agendas of Elizabeth.

Notes

1. See for instance Helen Hackett, *Virgin Mother, Maiden Queen: Elizabeth I and the Cult of the Virgin Mary* (Basingstoke: Macmillan, 1995).
2. I have found at www.assyriansocietycanada.org/legend_of_semiramis.htm the assertion that Queen Margaret of Denmark was compared with Semiramis in the fourteenth century, but I do not know of any confirmation of this.
3. George Sandys, in the argument of the Fourth Book of his *Ovid's Metamorphosis* (1632), ll. 1–2, declares 'Derceta, a Fish. Semiramis a Doue./ Transforming Nais equall Fate doth proue'.
4. Olaus Magnus, *Description of the Northern Peoples* [1555], translated by Peter Fisher and Humphrey Higgens (London: The Hakluyt Society, 1996), 3 vols, 1, p. 3. Magnus opens his account of the north by noting how Democritus 'directed his steps to Babylon, the capital of Assyria, perhaps to gaze on its walls, which had been constructed from brick baked with sulphur and iron at the expense and command of Queen Semiramis'. Magnus also speaks of how 'A temple … famous since the time of Ninus … stood by the River

Sala, where today the seat of the primate and archbishop of the Swedes and Götar lies' (p. 156), and in vol. 3 he writes how in her arrangements for her tomb, 'with sophisticated mockery this excellent woman reviled the sin of greed' (p. 819).

5. Magnus, *Description of the Northern Peoples*, 2, p. 583.

6. Samuel Butler writes in *Hudibras* that 'Loss of *Virilit*[y's] averr'd / To be the cause of loss of *Beard*, / That does (like *Embryo* in the womb) / Abortive on the Chin become. / This first a *Woman* did invent, / In envy of *Mans* ornament. / *Semiramis* of *Babylon*, / Who first of all cut men o'th'*Stone*: / To mar their *Beards*, and laid foundation / Of *Sow-geldering* operation.' (Second Part, Canto 1, ll. 709–718).

7. Gordon Kipling, *Enter the King: Theatre, Liturgy and Ritual in the Medieval Civic Triumph* (Oxford: Clarendon Press, 1998), p. 303.

8. Thus John Taylor, in 'Bull, Beare, and Horse, Cuts, Curtols, and Longtailes' (*Works not in the volume of 1630* (1870), ll. 21–2, follows a discussion of Pasiphaë with the remark that ''Tis said *Semiramis* (King *Ninus* Mother) / Did love a Bull, which is as true as 'tother', while Laurence Ramsey, in *The practise of the Divell* (1577?), ll. 409–13, writes of how 'Many a mynsing Nunne, and many a noble Dame, / In hell is nowe resident, which dines and suppes with me: / As Semiramis and Cleopatra, which liued in all glorie, / Flora and Lais, gyrles of such report, / That since their time, the proudest may come short'. Semiramis is also coupled with Lais in Marlowe's Elegy 5, 'On Corinna Going to Bed', from *All Ovids Elegies*: 'Then came *Corinna* in a long loose gowne, / Her white neck hid with tresses hanging downe. / Resembling fayre *Semiramis* going to bed, / Or *Layis* of a thousand woers sped' (ll. 9–12).

9. Thus George Whetstone, in *An Heptameron of Ciuill Discourses* (1582), writes of how in the course of discussing 'The Question that arose at Supper vpon the fourth Dayes exercise': 'Aluisa vechio, tooke vpon her, to mayntaine a woman, to be a creature euery way, as execellent and perfecte as Man … For naturall shape (quoth she) they are more beautifull, of a better temperature, and complection then men. In valiaunt exploytes, what difference was there betweene Semiramis and her Husbande Ninus?' Similarly George Pettie in *A petite Pallace* (1576), writing on Alexius, asks 'what man was euer more couragious then Semiramis, who in the habite & apparell of a man gouerned ye Assirians, most couragiously?' (p. [228] 221, Ffiij), and William Warner in *Pan his Syrinx* (1584) describes how 'Staurobates at his home comming, found his country inuaded by ye armipotent Virago Semiramis, whom (which neuer hapned her else-where) he incountred, wounded, & lastly chased her mighty troupes fro out his Territories. wholy deliuering himself in a short time of ye *Assrians*' (Pheone. Calamus quartus. Cap. 20, p. 65, 12).

10. Richard Rainolde, *The Foundation of Rhetoric*, 1563 (Menston: Scolar Press, 1972), fols xiiv–xiiir.

11. Anthony Munday, *Zelavto* (1580), Part 3, p. [129], 125, Qiij.

12. Edmund Spenser, *The Faerie Queene*, edited by A.C. Hamilton (Harlow: Longman, 1997) I.5.50.

13. Christopher Marlowe, *Tamburlaine, Part Two*, in *Christopher Marlowe: The Complete Plays*, edited by J.B. Steane (Harmondsworth: Penguin, 1969), III.5.35–39.

14. Lisa Hopkins, *Christopher Marlowe: A Literary Life* (Basingstoke: Palgrave, 2000), pp. 107–116.

15. William Warner, *Syrinx: or a sevenfold history* [1584], edited by Wallace A. Bacon (New York: AMS Press, 1950), p. 74.

16. Ronald B. McKerrow, ed., *The Works of Thomas Nashe*, 5 vols, revised by F.P. Wilson (Oxford: Basil Blackwell, 1958), III, p. 112.

17. Thomas Nashe, *The Unfortunate Traveller and Other Works*, edited by J.B. Steane (Harmondsworth: Penguin, 1972), p. 428.

18. For the events at Tilbury see Chapter 2 above.

19. Robert Greene, *James the Fourth*, edited by Norman Sanders (Manchester: Manchester University Press, 1970), Additional Chorus VI, 7–13.

20. Lloyd's work has recently been extensively explored by Sally Harper, '"A Dittie to the tune of Welsh Sydannen": A Welsh image of Queen Elizabeth', *Renaissance Studies* 19.2 (April 2005), pp. 201–228.

21. Barnabe Barnes, *The Devil's Charter* [1607], edited by Nick de Somogyi (London: Globe Quartos, 1999), IV.4.

22. W.S., *The Lamentable Tragedy of Locrine* (London: Thomas Creede, 1595), II.2. The authorship of *Locrine* is uncertain, but the play in its revised form is generally attributed wholly or partly to Greene (see C.F. Tucker Brooke, *The Shakespeare Apocrypha: Being a collection of fourteen plays which have been ascribed to Shakespeare* (Oxford: Clarendon Press, 1908), preface, p. xiii; Peter Berek, '*Locrine* Revised, *Selimus*, and Early Responses to *Tamburlaine*', *Research Opportunities in Renaissance Drama* 23 (1980), pp. 33–54, p. 35; Baldwin Maxwell, *Studies in the Shakespearean Apocrypha* (New York: King's Crown Press, 1956), p. 62; and Kay B. Michael, 'The Lamentable Tragedy of *Locrine*: An Edition', (unpublished Ph.D. thesis, University of Maryland, 1972), introduction, p. 46.

23. William Shakespeare, *A Midsummer Night's Dream*, in *The Norton Shakespeare*, edited by Stephen Greenblatt, Walter Cohen, Jean E. Howard, and Katharine Eisaman Maus (London: W.W. Norton, 1997), II.1.158. All further quotations are taken from this edition.

24. For comment on the links between *The Faerie Queene* and *A Midsummer Night's Dream* see Susan Frye, *Elizabeth I: The Competition for Representation* (Oxford: Oxford University Press, 1993), p. 145.

25. There are also references to Semiramis in *Titus Andronicus*, where Aaron the Moor compares his lustful mistress Tamora with Semiramis, and in *The Taming of the Shrew*, where the Lord promises Christopher Sly 'a couch / Softer and sweeter than the lustful bed / On purpose trimmed up for Semiramis' (William Shakespeare, *The Taming of the Shrew*, edited by G.R. Hibbard (Harmondsworth: Penguin, 1968), Induction 2.36–38).

26. Kipling, *Enter the King*, p. 303.

27. William Shakespeare, *Titus Andronicus*, edited by Jonathan Bate (London: Routledge, 1995), II.2.21–22. All further quotations from the play are taken from this edition.

28. Robert S. Miola, *Shakespeare's Rome* (Cambridge: Cambridge University Press, 2004), p. 60.

29. Heather James, *Shakespeare's Troy: Drama, Politics, and the Translation of Empire* (Cambridge: Cambridge University Press, 1997), p. 48.

30. Matthew Woodcock, 'The Fairy Queen Figure in Elizabethan Entertainments', in *Elizabeth I: Always Her Own Free Woman*, edited by Carole Levin, Jo Eldridge Carney, and Debra Barrett-Graves (Aldershot: Ashgate, 2003), pp. 97–115, pp. 98 and 100.

31. Marion A. Taylor, who suggests Alençon as source for Bottom, proposes a link between *Dream* and *The Faerie Queene* on the grounds that 'Alençon appears at least two times in *The Faerie Queene* and is symbolized as two disreputable villains, Braggadochio and the witch's son' (Marion A. Taylor, *Bottom, Thou Art Translated: Political Allegory in* A Midsummer Night's Dream (Amsterdam: Rodopi, 1973), pp. 31 and 73).

32. Richard Wilson, 'A World Elsewhere: Shakespeare's Sense of an Exit', *Proceedings of the British Academy* 117 (2002), pp. 165–199, pp. 182–183.

33. See Alison Shell, *Orality and the Old Religion* (Cambridge: Cambridge University Press, forthcoming).

34. Pamela Allen Brown, *Better a Shrew than a Sheep: Women, Drama, and the Culture of Jest in Early Modern England* (Ithaca and London: Cornell University Press, 2003), p. 161.

35. Reginald Scot, *The Discoverie of Witchcraft*, ed. Rev. Montague Summers (John Rodker, 1930; repr. New York: Dover, 1972), p. 87.

36. Regina Buccola, 'Virgin Fairies and Imperial Whores: The Unstable Ground of Religious Iconography in Thomas Dekker's *The Whore of Babylon*', forthcoming in *Marian Moments in Early Modern Drama*, edited by Regina Buccola and Lisa Hopkins (Burlington: Ashgate, 2007).

37. Shell, *Orality and the Old Religion*.

38. Charles Nicholl, *A Cup of News: The Life of Thomas Nashe* (London: Routledge and Kegan Paul, 1984), p. 81.

39. Regina M. Buccola, 'Shakespeare's Fairy Dance with Religio-Political Controversy in *The Merry Wives of Windsor*', in *Shakespeare and the Culture of Christianity in Early Modern England*, edited by Dennis Taylor (New York: Fordham University Press, 2003), pp. 195–219, p. 163.

40. Writing of *Macbeth*, Richard Wilson says of *The Whore of Babylon* that 'Dekker's text reads like an X-ray of Shakespeare's intentions' (*Secret Shakespeare: Studies in Theatre, Religion and Resistance* (Manchester: Manchester University Press, 2004), p. 193).

41. On the connections between *Dream* and *The Whore of Babylon* see also Taylor, *Bottom, Thou Art Translated*, p. 153.

42. Thomas Dekker, *The Whore of Babylon*, edited by Marianne Gateson Riely (London: Garland, 1980), Prologue, l. 19. All further quotations from the play are taken from this edition.

43. See for instance K.M. Briggs, *The Anatomy of Puck* (London: Routledge and Kegan Paul, 1959), p. 44.

44. Thomas Herron, 'Irish Den of Thieves: Souterrains (and a Crannog?) in Books V and VI of Spenser's *Faerie Queene*', *Spenser Studies* 14 (2000), pp. 303–317, p. 303.

45. Edmund Spenser, *A View of the Present State of Ireland*. Online: http://darkwing.uoregon.edu/~rbear/veue1.html, Part I, p. 35. All further references to the text are taken from this edition.

46. William Shakespeare, *The Tempest*, edited by Virginia Mason Vaughan and Alden T. Vaughan (London: Thomas Nelson, 1999), V.1.295–296.

47. See for instance Paul Hentzner, *Travels in England during the reign of Queen Elizabeth*. Online: http://etext.library.adelaide.edu.au/h/hentzner-travels/, p. 30, accessed 28 April 2004.

48. Annabel Patterson, *Shakespeare and the Popular Voice* (Oxford: Basil Blackwell, 1989), p. 55.

49. On the relationship between the two plays see Ernest Schanzer, 'A Neglected Source of "Julius Caesar"', *Notes and Queries* (May 1954), pp. 196–197, and William Poole, '*Julius Caesar* and *Caesars Revenge* Again', *Notes and Queries* 49.2 (June 2002), pp. 226–228; also of interest is René Weis, '*Caesar's Revenge*: A Neglected Elizabethan Source of *Antony and Cleopatra*', *Shakespeare Jahrbuch* (1983), pp. 178–186.

50. The Arden 2 editor points out the many debts of Titania's speech about the weather (II.1.85–102) to *The Shepheardes Calender*, which might indeed seem to be directly glanced at in the call for 'A calendar, a calendar!' (III.1.49). See William Shakespeare, *A Midsummer Night's Dream*, edited by Harold Brooks (London: Methuen, 1979).

51. Edmund Spenser, *The Faerie Queene*, edited by A.C. Hamilton (Harlow: Pearson Education, 2001), V.5.3. All further quotations from the poem are taken from this edition.

52. Louis Montrose, '*A Midsummer Night's Dream* and the Shaping Fantasies of Elizabethan Culture: Gender, Power, Form', *Representations* 2 (1983), pp. 65–87, reprinted in *New Historicism and Renaissance Drama*, edited by Richard Wilson and Richard Dutton (London: Longman, 1992), pp. 109–130, pp. 120–121.

8

Evaluating virginity:
A Midsummer Night's Dream
and the iconography of marriage

ANNALIESE CONNOLLY

A Midsummer Night's Dream is a play which is heavily imbued with the iconography of virginity which had been developed by and for Elizabeth I in the final phase of her reign. The play includes a number of the personae used to celebrate her status as a Virgin Queen, and the play's emphasis upon the influence of Diana and the figure of the 'imperial votress', for example, has often been interpreted as praise for Elizabeth.[1] More recently critics such as Louis Montrose have suggested that the play encodes a much darker and less complimentary response to the queen.[2] By the 1590s the gap between Elizabeth as mythical and perpetual virgin and the reality that she was an ageing queen who refused to name her successor was widening.[3] The celebration of chastity which was a feature of so much of the literature of praise served in many ways to underline the associated quality of sterility, so that as the decade continued images of panegyric became used as the criterion by which to assess the consequences of Elizabeth's virginity.

This chapter is concerned with several strategies of retrospection employed by Shakespeare in *Dream* in order to critique Elizabeth and her iconography of virginity. The first example of this is the relationship between *Dream* and Marlowe's *Dido, Queen of Carthage*. Here Shakespeare deliberately alludes to Marlowe's play in order to establish a number of visual and thematic parallels between Dido and Titania and to align himself with Marlowe's response to earlier entertainments in which myths of queens and cupids were adapted to present allegories of praise for the queen.

The second strategy of retrospection is Shakespeare's use of the figure of Titania to reassess Elizabeth's status in the 1590s as perpetual virgin. One of the consequences of Titania's childlessness is her attachment to the Indian boy, which in turn has an apocalyptic effect on the natural world as a result of her quarrel with Oberon. The images of the long-term impact of this dispute on the fairy world echo the sentiments of those speeches delivered to Elizabeth in the 1560s which exhorted the queen to marry and emphasised the consequences of her failure to provide England with an heir of her body. Indeed the play's emphasis upon specific fruits recalls the metaphor of fruit used by Elizabeth's subjects to appeal to her own fruitfulness as they encouraged the queen to marry, but the effect in *Dream* is sharply ironic as the fruits are juxtaposed with the portrait of a barren queen, who can now only offer fruit but cannot bear any herself. The play therefore offers a rather bleak assessment of Elizabeth's reign.

The case has often been made for the influence of Marlowe's *Dido, Queen of Carthage* on a range of Shakespeare's plays, including *Hamlet*, *Antony and Cleopatra*, and *The Tempest*.[4] In instances where critics have identified allusions to Marlowe's play in Shakespeare's work it has been suggested that these echoes are primarily for the purposes of parody, with Shakespeare recalling Marlowe's *Dido* in order to send it up.[5] One play rich in allusions to Marlowe's *Dido*, which has been comparatively overlooked, is *A Midsummer Night's Dream*. Here Shakespeare invokes *Dido* not for parody but to establish links between the experiences of the two queens.

The first critic to identify similarities between the two plays, in his critical study of Marlowe, was J.B. Steane, who makes passing reference to the similarity in the lyrical tone of the scene in which Venus sings Ascanius asleep in the wood. Steane remarks that 'The whole passage is akin to the fairy world of *A Midsummer Night's Dream*',[6] but limits his enquiry to this remark, as he is concerned with simply outlining the shifts of tone and mood within Marlowe's *Dido*. Later Jackson Cope developed the argument for the influence of *Dido* on *Dream* by noting the thematic links between the two plays, outlining the parallels between the two queens, Dido and Titania, each of whom is caused to dote as a result of the work of Cupid's arrow.[7] Cope also comments on the 'stylistic juxtapositions of the lyric and the laughable' in both plays, in Dido's wooing of Aeneas in the cave and Titania's courting of Bottom. He concludes that 'the mixed farce and romance of *Dido, Queen of Carthage* is Marlowe's most significant gift to Shakespeare, progenitor of that strange crossbreeding of Puck and Oberon and Theseus and Bottom's players, *A Midsummer Night's Dream*'.[8] Once again, however, Cope's remarks on the thematic links between the two plays are made but not fully developed. More recently Fred B. Tromly has also observed the influence of *Dido*'s mix of tragedy and farce on *Dream*.[9] Shakespeare's blend of comedy and tragedy, however, is not as dark as Marlowe's, with Titania's punishment culminating in her humiliation rather than her death. Tromly also points out similarities of plot structure as both plays present two pairs of lovers whose behaviour in the wood is characterised by flight and pursuit.[10] In *Dido*, Iarbas, one of Dido's suitors, pursues her on the hunt, despite being spurned in favour of Aeneas; he, in turn, is then chased by Dido's love-lorn sister, Anna. Similarly Helena follows Demetrius into the wood as he chases Hermia and Lysander.

Shakespeare signals his interest in the story of Queen Dido in the opening scene of *A Midsummer Night's Dream* when Hermia makes her avowal to Lysander:

> I swear to thee by Cupid's strongest bow,
> By his best arrow with the golden head,
> By the simplicity of Venus' doves,
> By that which knitteth souls and prospers loves
> And by that fire which burn'd the Carthage queen.
> When the false Trojan under sail was seen[11]

It is noteworthy that Hermia, in swearing by the bow and arrow and Venus's girdle, is pledging her love by those very things that prompt a love madness: dotage. This unusual choice of objects to swear her constancy and fidelity by is underlined by her invocation of the story of Dido and Aeneas. This series of items offers a condensed account of Dido's story as they are the items which both facilitated and symbolise her love for Aeneas. Whilst the pair may well be famous as lovers, Dido's story is also one of the more disturbing issues of fickleness and abandonment. Shakespeare thus combines the two images of Dido as a queen transformed by Love's arrow and as an abandoned lover to prefigure the behaviour of the lovers and Titania in the wood.[12]

The introduction of the fairy world in *Dream* establishes a series of thematic links with Marlowe's story of Dido. In Marlowe's opening scene between Jupiter and Ganymede, it is Jupiter's infatuation with this young boy that has caused him to neglect his care of Aeneas, as Venus is quick to remind him: 'Ay, this is it! You can sit toying there / And playing with that female wanton boy, / Whiles my Aeneas wanders on the seas, / And rests a prey to every billow's pride.'[13] Similarly, strife in the fairy world is caused by Titania's love for the Indian boy as she abandons her role as Oberon's wife and the Fairy Queen with dire consequences for the natural world.

Shakespeare builds a series of connections between the two plays and the identification of stylistic similarities noted by Jackson Cope between the two plays is, I will argue, deliberately done in order to underline the thematic links. Cope's identification of parallels between Dido's wooing of Aeneas in the cave and Titania's infatuation with Bottom in the fairy bower suggests that we are invited to draw a comparison between the two queens. Both women, as a result of Cupid's arrow, are forced to woo a beloved who appears oblivious to their affections. Aeneas, for example, fails to pick up on a series of hints from Dido about her love for him until finally she suggests that he cannot love her, which prompts the desired response. In *Dream*, however, Bottom remains unaware of Titania's love for him, concentrating instead on the treats offered him by the fairies.

The myth of Dido was one which had been used in Elizabethan entertainments as early as 1564. One version of the story which has not survived was written by Edward Helliwell, formerly a fellow of King's College, Cambridge, and was performed in the College chapel for the queen in August 1564. The use of the myth increased significantly, however, during the period 1579 to 1583 which coincided with the marriage negotiations between Elizabeth and Francis, Duke of Anjou. Susan Doran has noted that those subjects who opposed the match actively cultivated a range of personae for the queen which celebrated her virginity rather than her marriageability.[14] The story of Dido forms part of this political impulse, as Elizabeth is invited by her subjects to align herself with her mythical forebear Aeneas and reject what Dido cannot, namely the personal considerations of love.

There are a number of entertainments which demonstrate how the myth of Dido was adapted for the purposes of flattery and in response to the developing mythos of Elizabeth as Virgin Queen. The entertainments for Elizabeth on her progress to Norwich in 1578, by Thomas Churchyard and Henry Goldingham, provide examples of the recurring motif of the surrender of Cupid's arrows. Churchyard's device *The Shew of Chastitie* depicts Cupid's disgrace at the hands of Chastity and her women, with his bow and arrows being surrendered to the queen. The piece not only compliments the queen by presenting her as immune to the arrows of Cupid but in giving her the arrows advises her 'to learn to shoot at whom best she pleased', thus leaving the question of marriage up to the queen.[15] In Goldingham's show Cupid is more submissive and offers his arrows to Elizabeth without resistance.

The entertainment for the state visit of the Polish Count Alasco in 1583 also affords further example of the adaptation of the story of Dido. William Gager dramatised Virgil's account of Dido and Aeneas to entertain the Count and other dignitaries at Christ Church, Oxford. Gager invokes the Eliza–Elissa comparison, but is also keen to suggest both how like and unlike Elizabeth is to Elissa. The epilogue sums this up:

> But Dido (Elisa), one woman surpasses you by far: our virgin queen (regina virgo). In her piety, how many reversals has she endured! What kingdoms has she founded! To what foreigners has she plighted her trust! But she has not condescended to marry any Sychaeus, and may no Aeneas sway her affections![16]

As Michael Pincombe concludes, Gager's point is that 'Elizabeth is an Elissa who is so much in command of her own affections that she has never even married, far less entered into a disastrous liaison with a foreigner'.[17]

Marlowe's play in its handling of the myth of Dido, I will argue, was a calculated departure from previously dramatised accounts, offering instead an antidote to those plays in which Dido and Cupid were repeatedly presented as a compliment to the queen.[18] Marlowe, unlike Gager, avoids adding any material which might qualify his play's representation of female rule. Dido is not used as the means of underlining Elizabeth's qualities as a ruler. In fact the absence of any use of allegory for the purposes of praise implies the exact opposite. Criticism of the queen is implicit in the text. Marlowe, like Gager, makes use of Dido's other name, Elissa, which Marlowe spells Eliza, but the invocation of her name is described as a 'hideous echo' rather than a hymn of praise.[19] Aeneas also refers to her using the title favoured by Elizabeth when he calls her 'princely Dido'.[20] The final image of Dido on a burning pyre is also suggestive of one of Elizabeth's favourite symbols, the phoenix.[21] Dido's death, however, is tainted by the comic succession of bodies on to the pyre after her, as she is swiftly followed by Iarbas, the disappointed suitor, and her sister; and unlike the phoenix, Dido serves to emphasise the mortal nature of queens, as she cannot rise from the ashes.

In 1584 the Children of the Chapel and St Paul's performed John Lyly's *Sapho and Phao* at court.[22] Lyly's play is significant as it demonstrates another variation on the Dido story. Lyly's source was the classical myth of the unrequited love of Sappho for the ferryman Phao, whom Venus had made beautiful, and her suicide. Lyly, however, adapts the story to one more in keeping with the attitudes of Elizabeth's court, transforming Sappho from the historical poetess into a young, beautiful, and wise princess, rather than the older and darker figure of the sources. The relationship between Sappho and Phao is altered to stress the difference in rank between the lovers; it is love now between a ruler and her subject. Phao is not simply beloved, but reciprocates Sapho's affections, and it is as a result of this that Sapho, despite falling in love, is able to conquer her emotions and continues to govern, rather than suffering the pangs of rejection and eventually taking her life, as she does in Ovid.

It is Lyly's invention that Sapho falls in love as a punishment from Venus for successfully resisting love: Sapho, like Elizabeth, appears to have successfully combined both her body natural and her body politic, thus threatening the supremacy of Venus on earth. Cupid himself doubts whether Sapho is susceptible to his arrows: 'they say she hath her thoughts in a string, that she conquers affections and sendeth love up and down upon errands. I am afraid she will yerk me if I hit her.'[23] Cupid is successful and Sapho does fall in love with Phao. Venus, however, intervenes again, as she too has become enamoured of the ferryman and cannot brook a rival. She uses her charms to persuade Vulcan to make a set of arrows for Cupid that will make Sapho disdain Phao and another to make Phao dote on Venus. Cupid, however, betrays his mother and instead of making Phao love Venus, he shoots an arrow which makes him hate her. Sapho recovers from her love sickness, having realised that, as Phao is not her equal, she can never truly love him.

The fact that Venus herself succumbs to Phao's beauty makes Sapho's triumph complete; she has shown the goddess to be at the mercy of nothing more than physical attraction. For there to be love there must also be virtue, and so the play becomes an allegory of the triumph of virtue over desire. This reading is reinforced in the final scene of the play as Sapho adopts Cupid for her son so that she can use his arrows to usurp Venus's position on earth: 'I myself will be the queen of love. I will direct these arrows with a better aim, and conquer mine own affections with greater modesty.' (V.2.28–30) The play concludes with Venus temporarily outwitted, threatening to revenge herself on them both. Sapho's victory over Venus elevates her to the position of earthly deity, which in turn suggests Elizabeth's own mythos of virginal goddess. In Act V of *Sapho and Phao*, Lyly fuses the images of Cupid and his arrows with those of Dido with Cupid on her lap to produce the ultimate compliment. The surrendering of the arrow signals triumph over love, whilst the tableau of Sapho as mother of the god of love recalls Dido and again invites the audience to consider this particular Elissa's victory.

In the context of these depictions of Cupid, Marlowe's Cupid may well have seemed an alarming prospect as he describes how he will effect his mother's plan:

> Convey this golden arrow in thy sleeve,
> Lest she imagine thou art Venus' son;
> And when she strokes thee softly on the head,
> Then shall I touch her breast and conquer her.
>
> (III.1.3–6)

Marlowe shows Cupid actively piercing the queen on stage, whereas in Lyly this action takes place offstage and is a comic blend of the literal and the figurative. Sapho falls in love at first sight with Phao, apparently without the physical intervention of Cupid's arrow. Later, although Lyly presents Sapho languishing from the effects of the arrow, their impact is defused by placing emphasis on the creation of a new set of arrows for Cupid as a comic interlude between Vulcan and Venus and finally by their surrender. In Lyly the arrows are presented on stage, and we see their effect on Sapho, but we do not see her being pierced and we are left with the image of her controlling their use.[24]

It is noteworthy that in Act III, scene 2, following Dido's encounter with Cupid, Marlowe uses the image of Cupid surrendering his arrows to ironic effect. Venus is alerted by her doves that Ascanius is in danger. He is threatened by Juno, whose dislike of the Trojans means that she is keen to sabotage Venus's plans for her son to found Rome. In a series of comic exchanges Juno protests that she regrets her attempts to harm Aeneas and as a pledge Venus resolves that.

> Cupid shall lay his arrows in thy lap,
> And to a sceptre change his golden shafts,
> Fancy and modesty shall live as mates.
>
> (III.2.56–58)

Here Cupid will transform his arrows into a sceptre and serve Juno. This is surely uttered with irony, as Venus knows that Juno's position has shifted only because she can see that Dido will serve at least as a mechanism to delay Aeneas from reaching Italy. It is clear that there is little chance of Cupid serving Juno and this self-imposed regulation by Venus is simply politic. The suggestion of Cupid surrendering his arrows to Juno is, I think, very telling in view of its popularity as a motif in court comedies and entertainments. The fact that we see the very opposite and actually witness Dido being pierced on stage suggests that Marlowe's play is his response to this kind of drama and its appropriation of this Virgilian icon.

Michael Pincombe has suggested that Marlowe's *Dido* is in part a response to Lyly's *Sapho and Phao* and its appropriation of the Virgilian icon of Cupid on Dido's lap. Marlowe's opening scene of *Dido*, Pincombe argues, parodies Lyly's version of the

Virgilian icon of Dido and Cupid, which he presents in the penultimate scene when Cupid climbs into Sapho's lap.[25] Pincombe does not elaborate on why Marlowe might choose to recall Lyly's *Sapho* in his play and why he repeatedly stages his own variations on the Virgilian icon. I argue that Marlowe, in using the image of Jupiter with Ganymede on his knee to replicate that of Sapho and Cupid, recalls the image of Dido with Cupid in her lap to undermine the compliment that Lyly's play intended to offer Elizabeth. Lyly suggests the Virgilian icon of Dido and Cupid in his penultimate scene to highlight how *unlike* Dido his Sapho is. Marlowe instead offers his own version to debunk not just the gods but also Lyly and those plays in the service of royal flattery.

The tableau in the induction in which a younger boy is held in the arms of an older one is repeated throughout the play, firstly with Jupiter and Ganymede, then with Venus and Ascanius, followed by Cupid with Dido and the Nurse. The repetition of the image is a calculated one, an example of what Cope calls 'reflexive satire' in which Marlowe utilises the reputation of the boy actors as catamites in order to capitalise on the potential for risqué humour.[26] The play, which begins with a sodomitical framework, draws comparison between the boys who were pressed into service in the child companies and the story of Ganymede, who was kidnapped by Jupiter to be his cupbearer. The suggestion is repeated in Act IV, scene 4, when Dido gives Aeneas her sceptre and crown and says: 'Now looks Aeneas like immortal Jove: / O where is Ganymede, to hold his cup' (IV.4.45–46). By underlining the physicality and sexual reputation of the boys, Marlowe once again reduces the possibility for flattery by heightening the play's potential for risqué humour.

Shakespeare, like Marlowe, uses Titania's treatment of Bottom in the fairy bower to offer his own satirical tableau. This culminates in Act IV, scene 1, when Titania holds Bottom in her arms and they fall asleep together: 'Sleep thou, and I will wind thee in my arms' (IV.1.39). *Dream* re-enacts the carnival inversion of *Dido* when queens, commoners, and gods are manipulated by the children in their arms, so Titania's love for the changeling boy causes her to dote upon an artisan turned ass. Shakespeare's version of the Virgilian icon not only serves as device to critique the queen but also recreates the humour of Marlowe's play by entering into the spirit of the risqué comedy of the boys' companies. The image of a boy actor playing Titania holding the adult who played Bottom offers a silhouette, which immediately returns us to those self-reflexive visual jokes of the boys' companies and their reputation as catamites. This humour is doubly invoked by the comic potential of the wordplay on ass/arse. There has been cautious speculation as to the significance of Bottom's name, particularly the currency of the pun on ass/arse. Annabel Patterson, in discussing the visual pun of Bottom's transformation into an ass, remarks of this trend that:

> It is typical of the Oxford English Dictionary's conservatism that it does not sanction this meaning of the word in Shakespeare's day, with the result that generations of editors have been satisfied with 'bottom' as a technical term for the bobbin in weaving.[27]

Shakespeare uses the pun on Bottom's name, together with the suggestion of his seduction by Titania, to purposefully recreate the tongue-in-cheek satire of the boys' companies. Titania's speeches to Bottom are riddled with puns on intercourse and male and female genitalia. Titania's metaphor certainly suggests her desire for coitus:

> So doth the woodbine the sweet honeysuckle.
> Gently entwist; the female ivy so
> Enrings the barky fingers of the elm.
>
> (IV.1.41–43)

Shakespeare's choice of 'enrings' is significant as it not only suggests intercourse, but also 'ring', punning on the anus. This series of meanings suggests not only copulation between Titania and Bottom, punning on his name, but also between the boy playing Titania and the man playing Bottom, replicating the reflexive humour of Marlowe's play.[28]

Marlowe similarly exploits the names of Dido and Aeneas for comic purpose as they both offer a sexual pun. Dido's name, for example, puns on Die-do, with 'die' referring to orgasm. It seems unlikely that Marlowe would have overlooked this opportunity for further comedy. There are several instances when Marlowe seems to have his queen deliberately punning upon her own name during the play. In Act III, scene 4, Dido tries to hint of her love for Aeneas: 'The thing that I will die before I ask, / And yet desire to have before I die' (III.4.8–9). These lines appear to be Dido's attempt to employ another device from her rhetorical armoury. The repetition of 'die' in each line suggests an example of imperfect chiasmus that Dido, in her desperation to suggest her real meaning to Aeneas, is unable to pull off.[29] The effect instead is one of comic frustration. The argument for punning is further strengthened by the fact that in this scene Dido tries to preserve her modesty and fails. She wrestles with seeming immodest, but is faced by a rather dull-witted Aeneas who fails to pick up on her hints. Her modesty is, therefore, compromised not only by Aeneas, but also by her own name as it becomes synonymous with sexual passion. Later in the scene, when she reveals her love for Aeneas, Dido attempts to ensure a positive response by suggesting that he cannot love her, as he prefers the pursuit of fame and would rather appear 'fair to Sirens' eyes / Than to the Carthage Queen that dies for him' (III.4.38–39). This attempt at female manipulation and the note of desperation suggests the comedy to be gained from the older boy playing Dido attempting to bully into submission a smaller one playing the Trojan hero Aeneas.[30]

Like Marlowe, Shakespeare offers his own variation on the traditional story of love caused by Cupid's arrow in *Dream* to offer his own appraisal of the queen. It has been customary for critics to suggest that the play's references to the 'fair vestal throned by the west' (II.1.158) and the 'imperial votress' (II.1.163) are flattering analogies for the queen, particularly in view of the fact that Cupid's arrow is successfully deflected.[31]

The 'fair vestal' is like Lyly's Diana in *Gallathea*, 'whose heart abateth the point of Cupid's arrows'.[32] The play's insistence upon the influence of Diana reinforces the suggestion that Shakespeare's aim is to compliment the queen as he incorporates the iconography of the queen's mythos, which served to underpin it. More recently, however, it has been suggested by Louis Montrose that this complimentary framework is in fact a smokescreen, as virtuous impenetrability is quickly undermined. Although the arrow misses its target, it hits a flower, whose juice goes on to have the same effect as the arrow. Oberon describes the flower's transformation:

> That very time I saw (but thou couldst not),
> Flying between the cold moon and the earth,
> Cupid all arm'd: a certain aim he took
> At a fair vestal, throned by the west,
> And loos'd his love-shaft smartly from his bow
> As it should pierce a hundred thousand hearts.
> But I might see young Cupid's fiery shaft
> Quench'd in the chaste beams of the watery moon;
> And the imperial votress passed on,
> In maiden meditation, fancy-free.
> Yet mark'd I where the bolt of Cupid fell:
> It fell upon a little western flower,
> Before milk-white, now purple with love's wound:
> And maidens call it 'love-in-idleness'.
> Fetch me that flower; the herb I show'd thee once.
> The juice of it, on sleeping eyelids laid,
> Will make or man or woman madly dote
> Upon the next live creature that it sees.
>
> (II.1.155–172)

The effect of Cupid's arrow on both Dido and Titania is to make them dote. Titania exclaims to Bottom 'O how I love thee! How I dote on thee!' (IV.1.44), while Venus instructs Cupid to visit Dido and 'touch her white breast with this arrowhead, / That she may dote upon Aeneas's love' (II.1.326–327). In Titania's case the effect of the flower cannot be countered by an arrow of disdain, but by 'Dian's bud' (IV.1.72). These are in fact the means by which Oberon can reassert his patriarchal control over the Fairy Queen. Montrose concludes:

> The vestal's invulnerability to fancy is doubly instrumental to Oberon in his reaffirmation of romance, marital and parental norms that have been inverted during the course of the play. Thus, Shakespeare's royal compliment remythologises the cult of the Virgin Queen in such a way as to sanction a relationship of gender and power that is personally and politically inimical to Elizabeth.[33]

In *A Midsummer Night's Dream* I suggest that Shakespeare deliberately employs so many of the images associated with Elizabeth's personae as Virgin Queen in order to signal a re-evaluation of them. In those plays which dramatise the story of Dido and Aeneas or offer a variation on that story the choice which is repeatedly played out for Elizabeth and her dramatic female personae is the choice between the brothers Cupid and Aeneas, the pursuit of love or the establishment of an empire. Elizabeth is repeatedly shown in the act of rejecting Cupid's arrow and choosing a life given over to chastity and service. The use of this story as a political tool served its short-term aim of foiling the proposed marriage between Elizabeth and Anjou, but in *Dream*, specifically through the figure of Titania, Shakespeare considers the cost of the Queen's decision to choose Aeneas over Cupid and remain unmarried.

The obvious consequence of this decision was that the identity of her successor was a matter of speculation, with candidates including James VI of Scotland, Arbella Stuart, and the Infanta Isabella. It appeared likely that James would succeed to the throne, but Elizabeth continued to refuse to name an heir. During the first decade of Elizabeth's reign there were repeated appeals by her subjects that the queen marry and the reasons given included the desire to avoid a contested succession. As a providential monarch and defender of the Protestant faith the failure to marry is repeatedly described in apocalyptic terms. An example from c.1560 is indicated in a letter from Matthew Parker, the Archbishop of Canterbury, Edmund Grindal the Bishop of London, and Richard Cox of Ely, who considered it their pastoral duty to

> Be solicitous in that cause which all your loving subjects so daily sigh for and morningly in their prayers desire to appear to their eyes. Marriage we all wish to see your godly affection inclined to, whereby your noble blood might be continued to reign over us to our great joy and comfort, whereby the great fears of ruin of this your ancient empire might be prevented, the destruction of your natural-born subjects avoided. We cannot but fear this continued sterility in your Highness' person to be a great token of God's displeasure toward us.[34]

At the opening of Parliament in 1563 Alexander Nowell, the Dean of St Paul's, preached a sermon before the queen in which he concluded by encouraging the queen to consider matrimony and the continuance of the Tudor dynasty:

> And whereas the Queen's majesty most noble ancestors have commonly had some issue to succeed them, but her majesty yet none; which want is for our sins to be a plague unto us. For as the marriage of Queen Mary was a terrible plague to all England, and like in continuance to have proved greater; so now for the want of your marriage and issue is like to prove as great a plague.[35]

These images of a childless queen whose status is described in terms of natural disasters such as plague and famine are brought sharply back into focus in the 1590s through the figure of Titania. The appearance of the fairies is framed by the discussion of the marital discord between Oberon and Titania. The royal marriage has yet to produce children and Titania's attachment to the Indian boy can be seen partly as a consequence of her own childlessness. Titania acknowledges that their quarrel has had far-reaching effects upon the natural world:

> the winds, piping to us in vain,
> As in revenge have suck'd up from the sea
> Contagious fogs; which, falling in the land,
> Hath every pelting river made so proud
> That they have overborne their continents.
> The ox hath therefore stretch'd his yoke in vain,
> The ploughman lost his sweat, and the green corn
> Hath rotted ere his youth attain'd a beard;
> The fold stands empty in the drowned field,
> And crows are fatted with the murrion flock.
>
> (II.1.88–97)

The forces of nature have combined to create a world of pestilence and dearth:

> the moon, the governess of floods,
> Pale in her anger, washes all the air,
> That rheumatic diseases do abound.
>
> (II.1.103–105)

Whilst the description of the countryside in the play may offer an accurate account of England in the 1590s when there were a number of failed harvests owing to bad weather,[36] this portrait of the natural world echoes the apocalyptic images of a monarch who has failed to provide England with an heir.

The less than flattering portrait of a barren Elizabeth offered by Titania is reinforced in the play as Shakespeare recalls Marlowe's play to identify Titania with the character of the Nurse. In Act III, scene 1, Titania's inducements for Bottom are suggestive of those used by the Nurse to entice Cupid as Ascanius away from the court. Titania instructs her fairies to.

> Feed him with apricocks and dewberries,
> With purple grapes, green figs, and mulberries;
> The honey bags steal from the humble-bees.
>
> (III.1.159–161)

This list directly echoes Marlowe's Nurse:

> I have an orchard that hath store of plums,
> Brown almonds, services, ripe figs, and dates,
> Dewberries, apples, yellow oranges;
> A garden where are bee-hives full of honey.
>
> (IV.5.4–7)

Clifford Leech suggested that Marlowe included the scene between Cupid and the widowed Nurse as it offered a parallel with her mistress as 'Dido's infection is mirrored and exaggerated in the Nurse's'.[37] The Nurse, like her mistress, is a widow who quickly becomes infatuated with Cupid disguised as Ascanius. The discrepancy between the age of the Nurse and the youthfulness of Cupid is made explicit to underline the ridiculous nature of her passion:

> That I might live to see this boy a man!
> How prettily he laughs! Go, ye wag!
> You'll be a twigger when you come to age.
> Say Dido what she will, I am not old;
> I'll be no more a widow, I am young;
> I'll have a husband, or else a lover.
>
> (IV.5.18–23)

To which Cupid spitefully responds 'A husband and no teeth!' (IV.5.24). The Nurse alternates between reason and fancy:

> O what mean I to have such foolish thoughts!
> Foolish is love, a toy. O sacred love,
> If there be any heaven in earth, 'tis love,
> Especially in a woman of your years.
> Blush, blush for shame, why shouldst thou think of love?
> A grave and not a lover, fits thy age.
>
> (IV.5.25–30)

The Nurse's role as an intermediary between Dido and the audience is significant; although the audience will laugh at her dotage as grotesque, her character, whilst serving as a reflection of Dido, generates a balanced response, as she is not allowed to undermine entirely our sympathy for Dido. Titania's allusion to Marlowe's Nurse reveals the absence of an equivalent Nurse figure in *Dream*. Shakespeare uses Titania's list of enticements to underline that the Fairy Queen is in fact a conflated version of both Dido and the Nurse and is therefore doubly ridiculous. By deliberately suggesting that Titania collapses within herself the identities of Dido and the Nurse, Shakespeare presents an extreme vision of female rule in which the queen is not only subject to Cupid's arrow but is also notably childless.

Critics such as A.L. Rowse and Steane have also remarked upon the scene between Cupid and the Nurse primarily in the service of a comparison with Shakespeare. Rowse praises the exoticism of the Nurse's fruit garden only then to dismiss it because it seems to lack the realism of an English Shakespearean garden. 'Unlike Shakespeare's, it is not a real English garden; it is a Renaissance garden out of a book.'[38] Similarly, Steane describes the Nurse's speech as presenting 'an Elizabethan version of the modern birthday-card rustic garden idyll'. In each case the speech is compared to Shakespeare and found wanting.[39]

The similarities between these two speeches, however, indicate that there is a deliberate strategy at work on Shakespeare's part and that this is not a chance echo. This is clinched by the way in which the speeches of both the Nurse and Titania refer to dewberries. References to dewberries are not readily found in the literature of the period outside botanical writing. The Revels edition of *Dido* notes that Marlowe only ever used the word 'dewberries' in this play, although H.J. Oliver does identify its use by Shakespeare in *Dream*, but without further comment.[40] The Chadwyck-Healey electronic database confirms that only Marlowe and then Shakespeare in *Dream* use this word in their plays. The word then appears only in later eighteenth- and nineteenth-century adaptations of Shakespeare's play.[41]

As has been noted, editors of Shakespeare have made more of his references to flora and fauna than those of Marlowe. Harold Brooks in the Arden *Dream* cites Henry Lyte's *A Niewe Herball, or Historie of Plantes*, of 1578, a translation of Dodoen's *Cruydeboeck*, as Shakespeare's source for the fruit; in this the dewberry is described as a blackberry.[42] In the Revels edition of *Dido* the note for dewberry echoes the *OED* definition as 'a species of blackberry or bramble berry' rather than suggesting a particular source.[43] The definition of the dewberry in the *OED* notes that

> In some earlier English writers, and mod. dialects, the name is applied to the gooseberry (dayberry). Shakespeare's dewberry, which is mentioned among delicate cultivated fruits, is supposed by some to have meant the gooseberry.[44]

What is significant, however, are the medicinal properties associated with the dewberry and the gooseberry in early modern herbals. Both the dewberry and the gooseberry are associated with female fertility as they are offered as remedies for either cravings in pregnancy or heavy periods. For example, in Lyte's *Niewe Herball* the fruit of the blackberry or bramble berry is described as the dewberry. Lyte suggests a decoction of the unripe fruit as a remedy to stop 'womens flowers and all other issue of blood'.[45] Nicholas Culpeper in *The English Physitian* suggested that a decoction of the leaves, brambles, and dried branches of the bramble or blackberry bush 'is good for the too much flowing of womens courses'.[46] If the dewberry is another name for the gooseberry the properties of this plant and particularly its fruit are suggestive. John Gerard, for example, claims in *The Herball or Generall Historie of Plantes* that the fruit stops 'the menses or monthly sickness'.[47] Culpeper advises

The practife of the new and old phificke,

wherein is cōntained the moft excellent Secrets of

Phificke and Philofophie, deuided into foure Bookes, In the which are the beft approued remedies for the difeafes as well inward as outward, of al the parts of mans body: treating very amplie of al diftillations of waters, of oyles, balmes, Quinteffences, with the extraction of artificiall faltes, the vfe and preparation of Antimony, and potable Gold. Gathered out of the beft & moft approued Authors, by that exeellent Doctor *Gefnerus.* Alfo the Pictures and maner to make the Vef= fels, Furnaces, and other Inftruments thereunto belonging. Newly corrected and publifhed in Englifh, by *George Baker,* one of the Queenes Ma= iefties chiefe Chirurgians in ordinary.

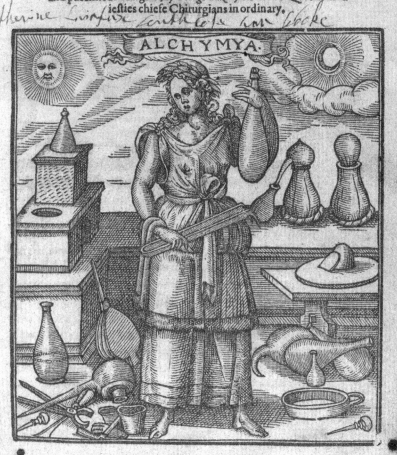

ALCHYMYA.

Printed at London, by Peter Short. 1 5 9 9.

1 llustrated frontispiece, George Baker, *The practise of the new and old phisicke* (London, 1599)

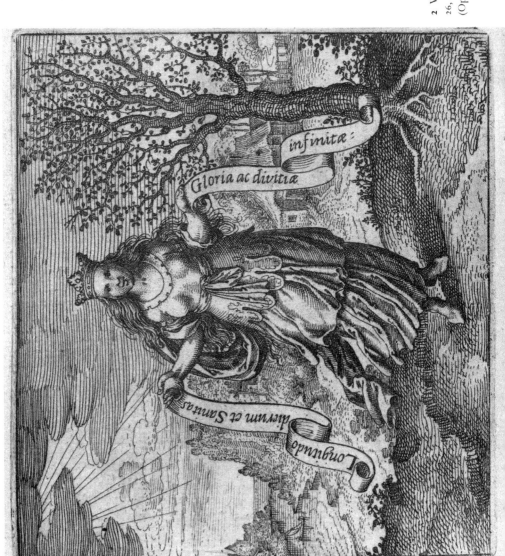

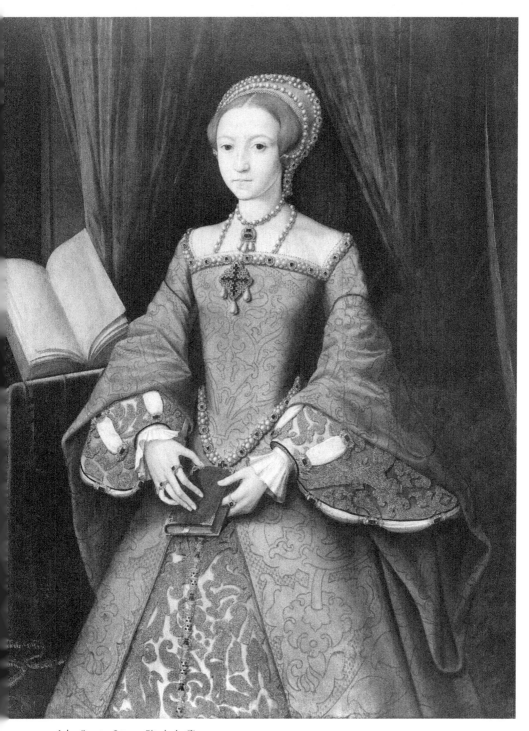

3 John Scrots, *Princess Elizabeth*. Circa 1542–47

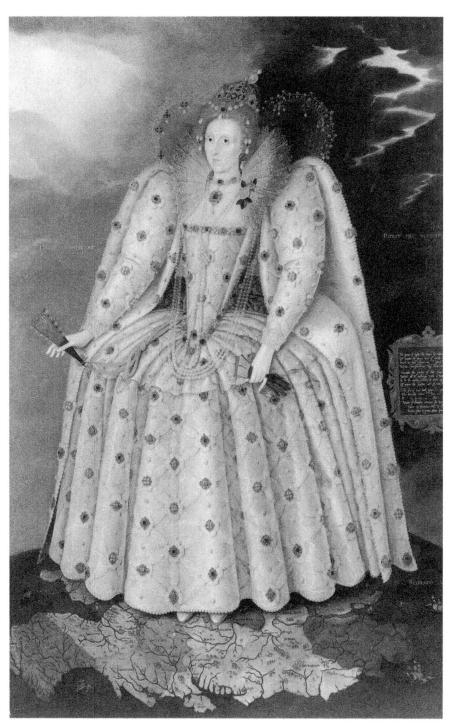

4 Marcus Gheeraerts, *The Ditchley Portrait*. Circa 1592

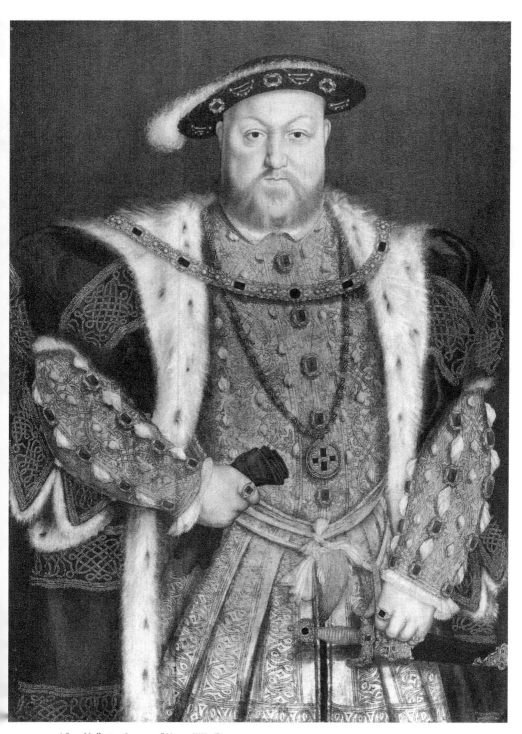

5 After Holbein, *Portrait of Henry VIII*. Circa 1540

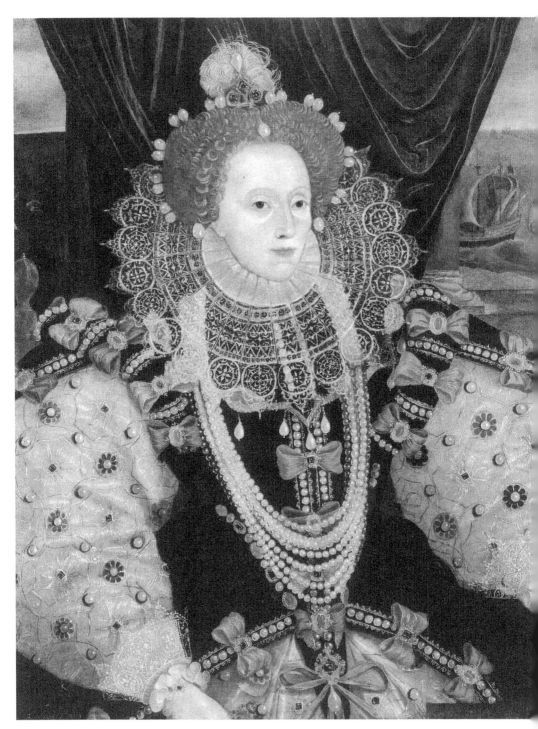

6 Attributed to George Gower, *The Armada Portrait*. Circa 1588

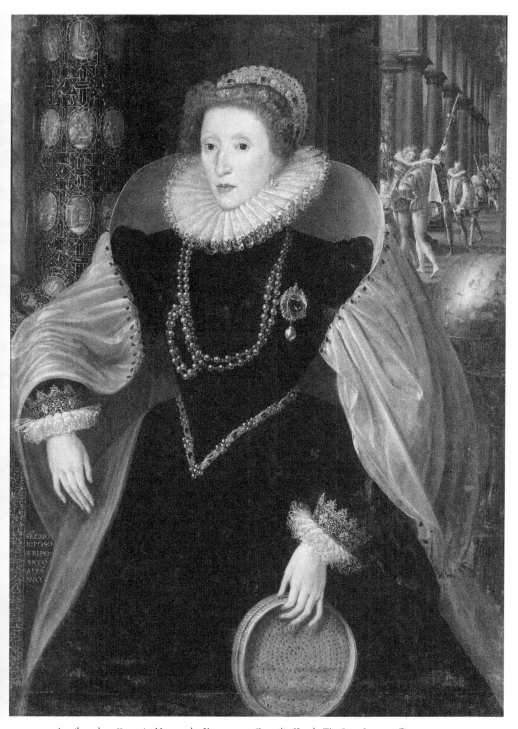

7 Attributed to Quentin Massys the Younger or Cornelis Ketel, *The Sieve Portrait*. Circa 1580

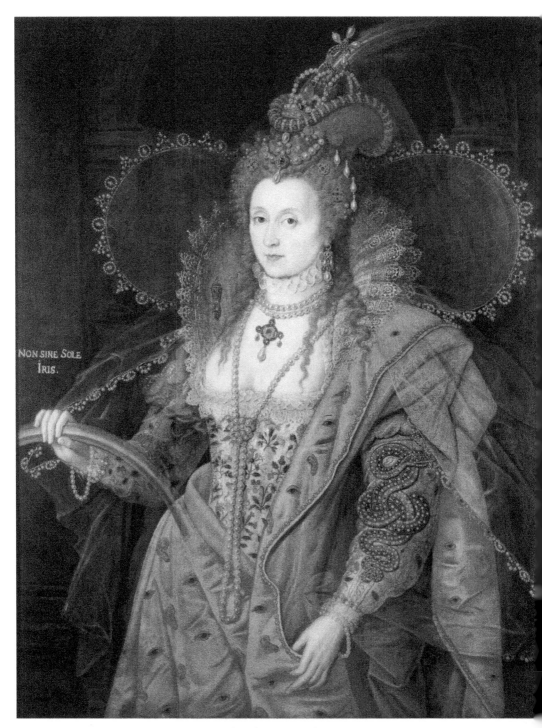

NON SINE SOLE
IRIS.

8 Attributed to Marcus Gheeraerts, *The Rainbow Portrait*. Circa 1600

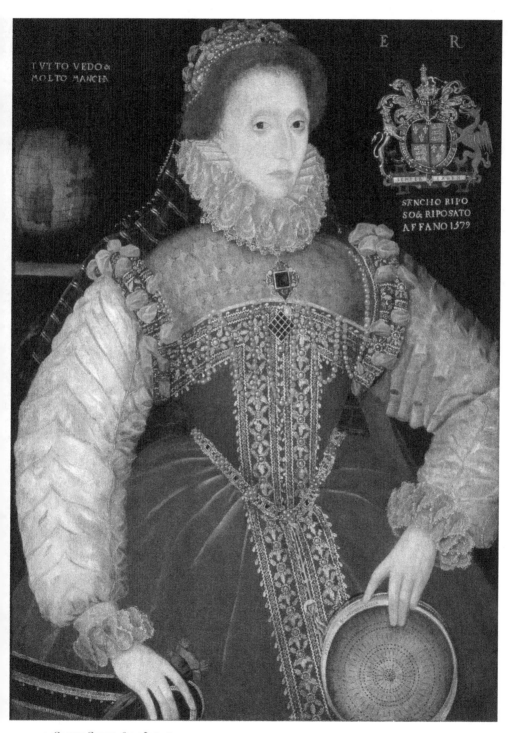

9 George Gower, *Sieve Portrait*. 1579

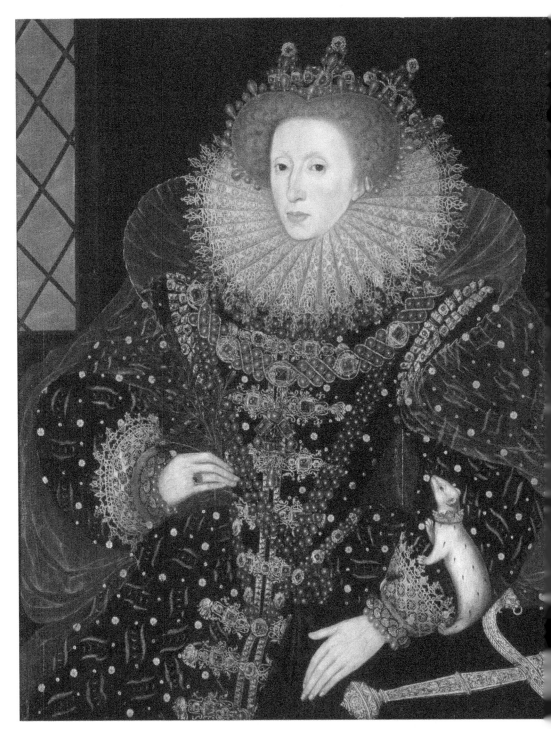

10 Nicholas Hilliard, *Ermine Portrait.* 1585

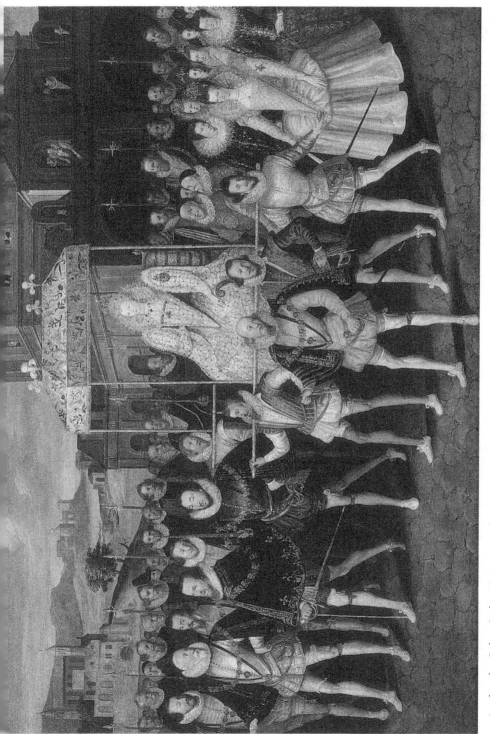

11 Attributed to Robert Peake, *The Procession of Queen Elizabeth I to Blackfriars*. Circa 1600

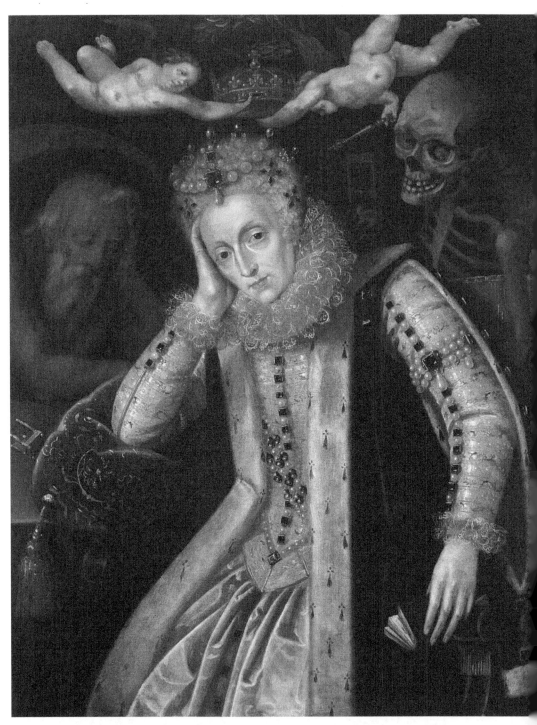

12 English School (seventeenth century), *Queen Elizabeth I (1533–1603) in Old Age*. Circa 1610

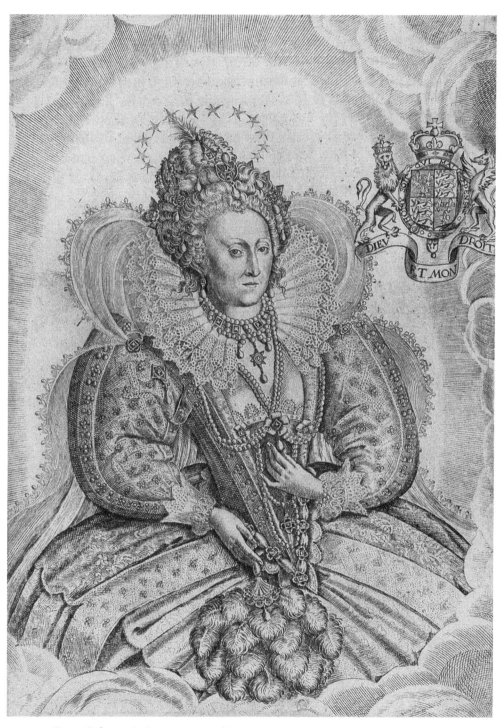

13 Francis Delaram, *Posthumous engraving of Queen Elizabeth I*. Circa 1617–19

14 Epitaph for King Arthur in Sir Thomas Malory, [*Le morte darthur*]. 15th century

15 Epitaph for John Brooke

The Body of
B. Franklin,
Printer;
Like the Cover of an old Book,
Its Contents torn out,
And stript of its Lettering and Gilding,
Lies here, Food for Worms.
But the Work shall not be wholly lost:
For it will, as he believ'd, appear once more,
In a new & more perfect Edition,
Corrected and amended
By the Author.

He was born Jan. 6. 1706.
Died   17

Dr. Franklin Epitaph in his own

16 Epitaph for Benjamin Franklin, London. Circa 1727

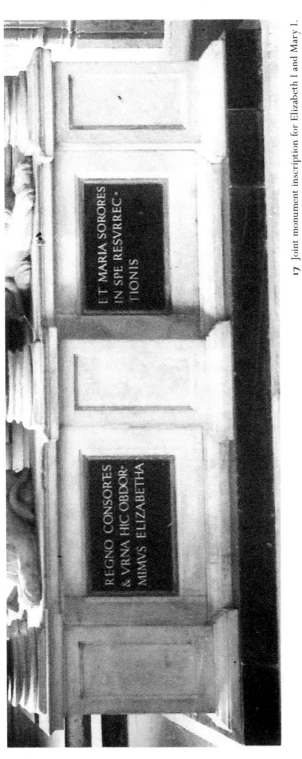

17 Joint monument inscription for Elizabeth I and Mary I.

that the fruit 'is excellently good to stay longings of women with child'.[48] John Parkinson also suggests that the gooseberries 'are a fit dish for women with child to stay their longings, and to procure an appetite unto meat'.[49] The identities of Titania's Fairy attendants Peaseblosssom and Mustardseed have also been remarked upon in the context of their medicinal properties.[50] Both plants were associated with fertility or the promotion of conception. In folklore the pea and its pod for example, were thought to contain a powerful love potion. The word peasecod was also associated with male genitalia, as a cod meant a bag of seeds and the word could also be inverted to produce 'codpiece'.[51] The mustard seed was also noted for its heat and according to Gerard its benefits for women, in particular, were that it 'prouoketh appetite', and 'prouoketh the tearmes'.[52]

Both plays' emphasis on those fruits and plants which promote conception and assist with the side effects of pregnancy serves to underline the sterility of Titania and the Nurse. Titania, from her celebration of the Indian votaress's pregnancy and love for her child, would seem to desire pregnancy herself, while the Nurse, who is clearly past child-bearing age, briefly deludes herself that she is young and amorous again. The use of fruit as a metaphor for fertility and children also recalls the earlier Biblical iconography employed by Elizabeth's Parliament as they attempted to persuade her of her obligation to marry. In February 1563 the Lords' petition to the queen urged:

> God (your highness knoweth) by the course of the Scriptures hath declared succession and the having of children to be one of His principal benedictions in this life; and of the contrary He hath pronounced otherwise. And therefore Abraham prayed to God for issue, fearing that Eleazar his steward should have been his heir, and had the promise that kings should proceed of his body. Anna, the mother of Samuel, prayed to God with tears for issue; and Elizabeth (whose name your majesty beareth), mother to John the Baptist, was joyful when God had blessed her with fruit, accounting herself delivered thereby of a reproach.[53]

The queen answered their request that she marry and name a successor with the following sharp retort:

> The two petitions that you presented me, expressed in many words, contained in sum as of your cares the greatest: my marriage and my successor, of which two I think best the last be touched, and of the other a silent thought may serve. For I had thought it had been so desired as none other tree's blossoms should have been minded or ever hoped if my fruit had been denied you.[54]

At the end of the Commons' petition to the queen in the same year and on the same subject, the speaker delivered a speech in the House of Lords in which he hoped that the question of the queen's marriage would soon be settled and he entreated 'God to encline your Majestie's hart to marriage, and that he will so blesse, and send such good successe thereunto that we may see the fruit and children, that may come thereof'.[55]

When Shakespeare comes to write *A Midsummer Night's Dream* nearly thirty years later, the final decade of Elizabeth's reign is characterised by critical assessment of her achievements as queen. Shakespeare's comedy reflects this political and cultural Zeitgeist by employing a series of retrospective strategies. The first is that *Dream's* allusions to Marlowe's play and the parallels established between Dido and Titania provide a referent to a pivotal moment in the manipulation of the queen's image. The use of Dido in the iconography of Elizabeth coincided with the marriage negotiations with Anjou, signalling the rejection of those images which supported the marriage-ability of the queen, in favour of her perpetual virginity. *Dream* then goes on to examine the political consequences of this ideological shift, by juxtaposing Titania with the Nurse, whose fruitlessness offers a stinging commentary upon Elizabeth's iconicity as a Virgin Queen.

Notes

1. See for example, Frances A. Yates, *Astraea: The Imperial Theme in the Sixteenth Century* (London: Routledge and Kegan Paul, 1975).

2. Louis Adrian Montrose, '"Shaping Fantasies": Figurations of Gender and Power in Elizabethan Culture', in *A Midsummer Night's Dream: Contemporary Critical Essays*, edited by Richard Dutton (Basingstoke: Macmillan, 1996).

3. Helen Hackett, *Virgin Mother, Maiden Queen* (Houndmills: Macmillan, 1995), pp. 163–197.

4. See for instance Maurice Charney, 'Marlowe and Shakespeare's African Queens', in *Shakesperean Illuminations: Essays in honour of Marvin Rosenberg*, edited by Jay L. Halio and Hugh Richmond (London: Associated University Presses, 1998), pp. 242–252, and Michael Hattaway, 'Christopher Marlowe: Ideology and Subversion', in *Christopher Marlowe and English Renaissance Culture*, edited by Darryll Grantley and Peter Roberts (Aldershot: Scolar, 1996), pp. 198–223.

5. H.J. Oliver in his introduction to the Revels *Dido* describes Shakespeare's treatment of the murder of Priam in the Pyrrhus speech as a 'good natured parody' of the same account in Marlowe's *Dido*. See Christopher Marlowe, *Dido, Queen of Carthage* and *The Massacre at Paris*, edited by H.J. Oliver (London: Methuen, 1968), p. xxxii. See also Dorothea Kehler, 'Shakespeare's Recollections of Marlowe's *Dido, Queen of Carthage*: Two Notes', *American Notes and Queries* 14 (2001), pp. 5–10, and Nicholas Brooke, 'Marlowe as Provocative Agent in Shakespeare's Early Plays', *Shakespeare Survey* 14 (1961), pp. 34–44.

6. J.B. Steane, *Marlowe: A Critical Study* (Cambridge: Cambridge University Press, 1965), p. 46.

7. Jackson I. Cope, 'Marlowe's Dido and the Titillating Boys', *English Literary Renaissance* 4 (1974), pp. 315–325.

8. Cope, 'Marlowe's Dido and the Titillating Boys', p. 325.

9. Fred B. Tromly, *Playing with Desire: Christopher Marlowe and the Art of Tantalization* (Toronto: University of Toronto, 1998), p. 58.

10. Tromly, *Playing with Desire*, p. 58.

11. William Shakespeare, *A Midsummer Night's Dream*, edited by Harold F. Brooks (London: Routledge, 1993), I.1.169–172. All further quotations from the play are taken from this edition.

12. Shakespeare employs the same strategy in *The Merchant of Venice* in the final scene of the play, when Jessica and Lorenzo exchange vows of love. They too select a series of classical lovers, including Dido and Aeneas, all notable for their unhappy endings.

13. Christopher Marlowe, *Dido, Queen of Carthage* and *The Massacre at Paris* (The Revels Plays), edited by H.J. Oliver. (London: Methuen, 1968), I.1.50–53. All further quotations from the play are taken from this edition.

14. Susan Doran, *Monarchy and Matrimony: The Courtships of Elizabeth I* (London: Routledge, 1996), pp. 10–11. See also Donald Stump, 'Marlowe's Travesty of Virgil: Dido and Elizabethan Dreams of Empire', *Comparative Drama* 34 (2000), pp. 79–107.

15. The full text of Churchyard's *A Discourse of The Queenes … entertainment in Suffolk and Norfolk (1578)* is available on the Chadwyck-Healey Database Literature Online. See also Michael Pincombe, 'Cupid and Eliza: Variations on a Virgilian Icon in plays by Gager, Lyly and Marlowe', in *The Iconography of Power. Ideas and Images of Rulership on the English Renaissance Stage*, edited by György E. Szönyi and Rowland Wymer (Szeged: University of Szeged, 2000), pp. 33–52.

16. William Gager, *Dido* in *William Gager: The Complete Works. Volume 1. The Earlier Plays* (London: Garland Publishing, Inc., 1994), p. 343.

17. Pincombe, 'Cupid and Eliza', pp. 38–39.

18. See Frederick S. Boas, *Christopher Marlowe: A Biographical and Critical Study* (Oxford: Clarendon Press, 1940), p. 52. For a detailed account of Marlowe's sources for *Dido* see *Christopher Marlowe: The Plays and Their Sources*, edited by Vivien Thomas and William Tydeman (London: Routledge, 1994), pp. 17–66.

19. Lisa Hopkins, *Christopher Marlowe: A Literary Life* (Basingstoke: Palgrave, 2000), p. 108.

20. Leah S. Marcus, 'Shakespeare's Comic Heroines, Elizabeth I, and the Political Uses of Androgyny', in *Women in the Middle Ages and the Renaissance*, edited by Mary Beth Rose (New York: Syracuse University Press, 1986), pp. 139–140.

21. Hopkins, *Christopher Marlowe: A Literary Life*, p. 108.

22. John Lyly, *Campaspe* and *Sapho and Phao*, edited by G.K. Hunter and David Bevington (Manchester: Manchester University Press, 1991), p. 152.

23. John Lyly, *Campaspe* and *Sapho and Phao* (The Revels Plays), edited by G.K. Hunter and David Bevington (Manchester: Manchester University Press, 1991), I.1.45–47. All further quotations from the play are taken from this edition.

24. For the suggestion that Sapho provides a flattering analogy for Elizabeth see Bernard Huppé, 'Allegory of Love in Lyly's Court Comedies', *English Literary History* 14 (1947), pp. 93–113. For an alternative view see Theodora A. Jankowski, 'The Subversion of Flattery: The Queen's Body in John Lyly's *Sapho and Phao*', *Medieval and Renaissance Drama in England* 5 (1991), pp. 69–86.

25. Pincombe, 'Cupid and Eliza', pp. 44–48.

26. Cope, 'Marlowe's Dido and the Titillating Boys', p. 318.

27. Annabel Patterson, *Shakespeare and the Popular Voice* (Oxford: Basil Blackwell, 1989), p. 66.

28. Frankie Rubenstein, *A Dictionary of Shakespeare's Sexual Puns and Their Significance* (Houndmills: Macmillan, 1989), pp. xv–xvi.

29. J.A. Cuddon, ed., *A Dictionary of Literary Terms and Literary Theory* (Oxford: Blackwell Publishers, 1998), p. 39.

30. Cope, 'Marlowe's Dido and the Titillating Boys', pp. 322–323. The boy playing Dido would have to be older from a practical perspective than the one playing Aeneas as Dido has more lines to learn.

31. See for instance William Shakespeare, *A Midsummer Night's Dream*, edited by Harold F. Brooks, p. lv. For an alternative view see Lisa Hopkins, *Writing Renaissance Queens: Texts*

by and about Elizabeth I and Mary Queen of Scots (London: Associated University Presses, 2002), p. 105.

32. John Lyly, *Gallathea and Midas*, edited by Anne Begor Lancashire (Lincoln: University of Nebraska Press, 1969), III.4.33–34.

33. Louis Adrian Montrose, '"Shaping Fantasies": Figurations of Gender and Power in Elizabethan Culture', in *A Midsummer Night's Dream: Contemporary Critical Essays*, edited by Richard Dutton (Basingstoke: Macmillan, 1996), p. 102.

34. J. Bruce, ed., *Correspondence of Matthew Parker, Archbishop of Canterbury* (Parker Society) (Cambridge: Cambridge University Press, 1853), pp. 129–132, p. 131.

35. G.E. Corrie, ed., *A Catechism by Alexander Nowell* (Parker Society) (Cambridge: Cambridge University Press, 1853), pp. 224–229, p. 228.

36. See Marcus, *Puzzling Shakespeare*, pp. 96–105.

37. Clifford Leech, 'Marlowe's Humour', in *Marlowe: A Collection of Critical Essays*, edited by Clifford Leech (Englewood Cliffs, NJ: Prentice-Hall Inc., 1964), pp. 167–178.

38. A.L. Rowse, *Christopher Marlowe: A Biography* (London: Macmillan, 1964), p. 47.

39. See also Caroline Spurgeon, *Shakespeare's Imagery and What It Tells Us* (Cambridge: Cambridge University Press, 1966).

40. Marlowe, *Dido, Queen of Carthage*, p. 73 n.6.

41. The Chadwyck-Healey Literature Online Database details the following versions of Shakespeare's *Dream*. The first is *A Midsummer Night's Dream* by George Colman and David Garrick (1763), the second is called *A Fairy Tale in Two Acts* by George Colman (1763) and the third version by Frederick Reynolds is called *A Midsummer Night's Dream, WRITTEN BY Shakspeare: WITH ALTERATIONS, ADDITIONS, AND NEW SONGS* (1816).

42. Shakespeare, *A Midsummer Night's Dream*, ed. Brooks, p. 60 n. 159.

43. *The Oxford English Dictionary*, second ed. (1989).

44. *OED*.

45. Henry Lyte, *A nievve herball, or historie of plantes* (London, 1578), pp. 660–662, cited from *Early English Books Online*, http://gateway.proquest.com/openurl?ctx_ver=Z39.88–2003&res_id=xri:eebo&rft_id=xri:eebo:image:7773:344

46. Nicholas Culpeper, *The English Physitian* (London, 1653), F3r, cited from *Early English Books Online*, http://gateway.proquest.com/openurl?ctx_ver=Z39.88–2003&res_id=xri:eebo&rft_id=xri:eebo:image:57702:30

47. John Gerard, *The herbal or Generall historie of plantes* (London, 1597), pp. 1143–1144, cited from *Early English Books Online*, http://gateway.proquest.com/openurl?ctx_ver=Z39.88–2003&res_id=xri:eebo&rft_id=xri:eebo:image:23253:591

48. Culpeper, *The English Physitian*, F3r, cited from *Early English Books Online*, http://gateway.proquest.com/openurl?ctx_ver=Z39.88–2003&res_id=xri:eebo&rft_id=xri:eebo:image:57702:30

49. John Parkinson, *Paradisi in sole paradisus terrestris, or, A choise garden of all sorts of rarest flowers* (London, 1656), pp. 560–561, cited from *Early English Books Online*, http://gateway.proquest.com/openurl?ctx_ver=Z39.88–2003&res_id=xri:eebo&rft_id=xri:eebo:image:46176:286

50. See Helen Hackett, *A Midsummer Night's Dream* in *A Companion to Shakespeare's Works Volume III The Comedies*, edited by Richard Dutton and Jean E. Howard (Oxford: Blackwell Publishing, 2005), pp. 338–357, and Lou Agnes Reynolds and Paul Sawyer, 'Folk Medicine and the Four Fairies of *A Midsummer Night's Dream*', *Shakespeare Quarterly* 10 (1959), pp. 513–521.

51. Reynolds and Sawyer, 'Folk Medicine and the Four Fairies of *A Midsummer Night's Dream*', p. 518.

52. Gerard, *The herbal*, p. 245, cited from *Early English Books Online*, http://gateway.proquest.

com/openurl?ctx_ver=Z39.88–2003&res_id=xri:eebo&rft_id=xri:eebo:image:23022:144

53. Leah S. Marcus, Janel Mueller, and Mary Beth Rose, eds, *Elizabeth I: Collected Works* (Chicago: University of Chicago Press, 2000), pp. 84–85.

54. Marcus, Mueller, and Rose, eds, *Elizabeth I: Collected Works*, p. 79.

55. Doran, *Monarchy and Matrimony*, p. 62.

Cynthia waning: *Cynthia's Revels* imagines the death of the queen[1]

Matthew Steggle

Cynthia, the goddess of the moon, was one of later Elizabethan literature's favourite surrogates for the figure of Elizabeth herself. As scholars including Philippa Berry and Helen Hackett have documented, Elizabeth appears in this guise in forms varying from *The Faerie Queene* to court pageants; from drama, such as Lyly's *Endymion* or Dekker's *Old Fortunatus*, to lyrics such as Ralegh's *The Ocean to Cynthia*. In particular there was a growing tension in lunar representations of the ageing Elizabeth in the last decades of her reign, as the prospect of her death started to come into view, and from this perspective, the moon is an especially interesting emblem, since it stands problematically on the celestial border between a sublunary, mortal world, subject to time and death, and the unchanging heavens above. Over the last years of her reign, different representations of Elizabeth attempted in different ways to negotiate the gap between Elizabeth's idealisation as a goddess, and the increasingly obvious evidence of her political vulnerability and personal mortality.[2]

This chapter is concerned with the political resonances of one of those represen-tations, although the play in the form in which it is usually read could perhaps be better considered as one-and-a-half of those representations: Ben Jonson's comedy *Cynthia's Revels*. First performed in 1600–1601, *Cynthia's Revels* was first published in quarto in 1601, but it is usually read, when it is read at all, in a text deriving from its appearance in Jonson's 1616 Folio *Works*. The two texts differ considerably, since F renames the central character from 'Criticus' to 'Crites'; alters the handling of the stage directions; and makes hundreds of minor cuts, additions, and alterations. It also adds around a thousand lines to the play in a series of substantial additions, mainly a sequence of four long scenes at the start of Act V set around the playing of a formalised duel of courtly etiquette. I would argue that this material is later in date than the original play – perhaps, indeed, as late as 1616. Herford and Simpson, though, argued that F's full version represents the play as acted in 1601, but that Jonson, as an afterthought, prepared a cut version, perhaps for performance at court, which was then printed as

Q. Footnotes to their edition temper this position by conceding that the F passages may contain minor retouchings of a later date, but their basic tenet is that the Folio has a unique authority as representing the 'real' *Cynthia's Revels*. In this case, though, Herford and Simpson are clearly wrong. Inconsistencies in the text of F demonstrate that the F additions are 'on top' of Q; such inconsistencies include the incompletely revised *dramatis personae*, the unrevised plot summary of the ensuing play presented in the Induction, and the disruption by the F additions of Q's carefully arranged time-scheme. The F text, then, is a composite, containing later revisions. If one is seeking to place *Cynthia's Revels* in its historical moment, then the version published in Q is clearly preferable, and that is the version which will be quoted here.[3]

One should start by conceding that most early Jonson critics, who saw *Cynthia's Revels* as 'a play evidently designed to shed lustre on [Elizabeth's] name', have plenty of evidence on their side.[4] Both Criticus, the sympathetic hero, and Arete, a personi-fication of Virtue, admire Cynthia unstintingly. One should also concede that a range of later readers have already found nuances, shades, and covert criticism in the panegyric of the play. Courtly compliment, as Janet Clare has argued of a group of early Jonson plays including this one, is capable of taking many subtleties, and Clare's essay is a formative influence on the argument here that the play is more hostile to, and indeed more dismissive of, Cynthia/Elizabeth than has generally been recognised hitherto.[5]

Cynthia's Revels was first performed by the Children of the Revels at the Blackfriars theatre, at some point in the interval between 2 September 1600, when that company acquired the lease of the theatre, and 23 May 1601, when the play was licensed for printing. This period spans a number of interesting political events, most obviously relating to the Earl of Essex. Essex had spent the summer of 1600 under house arrest, being released from that arrest, but still forbidden to attend court, on 26 August 1600. Through the autumn of 1600 his position worsened, with Elizabeth refusing to renew his monopoly on sweet wines, a moment identified by Paul E.J. Hammer as compounding his disgrace and financial ruin and precipitating his slide towards the armed rebellion which may (although this is uncertain) have been intended to install James VI as Elizabeth's successor — certainly in the 1590s Essex had presented himself as a 'champion of James's claim to the English throne'.[6] On 8 February 1601, Essex led three hundred armed men through the city of London in an inconclusive attempt at an armed uprising: arrested by the end of the day, he was beheaded on 25 February, and over the next month other followers of his were tried, found guilty, and executed.

All this is relevant to *Cynthia's Revels* because an important plot element within the play is the story of Diana and Actaeon, in which the young huntsman Actaeon surprises the goddess while she is bathing naked, and her response is to turn him into a deer and have him torn to pieces by his own hounds. This story is given prominence within Jonson's play, since Cynthia's desire to reject 'black and enuious slaunders' made against her after this incident is described as the immediate cause of the eponymous revels (B2v). When, in Act V, Cynthia herself enters the play, the fate of Actaeon is recalled both in the words of the sung lyric 'Queen and Huntress', which ask for mercy for the 'flying hart', and in Cynthia's own speeches justifying her actions against Actaeon. It is generally agreed that just as Cynthia, on some level at least, represents Elizabeth in this play, in accordance with the wider conventions of Elizabethan panegyric (and in accordance with the scene where she sees a seemingly miraculous vision of 'another *Cynthia*' — that is, Elizabeth, K4r), so Actaeon, to some extent, is open to being read as an allegorical version of the Earl of Essex. What remains unclear, however, is whether Actaeon represents an Essex who is merely disgraced, who is a rebel awaiting punishment, or who is already dead; and, if the last case applies, whether or not the allusions to him postdate the rest of the play (an argument first made by A.C. Judson, who notes that the Actaeon passages can relatively easily be detached from their dramatic context).[7] The Essex rebellion, or at least the circumstances leading up to it, are unquestionably part of the originary political moment of *Cynthia's Revels*, but, I will argue, they are not of themselves the whole story of the political content of this play.

A brief and necessarily partial plot summary will help readers orientate themselves around the argument that follows. *Cynthia's Revels* opens with an Induction, in which three boy actors describe the play that is to follow: we then meet the gods Cupid and Mercury, who decide to disguise themselves as pageboys and attend the revels to be held at Cynthia's court. First, though, Mercury conjures the nymph Echo, who bewails Narcissus's death by the nearby pool, and puts a curse on it to cause anyone who drinks its waters to be smitten with self-love. The ladies and gallants of the court, almost all foolish, hear of this water and send their pages to get some, and most of the play is taken up with their waiting, their practising witty repartee, and their playing of games. They drink the water, which has little discernible effect. Meanwhile, Criticus, the admirable scholar, is asked by his beloved Arete to prepare a masque for the revels, which he does, including parts for all the foolish courtiers, who perform it in front of Cynthia herself when she appears that evening. She praises the performance, and warns that she should not be regarded as too harsh, before discovering that the personified Virtues in the play were actually played by the foolish courtiers. She promises to reward Criticus, and punishes the foolish courtiers for their temerity by having them journey to Weeping Cross, singing a recantation of their follies.

Cynthia's Revels makes its first references to its eponymous goddess in the Induction, where she is described by the waggish boy actors, outlining the play to come, in terms which do not mention her deity at all, and instead treat her as if she was a mortal queen. Indeed, one of those references, interpreted by a member of the race of what Jonson elsewhere calls 'mice-eyed decipherers', might even be taken as a hostile reference to Cynthia. At her court, it seems, reward is given neither to Criticus the 'contemned' scholar nor to the figure he is in love with: 'Lady Arete, or Virtue, a poore Nymph of Cynthias traine, that's scarce able to buy her selfe a Gowne, you shall see her play in a Blacke Roabe anone: A Creature, that (I assure you) is no lesse scorn'd, then himselfe'

(A2v). Even allowing for the mock-acid tone of the boy actors' cynicism, this is not an idealising description of Cynthia's court. Here, for contrast, is a corresponding allegorical description of Cynthia's court offered in the Induction of Dekker's *Old Fortunatus*, a close contemporary of *Cynthia's Revels*:

> Euen to her temple are my feeble limmes trauelling. Some cal her Pandora: some Gloriana, some Cynthia: some Delphæbe, some Astræa: all by seuerall names to expresse seuerall loues: Yet all those names make but one celestiall body, as all those loues meete to create but one soule.

According to Dekker, all strangers offer Cynthia 'two eyes strucke blinde with admiration: Two lips (proud to sound her glorie:) Two hands held vp full of prayers and praises: What not, that may expresse loue? what not, that may make her beloued?'[8] Of course the two passages are not exactly comparable – Dekker's Cynthia is much more pointedly Elizabeth than Jonson's; both descriptions are further complicated by their setting in dramatic dialogue; and yet the first description of Cynthia's court in Jonson's play is quite a dismissive one. There is even a whiff of *lèse-majesté* about the Prologue which succeeds it, which starts:

> IF gratious silence, sweete Attention,
> Quick sight, and quicker apprehension,
> (The lights of iudgments throne) shine any wher;
> Our doubtful author hopes, this is their Sphaere.
>
> (B1v)

Jonson, in effect, displaces on to the theatre audience a description one might expect applied to a court, as representing the acme of intelligence and culture 'any wher'. The effect is compounded by the word 'throne', which, although perfectly capable of purely metaphorical application, might again remind spectators of monarchy. In Q this impression is reinforced by Jonson's enigmatic title-page motto: *Quod non dant Proceres, dabit Histrio*, 'What princes will not give, the actor will' (A1r).

If the Prologue offers a potentially hostile perspective on Cynthia's court *qua* court, then the first scene of the play offers a potentially hostile perspective on Cynthia *qua* goddess. The opening exchanges of Cupid (here a mischievous god of lust) and Mercury (an inveterate pickpocket) draw on Lucian's *Dialogues of the Gods* to outline a picture of an Olympus full of drinking, cushion-fights, and adultery.[9] Conversely, the second scene of the play, in blank verse, and set beside a spring in the forest of Gargaphie, stresses the grandeur and the dangerous power of the immortals, but even here the moral perspective is troubled. The nymph Echo has spent three thousand years living without a body, paying for having incurred '*Iunoes* spite', a spite which even Jove seems scared of. Different versions of the Echo story current in the Renaissance explained her crime in different ways. According to Ovid, she was an attendant of Juno, who by holding her mistress in conversation helped to conceal Jove's infidelities from her, but other versions of the story held that her crime lay in repeating unpalatable truths about the gods. Renaissance interpretations of Echo, therefore, tended to moralise her as an example of empty flattery, of indiscreet talkativeness, or even of true fame.[10] In Jonson's version Echo's 'libertie of tongue' seems to be her most conspicuous, and blameworthy, characteristic.[11]

Echo, then, was punished directly by Juno. While no god was comparably directly responsible for the fate of her beloved Narcissus, turned into a flower there by his own self-love, Echo places the blame for this squarely on the deities: 'Why did the Gods giue thee a heauenly forme, / And earthy thoughtes to make thee proude of it?' (B3v). And Echo describes the fate of Actaeon, who also perished in the same location: 'Here young Acteon fell, pursu'd, and torne / By Cynthias wrath (more egar then his houndes;)' (B4r). Actaeon is, like Echo, a figure from Ovid's *Metamorphoses* and Ovid's text is ambiguous about whether Actaeon entirely deserves such a terrible punishment for a 'crime' he committed almost accidentally. Nor did that debate stop with Ovid, as Sarah Annes Brown has documented: Renaissance commentators on the passage frequently struggled with the morality of the episode.[12]

Also on stage here, and perhaps throughout the play, and explicitly linked to Actaeon by Echo is what remains of another victim of Cynthia's wrath, Niobe, transformed into a weeping stone. Niobe's crime was to boast about her fourteen children: her punishment, in the form of the slaughter of all fourteen by Apollo and Cynthia, followed by her own petrification, seems grotesquely to exceed the crime. Even worse from the point of view of Cynthia's public relations, the incident appears to indicate that Cynthia has something of a track record of extreme punishment. Mercury, of course, rejects Echo's complaints:

> Stint thy babling tongue;
> Fond Echo, thou prophanst the grace is done thee:
> So idle worldlings (meerely made of voyce:)
> Censure the powers aboue them.

> (B4v)

In part this is a mainstream Renaissance allegorisation of Echo, as Joseph Loewenstein has explored. But it is also awkward, in that Echo is only 'merely made of voice' because Juno has put her in that position, depriving her of a body, as we are reminded at the start of the scene. Even Mercury's own authority to deliver these lines is undercut by the Lucianic satire of the previous scene, which has shown himself and the other 'powers aboue' in a very poor light.'Grace' being such a theologically loaded word in the period, it is also striking how miserly Jove's grace is: not a permanent redemption or rescue, but a momentary and almost surreptitious respite from the punishment which has already lasted three thousand years and which has no end in sight.[13] It is not merely that Jonson is using figures — Actaeon and Echo — who are from morally ambiguous stories, but, in the way that the scene is constructed, Jonson stacks the deck against the dignity of immortals in general, and in particular against Cynthia, the killer of Actaeon and the destroyer of Niobe.

Even when the action switches to Cynthia's court, that court does not come out of the play well. The 'mother of the maids', in charge of the welfare of the young female courtiers, is Moria, whose name and whose actions mark her out as an allegorical representation of Folly. She leads a group of 'nymphs' (an ambiguous word which connotes both an immortal spirit from classical mythology and a young court beauty, and thus skilfully elides the immortal world with that of the court) who include allegorical representations of Self-Love, Fantasticness, Money, and Laughter.[14] Their male counterparts, whose names allegorise the traits of being Pleasure-loving (Hedon), Impudent (Anaides), Beyond Recovery (Asotus) and Formless (Amorphus), are no better.

This arrangement of eight bad courtiers is balanced, with mathematical evenness, by eight good courtiers, but we see very little of them. Criticus, for instance, is a virtuous male courtier, and he alludes on one occasion to three of his friends ('good *Chrestus, / Euthus,* or *Phronimus*', Frv) whose censure he would respect, in contrast to that of Hedon and Anaides. These friends' names allegorise, respectively, Honest, Straightforward, and Sensible: however, we do not hear any more of them in the play. Arete, although despised by the other court ladies, seems to be of a higher status than they are, as is indicated in an exchange between Cupid and Mercury (now disguised as pages) concerning Moria's nymphs:

> MER. But are these (*Cupid*) the starres of *Cynthias* Court? doe these Nymphs
>   attend vpon *Diana*?
> CUP. They are in her Court (*Mercury*) but not as Starres; these neuer come in
>   the presence of *Cynthia*: the Nimphes that make her traine, are the diuine
>   *Arete, Timae, Phronesis, Thauma,* and others of that high sort. These are
>   priuately brought in by *Moria* in this licencious time, against her knowledge;
>   and (like so many *Meteors*) will vanish when shee appeares.[15]

Timē (Honour), Phronesis (Thinking), and Thauma (Wonder) do indeed appear in the play in Act V, as mute attendants on Cynthia herself. Mercury's explanation exculpates Cynthia by alleging her ignorance of what is happening at her court, although in a sense that fact is double-edged, since it could also be argued that it shows that Cynthia is imperfectly policing her own court. What is less arguable, though, is that Jonson portrays the court as possessing an almost Manichean symmetry between admirable and foolish courtiers, and that the foolish courtiers get far more exposure in the play than the admirable ones.

If one scene illustrates the tension between the panegyric and the critical views of Cynthia's court in the play, it is Act III, scene 4. There Criticus offers a long and searching account of the follies and misbehaviour to be seen at 'The strangest pageant,

fashioned like a court', an account which finishes by comparing the foolish courtiers'
activities to insubstantial spiders' webs:

> such *Cob-web* stuffe,
> As would enforce the commonst sence abhorre.
> Th' *Arachnean* workers.
> A R E. Patience *Criticus*.
> This knot of Spiders will be soone dissolu'd,
> And all their webbes swept out of *Cynthias* Court,
> When once her glorious Deity appeares,
> And but presents it selfe in her full light.
>
> (F3r)

Arete instead asks Criticus to spend time with her 'In contemplation of our
Goddesse name', waiting for that moment. There is clearly a tension between the
current corruption of the court, and the promised reformation. But what is also
striking here is the double reference to spiders, and the clumsy periphrasis of
'*Arachnean* workers'. The effect of this is to draw attention to the story of Arachne,
whose story immediately precedes that of Niobe in Book VI of Ovid's *Metamorphoses*,
and who provides yet another example, to set beside those of Niobe, Actaeon, and
Echo, of the gods losing their tempers. Arachne, in Ovid, finds herself challenged
to a weaving contest by the goddess Pallas in which, if the goddess can show better
workmanship, she will have the right to determine Arachne's fate. In the contest
both weavers make tapestries depicting scenes from mythology in which the Gods
use their terrible powers against mortals. Arachne does not lose the weaving contest
– indeed, even the goddess envies her workmanship – but Pallas is so embarrassed
by the stories of divine immorality depicted in Arachne's tapestry that she decides
to destroy her anyway, beating her over the head with a weaver's shuttle, watching
her hang herself, and then transforming her into a spider.[16] Thus the episode of Ovid
concerning Arachne is not merely a narrative about the fickleness and dangerousness
of the gods, in which they are seen as not even keeping their own promises, but a
meta-narrative about the dangers of even discussing those stories in the presence
of the gods. This scene of Jonson's most Ovidian play goes out of its way to allude
to this Ovidian story about the dangerousness of even telling the truth. Indeed, in
a sense such a reading is applicable to the other three victims highlighted by the
play. Some versions of Echo's story indicate that her crime was unwise repetition
of unpalatable truths; Niobe's statement about having more children than Leto was
not, at the moment it was made, untrue, merely unwise: and Actaeon's crime,
comparably, was merely to see something clearly that he ought not to have seen.
All of these four stories are about knowledge of unpalatable truths, and about the
dangers of even knowing them.

Cynthia's own justification, at the end of the play, of her actions towards Niobe and Actaeon stresses that their crimes could almost be considered thoughtcrimes, a form of inappropriate hubris:

> For so *Actaeon* by presuming farre,
> Did (to our griefe) incurre a fatall doome;
> And so, swolne *Niobe* (comparing more
> Then he presum'd) was *trophaeed* into stone.
> But are we therefore iudged too extreame?
> Seemes it no Crime to enter sacred Bowers,
> And hallowed Places with impure aspect
> Most lewdly to pollute? Seemes it no crime,
> To braue a Deity? let Mortalls learne
> To make Religion of offending Heauen;
> And not at all to censure powers diuine:
> To Men, this *Argument* should stand for firme,
> "A Goddesse did it; therefore it was good:
> "We are not cruell, nor delight in blood.

> > (L3r–L3v)

Uneasily defensive (and compared by Sarah Annes Brown to Milton's God) Cynthia avoids taking grammatical agency for the destruction of either Actaeon or Niobe. On the wider issue, she forecloses all discussion: men are 'not at all to censure' powers divine – a phrasing which could cover both goddesses and queens – and anyone doubting whether that proposition is valid is committing a crime even in doubting it. And yet even that proposition is presented in a form which seems to make it deliberately hard to swallow: Cynthia is a huntress, so that she does in a literal-minded sense delight in bloodshed. And her last lines can, in effect, be paraphrased as a tautology: 'I am not violent, and, if you say I am, I will kill you.'

As for her exposure and punishment, in Act V, of the fools, this too is problematic. Arete, again, appears to rule out any 'subversive' reading of Cynthia, warning Criticus in advance that Cynthia's appearance that evening

> is not done (my *Criticus*) without
> Particular knowledge of the Goddesse minde;
> Who (holding true intelligence, what Follyes
> Had crept into her *Pallace*) she resolu'd,
> Of sports, and Triumphs; vnder that pretext,
> To haue them muster in their Pompe and Fulnesse:
> That so she might more strictly, and to roote,
> Effect the Reformation she intends.

> > (I4v–K1r)

A reading 'against the grain' of this speech can find problems in the model it proposes, in which Cynthia is cast almost as a precursor of Adam Overdo. We are told that the follies entered her palace before the time of revels, which sits uneasily with Cupid's earlier remark that they entered her palace during and as a result of the revels. The revels were explicitly supposed to be a demonstration of Cynthia's lack of 'austerity', so that there is something unsporting about using them as a means of carrying out reformation 'strictly, and to roote'. Cynthia is, in effect, acting as an *agent provocateur*. And this speech can also be carried forward to compromise Cynthia when she claims surprise at the discovery of the follies in her midst. Arete's speech here makes that behaviour disingenuous, at least, and opens the way for a reading of Cynthia not so much in terms of Adam Overdo as in terms of the calculatedly surprised Tiberius of Jonson's *Sejanus*.

The word 'unsporting' perhaps seems anachronistic here: we can't expect Renaissance goddesses to have a sense of fair play. And yet this is precisely what Cynthia is asked to have, and using a metaphor from hunting, in 'Queen and Huntress', the great lyric which sets the scene for the final act, well described by Loewenstein as enacting 'the play's most grave transition ... a shift into the lyrical mode'.[17]

> *Queene and Huntresse*, chaste, and fayre,
> Now the *Sunne* is layde to sleepe,
> Seated, in thy siluer Chayre,
> State in wonted maner keepe:
> *Hesperus* intreats thy light,
> Goddesse excellently bright.
>
> Earth, let not thy enuious shade
> Dare it selfe to interpose;
> *Cynthias* shining Orbe was made
> Heauen to cleare, when day did close:
> Blesse vs then with wished sight,
> Goddesse excellently bright.
>
> Lay thy Bowe of Pearle apart.
> And thy Christall-shining Quiuer;
> Giue vnto the flying Hart,
> Space to breath, how short soeuer.
> Thou, that makst a day of night,
> Goddesse excellently Bright.

(K1v)

'Giue vnto the flying Hart, / Space to breath'; the lyric asks Cynthia to show some respite, and the irony of her turning her own revels into an opportunity for 'reformation' is precisely that it does not respect the space she has herself allotted to respite and holiday. One of the tenets of New Historicist criticism of Renaissance drama has been that licensed misrule can in itself be read as an instrument of the dominant authority, but Cynthia does not even honour her own licensing of that misrule, something which is made much more pointed by this lyric's direct appeal to her, at this moment in the play, to allow moments when her subjects can be off duty.

'Queen and Huntress' is also at the centre of the play's allusions to Essex, since there are a series of similarities between Essex and Actaeon. Like Actaeon, Essex was an active young man who offended a powerful woman; like him, part of his crime was to 'enter sacred Bowers', in that Essex had famously and disastrously stormed into Elizabeth's bedchamber on his return from Ireland in September 1599, surprising her before she was fully ready to be seen. One can certainly show that Jonson may at this date have been close to several members of the Essex circle. For instance, his first *Ode*, which also addresses a man facing misfortunes who is counselled to maintain his poise and loyalty until Cynthia intervenes to improve things, was composed at around the same date as *Cynthia's Revels*. There is uncertainty about whether its original dedicatee was Essex himself (as argued by Mark Bland), or, as is more usually thought, his ally James, Earl of Desmond: but it locates Jonson in these circles at this date and using this sort of imagery to them.[18] Furthermore, as Hester Lees-Jeffries notes, Hesperus, who sings 'Queen and Huntress', is a mythological figure with particular resonances of Essex, being used to figure him in, for instance, Spenser's *Prothalamion*.[19] If one were looking to construct a reading of *Cynthia's Revels* as a play from before Essex's execution, this song's plea for mercy is the best evidence available.

And yet what is striking here is just how oblique the references to Essex are. For Actaeon, within the play, it is clearly too late: he has already been torn to pieces, and is finished. There is no sense that Actaeon might be able to come back from his disgrace. The 'flying hart'/heart is a symbol applicable to any subject under Cynthia's power as well as to a specific nobleman, and there is no possibility of talking about Essex's potential return to power. Even if one were to take it as read that *Cynthia's Revels* was written by an Essex apologist, then one could hardly say it was written by an Essex apologist who expected him to be a force in the land in the near future.

None of this, then, helps with the dating issue, because none of it establishes whether Essex is dead or merely terminally disgraced, and one of the play's most striking qualities is its detachment from the detail of that matter. Nor can one sustain a reading of the play unambiguously hostile to Cynthia/Elizabeth and pro-Essex, since the situation is analogous to that of criticism of *Paradise Lost*. One can draw attention (as this chapter has done) to apparent flaws in the omnipotence of Cynthia, and to apparent cruelties resulting from lesser beings' inability to match Cynthia, and moments when the narratorial voice seems implicitly to criticise Cynthia, but all this still runs up against the argument that Cynthia is a god, and we are not, and therefore we have no right to criticise – very much the argument that Jonson puts into the mouth of Cynthia herself in the passage quoted above. Ultimately, allegory proves to be only a blunt tool in the attempt to derive from the play a consistent position on the question of Elizabeth's dealings with her inferiors in late Elizabethan England.

There is a similar inevitable ambiguity about the imagery of waxing and waning associated with the phases of the moon. This is clearly a dangerous analogy to apply in connection with a monarch, but Jonson's play contains the obviously subversive possibilities by insisting on the shortsightedness of not seeing the perpetual renewal of the cycle. Only when Cynthia describes Elizabeth directly, whose glory, in a pregnant phrase, 'seems ignorant of what it is to wane' (K4r), does this analogy start to become dangerous.

But one note is sounded, I think, quite clearly and harshly in *Cynthia's Revels*, for anyone who cares to listen, and it is a note which gets round the problem of mortals' insufficiency discussed above by comparing Cynthia not against mortals but against another god, and which subverts the perpetual renewal of the monthly cycle by thinking on a timescale of hours rather than weeks. In this play the really subversive allusions are not to Cynthia's waning – that is almost a red herring – but to her setting. Apollo is named in passing within fifteen lines of the start of the play proper, and the play frequently alludes to him and to his relationship to Cynthia. It is Apollo to whom Criticus prays for poetic inspiration, as is appropriate. The masque that Criticus writes, although addressed to Cynthia, comes close to calling her a temporary substitute for her brother: 'Sister of Phoebus to whose bright Orbe we owe, that we not complaine of his Absence' (L1r). Even 'Queen and Huntress' praises her as a temporary stand-in for the sleeping sun, and, in the phrase 'thou that mak'st a day of night', praises Cynthia by saying that her light is almost, but not quite, that of the day. The point about revels is that they are only temporary, and, by imaging Cynthia's court in terms of a temporary nocturnal festival, Jonson's play is casting its eyes forward to a time when, to borrow a phrase from his colleague Shakespeare, 'our revels now are ended'.

The folio preface, of course, makes explicit one possible allegorisation of this. Dedicating the play to the court in 1616, Jonson says the honest courtier possesses

> a mind, shining through any sute, which needs no false light, either of riches, or honors to help it. Such shalt thou find some here, even in the raigne of CYNTHIA (a CRITES and an ARETE.) Now, under thy PHOEBVS, it will be thy prouince to make more …[20]

The 'days' of the Jacobean court are contrasted with the 'nights' of Elizabeth's. But the idea of James as a sun god was present from the very start of James's reign: Jonson's poem *A Panegyre*, written in 1603, imagines the new king casting 'a thousand radiant lights' in all directions.[21] The material about Essex is in some ways a distraction from the really politically unsettling content of *Cynthia's Revels*, namely that it starts to look to a world after the queen.

This is a long way from the long-held view of the play as almost nauseating flattery of Elizabeth – so far, indeed, that we should stop and review the argument. I am arguing, then, that *Cynthia's Revels* does indeed contain panegyric of the queen, but that this praise is tempered not so much by the material about Essex as by the use of the figure of Cynthia herself, and the inherent idea of her temporariness as a substitute for true day, to perform, in a sense, the old crime of imagining the queen's death. What gives this project its urgency, and makes the praise particularly compromised, is this play's use of figures from Ovidian myth — Echo, Actaeon, Niobe, Arachne — whose fates emphasise the danger of even having that momentary imagination of the limitations of a Cynthia. For Jonson, in this play, Ovidian myth is a vehicle for articulating concerns about the unaccountability of monarchy, and the relationship between power and justice: and Elizabeth's own iconography can be used as a way of starting to imagine and negotiate politics after she is gone.

Notes

1. This chapter arises out of my collaboration with Eric Rasmussen on an edition of *Cynthia's Revels* for the forthcoming *Cambridge Works of Ben Jonson*, under the general editorship of David Bevington, Martin Butler, and Ian Donaldson. I thank all three of the general editors for their generous, scholarly help; Donald F. Bailey, for close and careful reading of the material; and Eric Rasmussen, since working with him has been both a pleasure and an education. This chapter, however, should not be taken as representing the views of any of these other scholars.

2. Philippa Berry, *Of Chastity and Power: Elizabethan Literature and the Unmarried Queen* (London: Routledge, 1989); Helen Hackett, *Virgin Mother, Maiden Queen: Elizabeth I and the Cult of the Virgin Mary* (Houndmills: Macmillan, 1995).

3. Ben Jonson, *Ben Jonson*, ed. C.H. Herford, P. Simpson and E. Simpson, 11 vols (Oxford: Clarendon Press, 1925–1952), 4, henceforth H&S; the play is cited from Ben Jonson, *The fountaine of selfe-loue. Or Cynthias reuels* (London: Walter Burre, 1601); Henry De Vocht, *Comments on the Text of Ben Jonson's 'Cynthia's Revels': An Investigation into the Comparative Value of the 1601-Quarto and the 1616-Folio* (Louvain: Librairie Universitaire, 1950), provides a long and minutely detailed comparison of the texts, although not all of the conclusions drawn from the comparison are tenable; the best argument that the additions are very late is made by Ralph W. Berringer, 'Jonson's *Cynthia's Revels* and the War of the Theatres', *Philological Quarterly* 22 (1943), pp. 1–22.

4. A.C. Judson, ed., *Cynthia's Revels* (New York, 1912), Introduction, p. xxii.

5. Janet Clare, 'Jonson's Comical Satires and the Art of Courtly Compliment' in *Refashioning Ben Jonson: Gender, Politics and the Jonsonian Canon*, edited by Julie Sanders, with Kate Chedzgoy and S.J. Wiseman (London: Macmillan, 1998), pp. 28–47; see also Martin Butler, '"Servant, but not slave": Ben Jonson at the Stuart Court', *Proceedings of the British Academy* 90 (1995), pp. 65–93.

6. Paul E.J. Hammer, 'Devereux, Robert, Second Earl of Essex (1565–1601)', *Oxford Dictionary of National Biography*. Online: www.oxforddnb.com/view/article/7565

7. Judson, ed., *Cynthia's Revels*, Introduction, pp. xxix–xxxi; H&S 1, pp. 394–396, do not accept the argument that it necessarily refers to Essex's death.

8. Thomas Dekker, *The Pleasant Comedie of Old Fortunatus* (London, 1600), A1v.

9. See Douglas J.M. Duncan, *Ben Jonson and the Lucianic Tradition* (Cambridge: Cambridge University Press, 1979).

10. Ovid, *Metamorphoses*, 3.337; Ernest W. Talbert, 'The Classical Mythology and the Structure of "Cynthia's Revels"', *Philological Quarterly* 22 (1943), pp. 193–210; Joseph Loewenstein,

Responsive Readings: Versions of Echo in Pastoral, Epic, and the Jonsonian Masque (New Haven: Yale University Press, 1984); see also Robert Wiltenburg, *Ben Jonson and Self-Love: The Subtlest Maze of All* (Columbia: University of Missouri Press, 1990).

11. On the 'system of restraint' implied by this phrase see Loewenstein, *Responsive Readings*, p. 174; again, Dekker's *Old Fortunatus* is an interesting touchstone: it too features Echo, but is much less interested in her backstory than in her use as a stage device.

12. Sarah Annes Brown, 'Arachne's Web: Intertextual Mythography and the Renaissance Actaeon', in *The Renaissance Computer: Knowledge Technology in the First Age of Print*, edited by Neil Rhodes and Jonathan Sawday (London: Routledge, 2000), pp. 120–134. Brown's excellent account draws attention to the symbolic potency of Arachne, but does not specifically mention the allusion to her in *Cynthia's Revels*; *Latin Commentaries on Ovid from the Renaissance*, edited and translated by Ann Moss (Signal Mountain, TN: Summertown, 1998); on Actaeon in particular see Leonard Barkan, 'Diana and Actaeon: The Myth as Synthesis', *English Literary Renaissance* 10 (1980), pp. 317–359.

13. 'Grace' is a word which comes back frequently in the play to describe both frivolous courtliness and Cynthia's favour of Criticus (e.g., K4v): it is coloured by this strikingly weak use of it early on.

14. *OED*, nymph *n.*¹ 1, 2.

15. E3r; this conflicts with the passage from the Induction quoted above, in which Arete's status in the court appears to be far lower.

16. See Brown, 'Arachne's Web'.

17. Loewenstein, *Responsive Readings*, p. 87; for an antidote to politicised reading of the lyric see Phyllis Rackin, 'Poetry Without Paradox: Jonson's "Hymne" to Cynthia', *Criticism* 4 (1962), pp. 186–96; the *Early English Books Online* transcription of Q reads, not 'Christall-shining' but 'Christ all-shining', and, while this is probably an erroneous reading of how the words are laid out, it draws attention to a possible overtone. Even an oblique reference to 'Christ' would add a new layer of complexity to the play's pagan world and to the idea of forgiveness adumbrated in the lyric.

18. Mark Bland, '"As Far from All Reuolt": Sir John Salusbury, Christ Church MS 184, and Ben Jonson's First Ode', *English Manuscript Studies* 8 (2000), pp. 43–78; Tom Cain, '"Satyres, that Girde and Fart at the Time": *Poetaster* and the Essex rebellion', in Sanders, Chedzgoy and Wiseman, eds, *Refashioning Ben Jonson*, pp. 48–70, explores Jonson's links with the Essex circles, and also argues that *Poetaster* is concerned with issues of free speech and free thought not dissimilar to those which are explored here with reference to *Cynthia's Revels*.

19. Hester Lees-Jeffries, 'A New Allusion by Jonson to Spenser and Essex?', *Notes & Queries* 50 (2003), pp. 63–65.

20. H&S, 4, p. 33; this also appropriates and redeploys the light imagery of Q studied by Carl F. Zender, 'The Unveiling of the Goddess in *Cynthia's Revels*', *Journal of English and Germanic Philology* 77 (1978), pp. 37–52.

21. H&S, 7, p. 113.

Part IV

Coda: Elizabeth's afterlife

10

'Turn thy Tombe into a Throne':[1] Elizabeth I's death rehearsal

Scott L. Newstok

> At the burial of an epoch
> no psalm is heard at the tomb.[2]
>
> (Anna Akhmatova)

Scholars have long debated just precisely when Elizabeth I commenced her iconographical self-presentation as a Virgin Queen; recent criticism has frequently called for 'renewed discussion' of the (purportedly mistaken) 'popular assumption' that such a cult was established early in her reign.[3] Arguments about this matter can oscillate between polarised terms — virginal iconography was early / it was late; she never intended to get married / she actually did; she invoked virginity / she invoked marriage to the state. Yet while the welcome re-examination of the iconographical representations of Elizabeth reminds us that familiar images of virginal figures were not fully employed until the later 1570s, her *initial* figuration of her virginal intentions in her first speech to Parliament merits further consideration. This speech, which ended with a coy but forceful epitaphic gesture, effectively inaugurated a pattern of subsequent manifestations as Diana, Cynthia, Gloriana, and the Virgin Mary. My analysis focuses on this gesture as a rhetorical and performative move. By examining this self-declared (albeit never inscribed) tombstone inscription in light of other statements made by Queen Elizabeth I throughout her life (as well as in conjunction with the contemporary discourse surrounding epitaphs), we can more fully appreciate the ambivalent rhetorical impact of her declaration. This chapter thus explores the ways in which an epitaph might unexpectedly mark the beginning, and not only the termination, of a sovereign's reign. Playing out this epitaphic tension in the public sphere was somewhat risky, perhaps even treasonous. Towards the end of the chapter, I toy with a query: by invoking the iconography of epitaphic virginity, was Elizabeth somehow allowing others to imagine the iconography of her own mortality? Such an inauguration, as it were, might also entail consequences for the political theology of envisioning the death of the sovereign.

Once and future kings

What's the first 'Tudor' epitaph? With a little ingenuity, we might arguably unearth it in Sir Thomas Malory's account of *Le Morte Darthur*, published by Caxton just weeks before the Battle of Bosworth, and only months before the coronation of Henry VII, who notably annexed the figure of Arthur through implied Welsh filiations. When Malory closes his narration of King Arthur's death (Figure 14), he assiduously acknowledges the gaps in the biographical record, admitting, for instance, that 'Thus of Arthur I fynde neuer more wryton in bookes that ben auctorysed, nor more of the veray certente of his deth herde I neuer redde ... More of the deth of Kyng Arthur coude I neuer fynde'.[4] These qualifications precede the story he deems most trustworthy, of the three queens bringing Arthur to his grave. Immediately following this description of an interment, however, Malory admits a conflicting story:

> Yet somme men say in many partyes of Englond that Kynge Arthur is nat deed, But had by the wylle of our Lord Ihesu into another place. And men say that he shal com ageyn, and he shal wynne the Holy Cross. I wyl not say that it shal be so, but rather I wyl sey here in thys world he chaunged his lyf.

While Malory certainly hedges his assertions through the entire *Morte Darthur*, he displays a particular ambivalence here, not only presenting differing accounts but also inserting his own judgement, which manages to deflect the contradictions by redirecting attention to what Arthur's life was like 'in thys world'. Despite this redirection, however, Malory still returns to give the last word to those who 'say that he shal come ageyn', for 'many men say that there is wryton vpon his tombe this vers: HIC JACET ARTHURUS, REX QUONDAM REXQUE FUTURUS' – *Here lies Arthur, once and future king*. While there remains some debate as to whether or not Malory was the first to coin this epitaph,[5] it clearly became an invariable element of subsequent lore, with the phrase serving as a signature epithet for Arthur's character.

The haunting quality of this epitaph emerges from multiple elements. Twentieth-century editions by Spisak (cited above) and Vinaver, among others, offer us the typographical assurance of offset, capitalised Latin verse. The Caxton edition has a paraph to indicate a shift in the text; and the Winchester manuscript even rubricates the epitaph – significantly, the only inscription (and the final one, at that) written in red ink throughout the entire text.[6]

These quasi-marmoreal gestures somewhat mitigate the uncertainty expressed in the contradictory versions of Arthur's death – Malory can have it both ways, in effect. At the same time, the meaning of the epitaph itself oddly reinforces the ambiguity of the sources, for we do not know where 'HIC' is, nor do we know when 'FUTURUS' will be. Neither the body nor the date is located, and the epitaph thus fails in fulfilling these basic declarative functions. Yet perhaps in this failure lies its success – death does not seem to have triumphed over the body of the king, even without the mediation of Christ.[7] This borders on blasphemy, for presumably only the intervention of the once-and-future-Saviour could redeem even a ruler from mortality. Much the same sentiment is expressed in a seventeenth-century epitaph on King James:

> We justly, when a meaner subject dies,
> Begin his Epitaph with, Here he lyes.
> But when a King, whose memory remains
> Triumphant over death; with, here he reigns:[8]

Again, it is noteworthy that the language of 'reign[ing]' over death, usually ascribed to Christ, is here applied in commendation of the king's enduring authority. The death of the sovereign understandably creates great anxiety in the body of the nation, for at such moments the tenuous nature of succession becomes most apparent; thus the *topos* of a triumph over mortality serves to reassure a distressed nation.

The reaffirmation of an extended line of kings and queens can likewise provide some reassurance that the throne will not turn into a tomb. Camden's *The Remains Concerning Britain* (1605–1623) provides a good example of this practice. While he generally seeks to gather and categorise antiquarian material ('rude rubble and out-cast rubbish') in order 'to praise Britaine' as a long-enduring state, we sense a yearning for political continuity most overtly the final section of the volume (on 'Epitaphes'), which devotes many pages to reciting and examining royal funereal inscriptions in some detail, from those of Arthur through 'the Princes of our time'.[9] For James's mother Mary and his son Henry, two and one epitaphs are given, respectively. But the greatest attention is devoted to Elizabeth, to whom are devoted not only five separate epitaphs but also a laudatory paragraph of Camden's own composition, effectively another remembrance of her life. The section on 'Epitaphes' can be read as a kind of textual burial plot for illustrous rulers, stretching from distant Arthur to Elizabeth of recent memory, thereby confirming the nation's endurance as a polity.

One of the five poems which he cites for the queen reads:

> Weepe greatest Isle, and for thy mistresses death
> Swim in a double sea of brackish water:
> Weepe little world for great Elizabeth.
> Daughter of warre, for Mars himself begat her.
> Mother of peace; for shee brought forth the later.
> She was and is, what can there more be said?
> On earth the chief, in heaven the second Maide.[10]

The first 'Maide', of course, is the Virgin Mary, whose name was synonymous with 'maid' since at least the twelfth century (an identification that perhaps coincided with the contraction of the word itself from 'maiden').

As in Arthur's epitaph, we are vaguely reassured that Elizabeth continues to live on elsewhere, even if a return is not promised for her. This epitaph resonates suggestively with another printed only a few pages later in Camden, among the 'few conceited, merry, and laughing Epitaphes' provided to offer relief from the seriousness of his enterprise. The poem is addressed to a virgin who has not made much of time:

> Here lies, the Lord have mercy upon her,
> One of her Majesties maides of honour:
> Shee was both young, slender, and pretty,
> Shee died a maide, the more the pitty.[11]

These two poems quickly give a sense of the complex and ambivalent response to the queen's virginity – on the one hand, a fairly impermeable doctrine that dying a virgin was a 'pitty', for a whole host of reasons (economic, social, sexual – crudely, the 'maid' wasn't 'made'); and on the other hand, the apotheosis of Elizabeth as being a near equal to that other Virgin Queen, Mary, the Mother of God. Elizabeth foregrounded her own virginity by declaring her dedication to it early in her political career, through an epitaph she envisioned for herself.

Let no man write my epitaph

Many today would concur with the inclination that writing your own epitaph entails an act of hubris, since such an action presumes that you could fully anticipate your own posterity. There is the suspicion that finalising the epitaph would in turn finalise the life, or that writing your own epitaph means that, in some respects, you are already dead to the world. Presumably there should be a degree of self-evidence in your characterisation that would not require your shaping it for others – in other words, writing your own epitaph would ideally be superfluous, in that your life should naturally express the intentions that you had for it. This is one of the reasons that Milton so scornfully mocks Charles I's 'self-portrait' in *Eikon Basilike* – it too presumptuously gives itself its own title: 'He who writes himself *Martyr* by his own inscription, is like an ill Painter, who, by writing on the shapeless Picture which he hath drawn, is fain to tell passengers what shape it is.'[12] Despite all of these reasonable apprehensions about epitaphic self-declaration, the question of 'what would you like your epitaph to be' still remains prevalent, with self-epitaphing an almost commonplace event in corporate circles – some consulting firms require that employees write their own epitaphs, describing themselves both as they are and as they would like themselves to be remembered, in a particularly macabre but apparently effective attempt to encourage goal-setting. The trick about such epitaphic mind-games is that they force you to create a statement of retrospective *fact*, which thereby helps *consolidate* the very state purportedly *described*.

This peculiar manner of self-projection became prevalent in the Elizabethan period, partly in response to the Protestant reformations (often, destructions) of Catholic memorial practices for the dead. Indeed, Elizabeth herself appears to have been the first major public figure in England to declare this kind of anticipatory retrospection. To be sure, occasional instances of living-subject epitaphs can be found in classical literature — for instance, Trimalchio's elaborate funeral performance in the *Satyricon*.[13] And in sixteenth-century wills, an extraordinarily small percentage of testators provide explicit instructions for their tombstone inscriptions. One exceptional set of instructions reads as follows (Figure 15):

> And I will there a large marble stone to be laid over me with my arms engraved upon the same and under them this epitaph which followeth and also what day and year I died:

[The acrostic letters are rotated 90° clockwise down the left side]

'J   John Brooke of the parish of Ash
O   Only he is now gone:
H   His days are past, his corpse is laid
N   Now under this marble stone.
B   Brookstreet he was the honour of
R   Robbed now it is of name
O   Only because he had no seed
O   Or child to have the same.
K   Knowing that all must pass away
E   Even when God will none can deny.
     He passed to God in the year of grace
     A thousand five hundred   it was
     The   day of   I tell you plain
     The   year of Elizabeth's reign.'

And I will that the same stone thus engraved to be laid over me by my executrix within two years next after my decease or else she to forfeit twenty pounds to the churchwardens of Ash.[14]

The confidence in this anticipation is remarkable, not only for Brooke's presumption that he would die in the sixteenth century but also for his certainty that Elizabeth would still be ruling. Moreover, behind the hint of this promise ('I will') we sense the coercion of a threat from beyond the grave (the financial forfeiture). The circumstances of a will and testament, however, are comparatively confined in their publicity when contrasted to a twenty-five-year-old queen, newly crowned, announcing her epitaph in her first address to Parliament. This was an exceptionally forceful enunciation which, to my knowledge, was without political precedent. Yet both declarations have in common the secular anxiety of the heirless memorial: as Gittings speculates on the instructions from Brooke, perhaps 'the failure to leave heirs, the traditional way

to keep one's memory alive, prompted him to be so particular about his memorial'
— down to the detail of an acrostic to perpetuate the name.[15]

May be sufficient

Upon Elizabeth's accession to the throne, Parliament was preoccupied with her status
as a female ruler – this, in itself, was an unsettling prospect for them, compounded
by the fact that she was unmarried, with no children. With the previous century's
wars of succession remaining an uncomfortably close memory, and with Henry VIII's
will effectively establishing conditions for competing claims to the crown,[16] they
were understandably concerned with her intentions. The first petition the House of
Commons made to her, hardly two weeks after her coronation in January, respectfully
yet insistently enjoined her to consider marriage. In her response she gave them 'hartie
thankes for the good zeale and loving care yow seme to have, as well towardes me
as to the whole state of your countrie'.[17] She reminded them that she had long been
determined to remain single:

> from my yeares of understanding, syth I first had consideration of my self to be
> borne a servitor of almightie God, I happelie chose this kynde of life in which I
> yet lyve ... so constant have I allwayes contynued in this determynacion ... that at
> this daie I stand free from anie other meaninge ...

She affirmed that even if she were to get married some day,

> ye may well assure your selves my meaninge is not to do or determyne anie
> thinge wherwith the realme may or shall have iuste cause to be discontented. And
> therefore put that cleane out of your heades. For I assure you ... I will never in
> that matter conclud any thing that shallbe preiudiciall to the realme, ffor the weale,
> good and safetie wherof I will never shune to spend my life.

After this she offered a vague reassurance that despite her 'mynde to lyve out of the
state of mariage ... the realme shall not remayne destitute of an heire that may be a
fitt governor'. Her response concluded with the statement: 'And in the end, this shalbe
for me sufficient, that a marble stone shall declare that a Queene, having raigned such
a tyme, lived and dyed a virgin.'[18]

Seven manuscript copies are still extant of the speech, most of which are, on
the whole, similar in meaning; it was soon printed in accounts of the early years of
her reign by chroniclers such as Grafton, Holinshed, Stow, and others (these are all
documented meticuously in Hartley's edition of Elizabeth's parliamentary speeches).
The only version which differs significantly from this main one was included by William
Camden in his *True and Royal History of the Famous Empress Elizabeth*, a Latin edition of
which was published in 1615 with an English translation in 1625. Her speech here is

shorter, and more histrionic – this is the source for the anecdote that she displayed her ring 'with which she was given in marriage and inaugurated to her kingdom in express and solemn terms', calling the 'whole kingdom of England' her 'husband'. Her epitaph is more explicitly presented as well:

> Lastly, this may be sufficient, both for my memorie, and honour of my Name, if when I have expired my last breath, this may be inscribed upon my Tombe:
> Here lyes interr'd ELIZABETH
> A virgin pure untill her Death.[19]

Camden claims to have had access to the papers of the Queen's adviser Sir William Cecil; it seems more likely that he embellished the presentation of the inscription somewhat, a half-century later. After all, he himself was a collector of epitaphs, and was eager to present a compelling narrative for James I, who had encouraged him to complete his biography of Elizabeth.

Some of the revisionist accounts of Elizabeth's reign have used the somewhat melodramatic quality of Camden's account to dismiss entirely her assertion of her intended virginity; John N. King, for instance, in an otherwise meticulously argued essay, criticises Camden's version for being not only 'hagiographical' but an outright 'falsification'.[20] Because he wishes to demonstrate that the cult of Elizabeth's virginity was not established until the 1580s, he even misconstrues the original documentary records, claiming that they never refer 'to a queenly vow to remain a chaste virgin', and therefore 'one may presume that this promise is a later addition' of Camden's.[21] To the contrary, every version of the speech ends with her epitaphic declaration of her virginity. Indeed, one contemporary manuscript even 'has this emphatic underscoring: "a quene havynge Reygnede suche a tyme lyvyde and dyede *a vyrgyne*"'.[22]

King seeks to correct those readers who uncritically accept Camden's version; as the editors of the recently published *Collected Works* of Elizabeth note, 'this is the form in which the speech has been best known to later ages, but it freely embroiders upon and condenses that speech as we have it from early sources'.[23] Some critics have gone so far as to take this as a draft version of her subsequent presentation to Parliament, claiming that it displays a canny revisionary process in which her 'generally negative' response became more 'conciliatory'.[24] This is unlikely, and few would concur with this position. Much more arguable is the inference, made by a number of critics in the last few decades, that this epitaph essentially established her cult of virginity – in other words, that, just by describing her tombstone, she immediately brought into being an entire symbolic apparatus (e.g. 'it became an emblem for her reign').[25] This moment undoubtedly would hold particular appeal for a New Historicist critic, since it appears to offer an anecdotally precise moment in which the 'poetic' or 'literary' or 'aesthetic' wells up within 'culture' or 'history' or 'politics'.[26] And yet one needs to take care not to equate flatly these distinct discourses – such conflation both over- and under-estimates the particular power of this moment. I am trying to present a more subtle articulation of how exactly her epitaph actually functioned, steering a middle course between the celebration of it by some critics and the denigration of it by others.

The epitaph is best read as a significant public enunciation of intentions that none the less was part of an evolving official relationship to 'virginity'. That is to say, this *was* a decisive moment, yet we should place it along a continuum. For one thing, this was not a *new* decision for Elizabeth, as she herself reminded her audience in that first parliamentary speech. She would recurrently emphasise the constancy of her path in private negotiations as well — for instance, in 1558 she rejected Queen Mary's enjoinder that she accept the proposal of a foreign prince, recalling that

> when Edward VI was King, she had asked permission 'to remayne in that estate I was, which of all others best lyked me or pleased me … I am even at this present of the same minde … I so well like this estate, as I perswade myself ther is not anie kynde of liffe comparable unto it … I assure you upon my truthe and fidelitie, and as God be mercifull unto me, I am not at this tyme otherways mynded, than I have declared unto you; no, though I were offered the greatest Prince in all Europe.' [27]

And shortly after her first speech to Parliament, the Spanish ambassador de Feria reported 'that she did not thinking of marrying' when he broached the subject with her.[28] None the less, there is some indication that her epitaphic self-stylisation as a Virgin Queen was beguiling to her first Parliament ('her contemporaries did not really understand such terminology')[29] — in effect, what she presented was beyond their conception. It did not fully assuage their concern about her single state, for they petitioned her to marry again in 1563, 1566, and 1576. Yet while 'iconographical variations of the classical protectress of virginity … were conspicuously absent from her early literary and artistic praise', she was already insinuating the themes which would emerge in her later aesthetic cults.[30] She began 'to exploit the coincidence of her birth date, 7 September, with the feast of the Nativity of the Virgin Mary and claim a symbolic kinship with the mother of Christ'.[31] We also know

> from the portrait and the miniature of Elizabeth in her coronation robes that Elizabeth wore her hair long and flowing for her coronation. This denoted the statue of virgin and bride, and therefore implied that the coronation was also Elizabeth's marriage to the nation.[32]

Already in the first year of her reign, a popular ballad by William Birch celebrated this conceptual union: early in the song, 'B' (Bessie / Elizabeth) states:

> Here is my hand,
> my dere lover Englande.

I am thine both with minde and hart.
For ever to endure,
thou maiest be sure.
Untill death us two depart.[33]

Towards the end, England addresses her as 'O swete virgin pure', with the wish that 'longe may ye endure / To reign over us in the lande'. It is clear that her self-identification as a Virgin Queen, while not impervious to challenge, none the less was already in progress from the commencement of her rule, beginning with this epitaph.

Death rehearsal

Throughout her reign one of Elizabeth's most successful political strategies was to promise deferred responses to insistent pressure from Parliament – as, for instance, in her 1563 answer to the second petition that she marry: 'I am determined in this so great and weighty a matter to defer mine answer till some other time because I will not in so deep a matter wade.'[34] The virginal epitaph, in many ways, resembles one of these deferred promises – postponed in the sense that it cannot be entirely fulfilled until the moment of her death, but none the less presenting an apparently binding statement of intent. This resembles Benjamin Franklin's well-known epitaph, in which he compares his printer's body to that of a book (Figure 16).

Yet Franklin was only twenty-one when he composed this for himself, years before he had his own printing shop; 'the epitaph may thus be said to announce not his death but his intentions for a career'.[35] Nor is this the epitaph found on his tombstone – he 'lies with his wife under a simple inscription in Christ Church, Philadelphia: "Benjamin and Deborah Franklin 1790"'.[36] Likewise, Elizabeth's final tomb inscriptions do not cite her self-declared virginity. (In contrast, many of the printed epitaphs for her do – e.g. Samuel Rowlands: 'Yea let the very Stones where shee shall lie, / Tell ages following, this of ours gone by: / Within our marble armes we do enclose / The virgin Queene'). Instead, James re-buried her with her half-sister Mary in 1606, a gesture designed to assert an equivalence that Elizabeth persistently refused.[37] The fact that Elizabeth's final tomb inscriptions do not cite her first epitaph (they do not even hint at the virginity invoked in it[38]) only serves to demonstrate that announcing your epitaph is not necessarily 'announcing your epitaph', but rather a rhetorical move with perception-shaping potential.

Elizabeth inaugurated, in effect, a new kind of speech act: the 'preliminary auto-epitaph'. It seems to have struck her as an effective move, for she concluded three other speeches within the next decade by anticipating her death.[39] For instance, in answer to the 1563 petition that she marry, she chided the Lords that their 'belief is … awry' if they doubted her 'determination' to remain single, but tried to console their fears about succession: 'I hope I shall die in quiet with *Nunc dimittis*, which cannot be without I see some glimpse of your following surely after my graved bones.'[40] (Another version reads 'gravestone' in place of 'graved bones').[41] Her two addresses to the Universities both end with similar references to her mortality. She even scorned those bishops who had tried to frighten Parliament with the spectre of her death, implying that everyone was already quite familiar with this prospect through her own public acknowledgement of it.[42]

I am cautious about invoking the concept of 'speech acts' here, in part because I am taking care not to say that *merely* by asserting her intended virginity did Elizabeth make it a cultural fact; this seems to have been the implication of some recent readers.[43] Her statement lacks the institutional or societal authority of J.L. Austin's more typical examples – including the notorious 'I do' of the wedding ceremony.[44] Nevertheless, in its *promissory* quality, her epitaph presented a forward-looking *rehearsal* of a role that, through iteration, came to be accepted as factual; she was rehearsing the mode of her sovereignty which was eventually taken to be self-evident. In this approach I am largely following the sociologist Grant McCracken in his modification of the more typically flat equivalence made by New Historicists between early modern 'performance' and politics. In particular, McCracken reads Elizabeth's coronation as akin to a wedding ceremony: 'Both wedding and passage look forward to a condition that may or may not realize the promises to which the parties involved have committed themselves.'[45] While Austin would disagree with the claim that the wedding ceremony does not enact the marriage, McCracken's re-evaluation is useful in that it acknowledges the similarities between the theatre and the throne without completely assimilating them.

Not long after her death a certain prophetic quality *did* come to be associated with Elizabeth's virginity, as when Cranmer blesses the baby Elizabeth in *Henry VIII* (or *All Is True*):

> She shall be, to the happiness of England,
> An agèd princess. Many days shall see her,
> And yet no day without a deed to crown it.
> Would I had known more. But she must die –
> She must, the saints must have her – yet a virgin,
> A most unspotted lily shall she pass
> To th' ground, and all the world shall mourn her.[46]

There is a similar moment in Thomas Heywood's *If You Know Not Me, You Know No Bodie: Or, The Troubles of Queene Elizabeth* (1605): 'Her own testimony during imprisonment takes on the quasi-prophetic cast that would become famous through Camden's *Annales*: "If I miscarry in this enterprise, and ask you why, / A Virgine and a Martyr both I dy".'[47] The epitaph itself also attained an enduring anecdotal currency; Francis Bacon cites it in his *Apophthegms* as she supposedly related to her ladies-in-waiting:

I am no lover of pompous title, but only desire that my name may be recorded in a line or two, which shall briefly express my name, my virginity, the years of my reign, the reformation of religion under it, and my preservation of peace.[48]

We might even read her declaration as a precursor to the many epitaphs to virgins which became a popular sub-genre in the seventeenth century (as perfected by Robert Herrick).

Intimations of mortality

Yet the question remains, why resort to an *epitaph*? Why not just announce 'I will always be a virgin'? Why was it her task to display her body verbally with this death sentence, as it were, in her, on her, legible for all, the herald of her own demise?[49] Clearly she had long been interested in the philosophical issue of remembrance; at the age of twelve, for instance, she prefaced a translation of John Calvin with a fairly sophisticated analysis of 'the custom ... to preserve the memory of notable things that were done in the past', and noted how 'characters, figures, images ... effigies ... [and] sculpting' were used to this end; she reserves especial praise for 'the invention of letters [, which] seems to me the most clever, excellent, and ingenious'.[50] Most of her correspondence to her half-brother King Edward VI seems preoccupied with the fear that he might think she had forgotten his benevolence and that he in turn would forget her.[51]

Moreover, Elizabeth had a particular interest in the preservation of tombstone memorials. This is evidenced by her repeated attempts to stem the iconoclastic razing of inscriptions and destruction of monuments in the fervour unleashed by the Reformation. Her 1560 extension of an earlier statute enjoins her subjects to

forbear the breaking or defacing of any parcel of any monument, or tomb, or grave, or other inscription and memory of any person deceased being in any manner of place, or to break any image of kings, princes ...[52]

Some of her first acts as queen included the careful orchestration of funerals for her half-sister, Mary Tudor, and Emperor Charles V, which were 'performed with great pomp and solemnity', according to one contemporary observer;[53] she also quickly ordered the restoration of her father's tomb, which had been recently removed.[54] Additionally, Elizabeth was as keenly aware as her contemporaries were of the rapidly disintegrating memorial practices of the Church in the period.

But perhaps what most impressed upon her mind the power of an intimation of mortality was the suspicion that naming a successor, getting married, or bearing a child would each entail the effective disestablishment of her own reign. As the French Ambassador reported in 1566, 'She had no desire to be buried alive, like her sister'.[55] Elizabeth herself acknowledged this fear — for instance, in her 1561 conversation with the Scottish ambassador, William Maitland, she rebuffed his entreaties that she designate Mary to inherit the crown: 'this desire is without example – to require me in my own life to set my winding-sheet before my eye! … Think you that I could love my winding sheet? Princes cannot like their own children, those that should succeed them.'[56] Even her last years were characterised by the sense that others were waiting for her demise – in response to the 'many rumours … bruted of her' death in 1599, she replied with macabre aplomb: *'Mortua sed non sepulta'* – dead but not buried.[57] This notion of a designated heir as a premonitory epitaph was not unfamiliar to Elizabethan writers; Holinshed, for example, included in his *Chronicles* (1577, 1587) an account of the Emperor Constantius calling his son Constantine to his deathbed. He gave the crown to him, declaring 'Now is my death to me more welcome, and my departure hence more pleasant; I haue héere a large epitaph and monument of buriall, to wit, mine owne sonne'.[58]

By presenting her own funereal inscription in her very first public speech, she tacitly acknowledged that others, as W.C. Fields acidly put it, 'would like to write your epitaph',[59] and that she, understandably, was loath to relinquish such control. She positioned herself, as it were, on the scaffold, uttering her last words as her first.[60] This also allowed for a strange sense of corporeal integrity, in that she defined 'an image of divine wholeness that was to be achieved in the future', and thereby 'the textualized body of the Queen thus contributed to the national narrative, in that it rendered the nation as eternal and its territory sanctified'.[61] The declaration presented her character as already written in stone, as it were – marmoreal and invariable. Such a presentation had an especial relevance in light of Scots reformer John Knox's recent tract, *The First Blast of the Trumpet Against the Monstrous Regiment of Women* (1558). Knox, intending his critique for Mary but awkwardly having it published shortly before Elizabeth's accession, argued that women were constitutionally unfit for rule, for Kings 'oght to be constant [and] stable'. Women, in contrast, had 'vertues … not comon with men … [woman is] a tendre creature, flexible, soft and pitifull; whiche nature, God hath geuen vnto her, that she may be apt to norishe children'.[62] The rhetoric of Elizabeth's epitaphic self-presentation echoes this masculine constancy and stability, and rejects flexibility, softness, and the nourishment of children. In effect, Elizabeth's feminine body had to be 'mortified … for the sake of the body politic'.[63]

Two bodies

This division between two bodies – a physical, mortal one and a political, transcendent one – is an inheritance from medieval political theology, in turn derived from Pauline conceptions of the two bodies of Christ, as Ernst Kantorowicz has demonstrated.[64] However, it was not extensively articulated in legal writing until the first years of Elizabeth's reign, in part 'because the future stability of the realm seemed at stake during the succession controversy'; thus, 'a legal metaphor defining the relationship between sovereign and perpetual state reached out beyond the courts of law to influence writers, polemicists and playwrights'.[65] Indeed, Elizabeth herself referred to the doctrine in her accession speech to the Privy Council in 1558: while she was 'but one body naturally considered', she also had 'by His permission a body politic to govern'.[66] The declaration 'The king is dead! Long live the king' is a kind of commonplace shorthand for the theory – while the physical body of the sovereign may pass away, an eternal concept of sovereignty will continue through the physical body of the successor. A literary manifestation of this theoretical fiction proliferated in 1603, when a number of books jointly published epitaphs for Elizabeth with celebrations of the new King James, '*Lamenting the ones decease, and reioycing at the others accesse*'.[67]

One pro-Mary epitaph even anonymously prophesied that the 'natural death' of the Queen of Scots would in turn punish 'all surviving Kings, (now made common persons) … with civil death', thereby making

> A strange and unusual kind of monument this is wherein the living are included with the dead; for, with the sacred ashes of this blessed Mary, know the Majesty of all the Kings and princes, lieth here, violated and prostrate.[68]

In this epitaph the unjust natural death entails the justice of civil death. Normally the civil body never dies, which is why the 'two bodies' theory contributes a greater sense of stability during transitions as well as an authority to buttress successions which were not based on simple primogeniture. However, as Kantorowicz argues, it also provides an opening for theoretical revolt, in that it allows the distinction to be made between the ideal concept of the king and the fallible (and potentially replaceable) embodiment of the current king. From the lawyer Edmund Plowden's 'language of 1560 it is only another step to the Puritan slogan, "fighting the king to defend the King"'.[69] In this respect Elizabeth's self-epitaph can analogously be read as part of the process which led to the Puritan revolution.

Many early modern writers discouraged writing epitaphs on living subjects, and my general sense is that, even when this rule was not articulated, it was still largely observed; it might be helpful to consider it more of a *tension* than a *rule*. A characteristic instance of this tension is to be found in the medieval writings of John of Garland, the first Englishman I know of to offer a definition of the epitaph, and consequently the first to break it, for as soon as he describes an epitaph as 'a poem inscribed over a dead body', he proceeds to cite one for himself: 'Turned now to ashes, he used to turn verses. He sleeps in this bed on a pillow of bedrock. Virgin, holy mother, may you shine forever, and raise John's soul from the depths to the heights.'[70] All self-composed epitaphs must confront this fundamental paradox: while still alive, a complete retrospective remains impossible (recall the classical dictum: 'count no man happy until he is dead'); yet, once dead, the deceased can no longer be the author of her own life (or would have to be a ghost, dictating from beyond the grave).

The first-person epitaphic address is thus, on a technical level, impossible without a degree of fictional infusion – anticipatory retrospect from the writer himself ('thus speaks him'[71]), assumption of deceased's voice by a survivor, or even projection of an indifferent account onto the unidentified speaker of the tomb (which I take to be the enunciator of all of these 'here lies' statements). To make an epitaph 'WHILE HE WAS YET LIUING IN REMEMBRANCE OF HIS OWN DEATH'[72] was furthermore seen as a somewhat vain exercise in the period. Such a paradox is expressed in a purported epitaph for John Donne, which asserts that 'He that would write an Epitaph ... / Should first be dead'.[73] How else could we fully trust 'The authors epitaph, made by himselfe'?[74]

What are the consequences of deploying this epitaphic tension in the public sphere? It is somewhat risky, in the same way that allowing a split between a physical and transcendent royal corpus is risky. In other words, should you really allow anyone, even the queen herself, to envision the death of the sovereign? Ever since the fourteenth century, English law had been quite forceful in emphatically denying this proposition. The 1352 Statute of Edward III explicitly defines treason to include even merely 'compassing or imagining the King's death'.[75] E. Kay Harris provides a good overview of what led to the law, and its unintended consequences:

> In an effort to check the interpretive latitude of the Crown in the matter of high treason, Parliament sought to identify, in this law, the specific acts that constituted this crime. Within the statute's 'definitive' list of treasonous acts, however, Parliament included the act of imagining the death of the king ... Through its provision for an imagined act of treason, the statute transgressed the very boundaries it had been designed to impose and posed problems regarding the type of evidence needed to establish this crime ... Once its interpretive possibilities had been tapped, imagining the death of the king figured frequently in the prosecution of treason throughout the fifteenth century.[76]

This was not an outdated medieval concern, for 'we find ample evidence that treason was perceived as an increasingly serious threat, policed with new urgency, and publicized with fresh intensity during the sixteenth century'.[77] And 'the king's lawyers were able if they wished to construe a great many crimes as compassing the death of the monarch'.[78] Elizabeth herself passed an important extension of the Statute in 1571, reaffirming it to be high treason to 'compass, imagine, invent, devise, or intend the death or destruction' of the queen, whether by means of 'printing, writing, ciphering, speech, words, or sayings'.[79] The legislation, as Greenblatt notes, 'does not deem it useful or important to distinguish between "imagine" as a subjective, inner state and "imagine" as the designing of a "real" plot'.[80]

This was a very real component of the law, with long-lasting consequences – as recently as the 1790s there were in England extensive debates about whether it was treasonous merely to *dream* about the death of the king.[81] Whether or not Elizabeth's own epitaph technically could be construed as treason (and there is reason to believe so, since treason could be construed quite narrowly in the Tudor period),[82] the larger point remains that such a speech act is likely more slippery than it appears at first glance. Similar arguments have been made regarding the English martyrologist John Foxe and his *Actes and Monuments* (1563).[83] In his lengthy catalogue of Protestant martyrs Foxe included narratives about Elizabeth's youthful imprisonment and other tribulations; the goal was clearly to glorify the new queen. Yet, by invoking Elizabeth in the context of people who had been tortured and brutally executed, Foxe unwittingly allowed for the reader's inference that this was a potential end for the queen as well. In effect Elizabeth's epitaph drew attention to her physical body (and its medico-social status as 'virgin'), the transient and lesser of her 'two bodies'. It opened up the imaginative space of treason, which itself was 'popularly regarded as an attempt to murder the entire body politic'.[84] By presenting her own epitaph, Elizabeth contributed, no matter how incrementally, to the conditions that allowed the possibility of imagining the death of a still-living subject.

Kings for such a tomb would wish to die

The 'paradox of sovereignty', to use the terms of political theorists, requires that the sovereign is 'both inside and outside the juridical order', that 'the sovereign stands outside the juridical order and, nevertheless, belongs to it, since it is up to him to decide if the constitution is to be suspended *in toto*'.[85] If anyone was to be allowed to say an epitaph over Elizabeth, it had to be herself. Yet, precisely by standing outside of legal strictures, Elizabeth seems to have opened the opportunity for others to do the same. Franco Moretti makes an analogous argument with respect to Renaissance tragedy: 'Tragedy disentitled the absolute monarch to all ethical and rational legitimation. Having deconstructed the king, tragedy made it possible to decapitate him.'[86] This is, admittedly, my most extravagant claim, that Elizabeth imagining her own tombstone was in some sense a precursor to the aggressively satirical publications of the 1640s,[87] which saw the rise of epitaphs for composite fictional characters ('Sir James Independent', 'Sir John Presbyter', 'Jack Puffe Gentleman'), inanimate objects ('Cheap-side crosse'), institutions ('Sr. Pitifull Parliament'), and even states of being ('Contentment').[88] As a later epitaph put it, these were all epitaphs 'by anticipation';[89] no wonder one mid-seventeenth-century Earl scornfully willed that he 'have no monument, for then I must needs have an epitaph and verses over my carcass – during my life I had enough of these'.[90]

Yet it is difficult to read these epitaphs on 'living' entities without concluding that the conceptual environment was becoming increasingly open to the peculiar kind of rehearsing sovereignty which entails an inhearsing of the sovereign herself. While I have not yet discovered any epitaphs made for Charles I while he was still alive (and in fact 'an attempt was made to signal the end of the lineage by denying Charles any tomb'),[91] many critics have noted the simultaneity of Charles's execution and the appearance of *Eikon Basilike* – 'it literally took the place of the king'.[92] Later epitaphs for Cromwell, in turn, were produced with tones of brutal vengeance, 'written in hell' or simply declaring that 'since there may be no stone / Shall stand this Epitaph; *That he has none*'.[93]

This transposition of the physical corpse and the textual corpus at the end of his life was in some sense anticipated, however intangibly, by Elizabeth's first epitaph, a forceful enunciation which initiated her reign by envisioning the death of the sovereign. When John Hayward later recounted this first speech in 1627, he interpolated Parliament's supposed response: 'These were her wordes; there wanteth nothing but the grace wherewith shee delivered them, which gave such life to that which shee spake that not onely satisfied, but almost amazed, those that wer present.'[94] As in Milton's epitaph on Shakespeare (written only a few years later), the subject's overwhelming vivification (*gave such life*) nearly serves to astonish (*almost amazed*) the audience. Personification of an inanimate concept – whether sovereignty or a dead author – commands a degree of authority unimaginable at the conceptual level alone. But such personification is also an embodiment that makes the concept mortal, which means it can (conceivably) be killed: 'And so Sepulcher'd in such pomp dost lie, / That Kings for such a Tomb would wish to die'.[95]

Notes

1. My title's quotation comes from the epigram by Sir John Mennes, 'On King James his death', *Recreation for Ingenious Head-peeces* (London: M. Simmons, 1650) (sig. P2r). This chapter derives from my forthcoming study, *Quoting Death in Early Modern England* (Palgrave, forthcoming), which examines how epitaphs are quoted outside the putative cemetery in early modern England. While there are many to thank for their assistance with that larger project, I gratefully cite here those who have helped shape this chapter in particular: Marjorie Garber, John Guillory, Marc Shell, the Oberlin College English Department, Eric Carlson, the Ohio State University Department of English, Maija Jansson, John Watkins, Arnold Sanders, and Takako Kato. The Harvard English Department provided generous fellowships (Dexter, Mellon, and Packard) in support of my work, as did the Andrew W. Mellon Foundation through the Yale University Library's Special Collections, which also helped defray costs for images. I'm further indebted to the staff at the Harvard, Oberlin, Amherst, Gustavus Adolphus, and Yale libraries.

2. Anna Akhmatova, 'In 1940: 1', *Poems of Akhmatova*, translated by Stanley Kunitz with Max Hayward (Boston: Houghton Mifflin, 1973), p. 119.

3. Susan Doran, *Queen Elizabeth I* (New York: New York University Press, 2003), p. 125.

4. James W. Spisak, ed., *Caxton's Malory: A New Edition of Sir Thomas Malory's* Le Morte Darthur, *Based on the Pierpont Morgan Copy of William Caxton's Edition of 1485* (Berkeley: University of California Press, 1983), p. 592.

5. Larry D. Benson has argued for its originality (Larry D. Benson, *Malory's* Morte Darthur (Cambridge, MA: Harvard University Press, 1976), p. 241), whereas John Withrington has convincingly gathered numerous potential precedents, postulating Lydgate's *Fall of Princes* as a likely source ('His epitaphe recordeth so certeyn: "Heer lith kyng Arthour, which shal regne ageyn"') ('The Arthurian Epitaph in Malory's *Morte Darthur'*, in *Arthurian Literature VII*, edited by Richard Barber (Cambridge: D.S. Brewer, 1987), pp. 103–144, p. 131.

6. British Library Additional MS 59678 f 482v; my thanks to Arnold Sanders and Takako Kato for clarifying this information about rubrication in the Winchester MS. for me.

7. For an analysis of the largely non-Christian epitaphs in the French romances of the

Arthurian saga, see Régine Colliot, 'Les Epitaphes Arthuriennes', *Bulletin Bibliographique de la Société Internationale Arthurienne* 25 (1973), pp. 155–175.

8. 'On King James his death', Mennes, sig. P2r.

9. William Camden, *Remains Concerning Britain* (1605), edited by R.D. Dunn (Toronto: University of Toronto Press, 1984), pp. 3, 6, 351.

10. Camden, *Remains*, pp. 351–352; attributed in the margin to Hugh Holland.

11. Camden, *Remains*, p. 358.

12. *Eikonoklastes*, in *Complete Prose Works of John Milton*, edited by Don M. Wolfe et al., 8 vols (New Haven: Yale University Press, 1953–1982), 3, p. 575. Dennis Kezar notes the 'epitaphic significance' Milton attributes to this text (*Guilty Creatures: Renaissance Poetry and the Ethics of Authorship* (Oxford: Oxford University Press, 2001), p. 162.

13. *The Satyricon of T. Petronius Arbiter*, trans. William Burnaby (1694), p. 107.

14. I have the scholarship of Clare Gittings to thank for first locating this epitaph (*Death, Burial, and the Individual in Early Modern England* (Beckenham: Kent, Routledge, 1984), p. 145); her source was Maidstone: Kent Archives Office. John Brooke, PRC 32/35/19.

15. Gittings, *Death, Burial, and the Individual*, p. 145.

16. See Jennifer Loach, *Parliament under the Tudors* (Oxford: Clarendon Press, 1991), p. 109.

17. Text from BL Lansd, 94, copy, cited in *Proceedings in the Parliament of Elizabeth I, Volume I: 1558–1581*, edited by T.E. Hartley (Leicester: Leicester University Press, 1981), pp. 56–57. All remaining citations from Elizabeth's writings, unless otherwise noted, are from Leah S. Marcus, Janel Mueller, and Mary Beth Rose, eds, *Elizabeth I: Collected Works* (Chicago: University of Chicago Press, 2000).

18. As Hartley notes, the MS is torn (because of a fold); missing words from the epitaph are supplied from Rawlinson D723.

19. *Annales: The True and Royall History of the Famous Empresse Elizabeth, Queene of England, France, and Ireland, etc. True Faith's Defendresse of Divine Renowne and Happy Memory* (1625), bk. 1, 26 [STC 4497], translated from *Annales rerum Anglicarum et Hibernicarum regnante Elizabeth* (1615). This is the original from which Marcus et al. draw (p. 59).

20. 'Queen Elizabeth I: Representations of the Virgin Queen', *Renaissance Quarterly* 43.1 (1990), pp. 30–74, p. 35.

21. King, 'Queen Elizabeth I', p. 36. He reiterates, 'The manuscript version of the queen's speech records no vow of perpetual virginity' (p. 38). Susan Doran cites King's line of argument in *Monarchy and Matrimony: The Courtships of Elizabeth I* (London: Routledge, 1996), p. 1; see also Mary Beth Rose, 'The Gendering of Authority in the Public Speeches of Elizabeth I', *Publications of the Modern Language Association* 115.5 (2000), pp. 1077–1082, p. 1078.

22. Cited by Janel Mueller in 'Virtue and Virtuality: Gender in the Self-Representations of Queen Elizabeth', in *Form and Reform in Renaissance England: Essays in Honor of Barbara Kiefer Lewalski*, edited by Amy Boesky and Mary Thomas Crane (Newark: University of Delaware Press, 2000), pp. 220–246, p. 226, note 24; the original source is Cambridge University Library MS Gg.3.32, fol. 201.

23. Marcus et al., *Elizabeth I: Collected Works*, p. 58, note 1.

24. See Frances Teague, 'Queen Elizabeth in Her Speeches', in *Gloriana's Face: Women, Public and Private, in the English Renaissance*, edited by S.P. Cerasano and Marion Wynne-Davies (Detroit: Wayne State University Press, 1992), pp. 63–78, p. 74.

25. Allison Heisch, 'Queen Elizabeth I: Parliamentary Rhetoric and the Exercise of Power', *Signs* 1.1 (1975), pp. 31–55, p. 55.

26. E.g. Stephen Greenblatt, 'The secular cult of the virgin was born', in *Renaissance Self-Fashioning: From More to Shakespeare* (Chicago: University of Chicago Press, 1980), p. 168), and Louis Adrian Montrose, 'Gifts and Reasons: The Contexts of Peele's *Araygnement of*

Paris', *English Literary History* 47.3 (1980), pp. 433–461, p. 441; and '"Shaping Fantasies": Figurations of Gender and Power in Elizabethan Culture', *Representations* 2 (1983), pp. 61–94, p. 78.

27. Cited in Helen Hackett, *Virgin Mother Maiden Queen: Elizabeth I and the Cult of the Virgin Mary* (Houndmills: Macmillan, 1995), p. 52. Hackett cites the letter from Sir Thomas Pope to Queen Mary, 26.4.1558; BL MSS Harl.444.7, Cotton Vitell.xii., 16.8.

28. Martin A.S. Hume, ed., *Calendar of Letters and State Papers Relating to English Affairs, Preserved Principally in the Archives of Simancas*, Vol. 1: Elizabeth, 1558–1567, 4 vols (London: Public Record Office, 1892).

29. Mueller, 'Virtue and Virtuality', p. 226. Mueller cites Neale's study *Elizabeth I and Her Parliaments, 1559–1581* (New York: St Martin's Press, 1958), p. 33; Neale discusses this again on p. 50.

30. King, 'Queen Elizabeth I', p. 43.

31. Susan Doran, *Monarchy and Matrimony: The Courtships of Elizabeth I* (London: Routledge, 1996), p. 9.

32. See Hackett, *Virgin Mother*.

33. Quoted from *The Penguin Book of Renaissance Verse 1509–1659*, selected and introduced by David Norbrook, edited by H.R. Woudhuysen (London: Allen Lane-Penguin, 1992), p. 93. Some readers have chosen to emphasise the marital iconography of her reign over the virginal iconography; the most compelling, in this respect, is Marc Shell (*Elizabeth's Glass: With 'The glass of the Sinful Soul' (1544) by Elizabeth I, and 'Epistle dedicatory' and 'Conclusion' (1548) by John Bale* (Lincoln, NE: University of Nebraska Press, 1993), p. 71). None the less, the precondition for her 'marriage' to the state (a not uncommon trope in the early modern period, albeit more unusual for a queen to make than a king) required this metaphorical 'virginity', as the later lines in Birch's poem indicate.

34. Marcus et al., *Collected Works*, p. 72.

35. Michael Warner argues this in his essay 'Franklin and the Letters of the Republic', *Representations* 16 (Autumn 1986), pp. 110–130, p. 111.

36. Nigel Rees, *Epitaphs: A Dictionary of Grave Epigrams and Memorial Eloquence* (London: Bloomsbury, 1993), p. 94.

37. See Julia M. Walker's discussion of this posthumous move in her essay, 'Reading the Tombs of Elizabeth I', *English Literary Renaissance* 26.3 (1996), pp. 510–30; see also Nicola Smith, *The Royal Image and the English People* (Burlington, VT: Ashgate, 2001), pp. 92–97: Smith notes that 'versions of Elizabeth's epitaph ... had appeared in numerous parish churches' (p. 94).

38. One set of the inscriptions read, in side-by-side panels:

REGNO CONSORTES	ET MARIA SORORES
& VRNA HIC OBDOR	IN SPE RESVRREC=
MIMVS ELIZABETHA	TIONIS

translated, roughly, as: 'In throne and grave consorts both, here rest we two sisters, Elizabeth and Mary, in hope of our resurrection'. http://tudorhistory.org/elizabeth/gallery3.html. See Figure 17.

39. Two are to be found in her orations at Cambridge (7 August 1564) and Oxford (5 September 1566); the other is addressed to Parliament, cited below; Marcus et al., *Collected Works*, pp. 89, 91.

40. Marcus et al., *Collected Works*, p. 80.

41. Marcus et al., *Collected Works*, p. 80, note 15, note that D'Ewes's condensed printed version concludes with 'I cannot with *Nunc dimittis* end my life without I see some foundation of your surety after my gravestone'.

42. Marcus et al., *Collected Works*, p. 95.

43. For instance, Joshua Scodel, *The English Poetic Epitaph: Commemoration and Conflict from Jonson to Wordsworth* (Ithaca: Cornell University Press, 1991), p. 53.

44. This being, of course, a more problematic example than it initially appears, as Judith Butler has influentially argued in *Bodies that Matter: On the Discursive Limits of 'Sex'* (New York: Routledge, 1993).

45. 'The Pre-Coronation Passage of Elizabeth I: Political Theatre or the Rehearsal of Politics?', *Canadian Review of Sociology and Anthropology* 21.1 (1984), pp. 47–61, p. 58. For a historical analysis of Tudor marriage practices which differs sharply from McCracken's rather loose sense of the promissory nature of marriage, see Eric Carlson, *Marriage and the English Reformation* (Oxford: Blackwell, 1994).

46. *The Norton Shakespeare*, edited by Stephen Greenblatt, Walter Cohen, Jean E. Howard, and Katharine Eisaman Maus (New York: Norton, 1997), V.4.56–62.

47. King, 'Queen Elizabeth I', p. 66. For a discussion of the medieval Virgin Martyr legend see Karen A. Winstead, *Virgin Martyrs: Legends of Sainthood in Late Medieval England* (Ithaca: Cornell University Press, 1997).

48. Cited by Frederick Chamberlin in *The Sayings of Queen Elizabeth* (London: John Lane, 1923), p. 310.

49. To paraphrase Michel Foucault, *Discipline and Punish*, translated by Alan Sheridan (New York: Vintage, 1979), p. 43.

50. From the epistolary preface (to Queen Katherine) to her English translation of Chapter 1 of John Calvin's *Institution de la Religion chretienne* (Geneva, 1541), 30 December 1545; Marcus et al. list the source as Edinburgh, Scottish Record Office, National Archives of Scotland, MS NAS RH 13/78, fols 1r–7r; 'in French, in Elizabeth's youthful italic hand, on parchment' (p. 10, note 1).

51. Found in letters such as: 14 February 1547, Marcus et al., p. 13; 20 September 1547, Marcus et al., p. 14; summer or autumn 1548, Marcus et al., p. 21.

52. For Elizabeth's proclamation see Margaret Aston, *England's Iconoclasts: Volume I, Laws Against Images* (Oxford: Clarendon Press, 1988), vol. 1, p. 314; John Weever reproduced it in the introduction to his 1631 *Ancient Funeral Monuments* (pp. 52–54).

53. Don Tomás Gonzalez, *Documents from Simanacas Relating to the Reign of Elizabeth (1558–1568)*, translated and edited by Spencer Hall (London: Chapman and Hall, 1865), p. 48. Jennifer Woodward astutely notes that the new monarch's care for the burial of the previous monarch typically arose from self-interest. *The Theatre of Death: The Ritual Management of Royal Funerals in Renaissance England, 1570–1625* (London: Boydell Press, 1997), p. 2.

54. Hume, *Calendar of Letters and State Papers*, p. 6.

55. La Forêt to Charles IX, 21 October 1566. This is Sir John Neale's paraphrase of a letter in possession of the publisher John Murray; *Elizabeth I and Her Parliaments*, p. 136. Also cited in Marie Axton, *The Queen's Two Bodies: Drama and the Elizabethan Succession* (London: Royal Historical Society, 1977), p. 11, note 1.

56. Marcus et al., *Collected Works*, pp. 64–65.

57. Rowland Whyte to Robert Sidney, 29 August 1599, in Historical Manuscripts Commission, *Report on the Manuscripts of Lord De L'Isle & Dudley* (London, 1934), II, p. 386. Cited by Catherine Loomis, 'Elizabeth's Southwell's Manuscript Account of the Death of Queen Elizabeth [with text]', *English Literary Renaissance* 26.3 (1996), pp. 482–509, pp. 509, note 56.

58. Raphael Holinshed et al., *Chronicles of England, Scotland, and Ireland* (1587), second edition, edited by H. Ellis, 6 vols (London, 1807–1808), I, p. 529.

59. In *International House* (dir. A. Edward Sutherland, 1933), Fields responds to Gracie Allen's adulatory request ('Oh professor, before you go to sleep, will you write me your

autograph?') by muttering 'I'd like to write your epitaph'.

60. See Frances E. Dolan, '"Gentlemen, I have one more thing to say": Women on Scaffolds in England, 1563–1680', *Modern Philology* 92.2 (1994), pp. 157–178, p. 167.

61. Susanne Scholz, *Body Narratives: Writing the Nation and Fashioning the Subject in Early Modern England* (New York: St Martin's Press, 2000), p. 11.

62. John Knox, *The First Blast of the Trumpet Against the Monstrous Regiment of Women* (1558), sigs 24r, 25v.

63. Axton, *The Queen's Two Bodies*, p. 37.

64. Ernst Kantorowicz, *The King's Two Bodies: A Study in Medieval Political Theory* (Princeton: Princeton University Press, 1957).

65. Axton, *Queen's Two Bodies*, pp. 17–18.

66. Marcus et al., *Collected Works*, p. 52.

67. I.F., *King Iames his welcome to London. With Elizaes tombe and epitaph, and our Kings triumph and epitimie. Lamenting the ones decease, and reioycing at the others accesse* (London: [By R. Read?] for Thomas Pauier, 1603) (STC 10798). See also: Samuel Rowlands, *Aue Caesar. God Save the King. The ioyfull Ecchoes of loyall English hartes, entertayning his Maiesties late ariuall in England. With an Epitaph vpon the death of her Maiestie our late Queene* (London, Printed [by William White] for W[illiam]. F[erbrand]. and G[eorge]. L[oftus], 1603) (STC 21364); Robert Fletcher, *A briefe and familiar epistle shevving His Maiesties most lawfull, honourable and iust title to all his kingdomes. VVith an epitaph or briefe lamentation for the late Maiestie Royall* (Imprinted at London: [By R. Read] for Iohn Harrison, 1603) (STC 11086). These references are drawn from Charles Bazerman, 'Verse Occasioned by the Death of Queen Elizabeth I and the Accession of King James I', unpublished Ph.D. thesis, Brandeis University, 1971.

68. Quoted and translated in Woodward, *Theatre of Death*, p. 68.

69. Axton, *Queen's Two Bodies*, p. 14.

70. *The* Parisiana Poetria *of John of Garland*, edited by Traugott Lawler (New Haven: Yale University Press, 1974), p. 103.

71. This is how Payne Fisher introduces 'The Inscription on Sir FRANCIS WALSINGHAM' (*The Tombs, Monuments, Sepulchral Inscriptions Lately Visible in St. Paul's Cathedral* (1684), p. 7).

72. William Pole, 1674, Dorchester, MA. Reprinted by W.B. Trask, 'Epitaphs at Dorchester', *The New England Historical and Genealogical Register* 2 (1848), p. 381.

73. Adapted from Dr Corbet's epitaph on John Donne, reported in Izaak Walton, *The Lives of John Donne, Sir Henry Wotton, Richard Hooker, George Herbert & Robert Sanderson*, introduced by George Saintsbury (London: Humphrey Milford, 1927), p. 85.

74. See Abraham Holland, *Hollandi posthuma A funerall elegie of King Iames: With a congratulatory salve to King Charles. An elegie of the magnanimous Henry Earle of Oxford. A description of the late great, fearefull and prodigious plague: and divers other patheticall poemes, elegies, and other lines, on divers subiectes. The post-humes of Abraham Holland, sometimes of Trinity-Colledge in Cambridge. The authors epitaph, made by himselfe* (Cantabrigiae [i.e. London Printed by Bernard Alsop and Thomas Fawcet] imprensis Henrici Holland, M.DC.XXVI, [1626]) (STC 13579).

75. J.R. Tanner, *Tudor Constitutional Documents, A.D. 1485–1603, with an historical commentary* (Cambridge: Cambridge University Press, 1922), p. 375.

76. E. Kay Harris, 'Evidence against Lancelot and Guinevere in Malory's *Morte Darthur*: Treason by Imagination', *Exemplaria* 7.1 (1995), pp. 179–208, p. 180.

77. Karen Cunningham, *Imaginary Betrayals: Subjectivity and the Discourses of Treason in Early Modern England* (Philadelphia: University of Pennsylvania Press, 2002), p. 1.

78. J.G. Bellamy, *The Law of Treason in England in the Later Middle Ages* (Cambridge: Cambridge University Press, 1970), p. 137.

79. Tanner, *Tudor*, pp. 413 and 414. For early fifteenth-century examples of 'treason by words'

see Bellamy, *Law of Treason*, pp. 116–120.

80. Greenblatt, *Renaissance Self-Fashioning*, p. 277, note 11.

81. John Barrell, 'Introduction', in *Imagining the King's Death: Figurative Treason, Fantasies of Regicide, 1793–1796* (Oxford: Oxford University Press, 2000), pp. 30–44.

82. Lacey Baldwin Smith, 'English Treason Trials and Confessions in the Sixteenth Century', *Journal of the History of Ideas* 15 (1954), pp. 471–498, p. 472.

83. See, for instance, Thomas S. Freeman, 'Providence and Prescription: The Account of Elizabeth in Foxe's *Book of Martyrs*', in *The Myth of Elizabeth*, edited by Susan Doran and Thomas S. Freeman (New York: Palgrave, 2003), pp. 27–55.

84. James Walter Weingart, 'The Concept of Treason in Tudor England', unpublished Ph.D. thesis, Northwestern University, 1976, p. 1.

85. Giorgio Agamben, *Homo Sacer: Sovereign Power and Bare Life* (Stanford: Stanford University Press, 1998), p. 15; Carl Schmitt, *Political Theology: Four Chapters on the Concept of Sovereignty*, translated by George Schwab (Cambridge, MA: Massachusetts Institute of Technology Press, 1985), p. 13.

86. Franco Moretti, *Signs Taken for Wonders: Essays in the Sociology of Literary Forms*, translated by Susan Fischer et al. (London: Verso, 1983), p. 42. David Scott Kastan makes a comparable claim about the deposition scene of *Richard II*, '"Proud Majesty Made a Subject": Representing Authority on the Early Modern Stage', *Shakespeare after Theory* (New York: Routledge, 1999), p. 111.

87. Remarking upon a contiguous genre, Nigel Smith notes: 'The 1640s are littered with elegies on real and abstract subjects which ominously prophesy a cultural deluge' (*Literature and Revolution in England, 1640–1660* (New Haven: Yale University Press, 1994), p. 287).

88. *The last vvill and testament of Sir James Independent* (London, 1647); *The last vvill and testament of Sir Iohn Presbyter who dyed of a new disease called the particular charge of the army* (London, 1647); *The Birth, life, death, vvil, and epitaph of Iack Pvffe gentleman* (London: Printed for T.P., 1642); *The Downe-fall of Dagon, or, the taking downe of Cheap-side crosse this second of May, 1643.* ([London]: Printed for Thomas Wilson, 1642[?]); *Ding dong, or Sr. Pitifull Parliament, on his death-bed*. By Mercurius Melancholicus (London, 1648); 'In golden letters may be read, / Here lie Content's late King and Queen' (ll. 31–32), in J. Paulin's poem 'Love's Contentment', a response to Marlowe's 'The Passionate Shepherd to His Love'; cited in Patrick Cheney, 'Career Rivalry and the Writing of Counter-Nationhood: Ovid, Spenser, and Philomela in Marlowe's "The Passionate Shepherd to His Love"', *English Literary History* 65.3 (1998), pp. 523–555, p. 537.

89. I refer to one satirist's attempt to declare the Puritan cause dead in 1683, *The old cause's epitaph by anticipation*.

90. 'Will of Philip V, Earl of Pembroke and Montgomery', cited in John Proffatt, *The Curiosities and Law of Wills* (San Francisco: Sumner Whitney, 1876), p. 16.

91. Nigel Llewellyn, 'The Royal Body: Monuments to the Dead, For the Living', in *Renaissance Bodies: The Human Figure in English Culture c.1540–1660*, edited by Lucy Gent and Nigel Llewellyn (London: Reaktion, 1990), pp. 217–240, p. 225. In contrast, epitaphs on Louis XIV, 'both virulent and comical, circulated before and after the real event' (Kathryn A. Hoffman, *Society of Pleasures: Interdisciplinary Readings in Pleasure and Power during the Reign of Louis XIV* (New York: St Martin's Press, 1997), p. 160).

92. Elizabeth Skerpan Wheeler, '*Eikon Basilike* and the Rhetoric of Self-Representation', in *The Royal Image: Representations of Charles I*, edited by Thomas N. Corns (Cambridge: Cambridge University Press, 1999), pp. 122–140, p. 122.

93. *The case is altered. Or, dreadful news from hell* (London: printed, for John Andrews at the white Lyon, 1660); 'Cromwell's Panegyrick', in *Rump: Or an Exact Collection of the Choycest Poems and Songs relating to the Late Times* (London, 1662), p. 225.

94. John Hayward, *Annals of the first Four Years of the Reign of Queen Elizabeth*, edited by John Bruce (London: Camden Society, 1840), p. 33.

95. John Milton, 'On Shakespeare', ll. 15–16, *John Milton: Complete Poems and Major Prose*, edited by Merritt Y. Hughes (Upper Saddle River, NJ: Prentice Hall, 1957), pp. 63–64.

Index

Lightning Source UK Ltd.
Milton Keynes UK
UKOW06f1441260317

297501UK00006B/139/P